HERE'S THE BASIS for your modern metalworking shop. We've rounded up the greatest of the new metalworking tools, including this BernzOmatic oxygen and welding torch. See all these fine tools in the article starting on page 30.

WHAT A BEAUTY! You may think we mean the attractive mother or the beautiful child. Actually we're talking about the redwood chaise. Indeed it is a beauty, and you'll find complete plans on page 136.

COLORFUL, PRACTICAL and all Coast Guard approved—for use in certain situations—these new life preservers include the type or types you should have on your boat. Be aware that the throwable buoyant cushion (right) is safe only when worn across the chest as shown here. It floats the swimmer in a face-up position. Other life preservers shown above are for use in specific situations. Be sure you're safe—and obeying the law—by reading the article on page 22.

HERE ARE great shots by a fine wildlife photographer. To get such photos you need to know some of the tricks of the trade. They come with considerable experience. The outdoorsman who took these photos lets you in on many of his secrets in the article on page 156.

IMPORT OUTBOARDS are joining the big leagues. Tests show that they're mighty good, but do these engines from Sweden, Japan, Great Britain and Italy have what it takes to compete on the American scene with the well-known Evinrude, Johnson, Chrysler, and Mercury motors? The Japanese even are marketing a backpack motor (above right). For photos and data on the new imports, see the article on page 20.

THE LATEST winter challenge is overnighting outdoors, and manufacturers have come up with some exceptional gear to keep you comfortable. If you're at all involved in camping, see the article on page 18. You'll be surprised at how much topnotch cold-weather gear you can tote on a "Pak Rak" (right).

Popular Mechanics
do-it-yourself yearbook
1979

Exciting new products

- for your home
- for your shop
- gear for outdoorsmen
- the best of the new tools
- what's new for photographers
- newsmakers in electronics

Great projects of the year

- to improve your home
- shop know-how
- challenging craft projects
- how-to in the great outdoors
- photo projects
- electronics know-how
- projects just for fun

Popular Mechanics, 250 W. 55th St., New York, NY 10019

EDITOR
Clifford B. Hicks

MANAGING EDITOR
Paul Hilts

ASSOCIATE EDITOR
Anne T. Cope

ART DIRECTOR
Ralph Leroy Linnenburger

ASSISTANT EDITOR
Tom Balow

PRODUCTION EDITOR
Dorothy Winer

PHOTOGRAPHY
Joe Fletcher

ART ASSISTANTS
Marian C. Linnenburger
Sue Sevick

CONTRIBUTING EDITORS
David Paulsen
Benjamin Lee
Ed Nelson

**EDITORIAL ADVISORY BOARD
POPULAR MECHANICS**
John A. Linkletter,
Editor
Robin C. Nelson
Executive Editor
Arthur J. Maher
Managing Editor
Harry Wicks
Home and Shop Editor
Ira Herrick
Art Director

ISBN 0-910990-71-9
Library of Congress Catalog Number 78 69987

©1979 The Hearst Corporation
all rights reserved

CONTENTS

Flooring by the roll: a quick put-down

Transform a room with cushioned vinyl flooring at do-it-yourself savings. The 15-ft.-wide rolls make it easy to install. You need only a few tools to give any room a new floor. Here's all you need to know

TO "RELAX" flooring, roll it backing side out. Roll it once from each end.

FROM FLOORING'S butting edge, mark off three other edges and cut oversize.

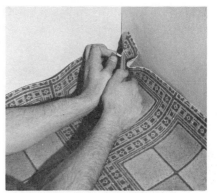

FLOORING will overlap walls. Make corner cuts so vinyl lies flatter.

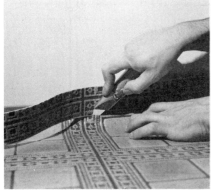

GRADUALLY TRIM down the excess flooring, testing for a neat fit.

PRESS a metal rule into the floor-wall angle. Use a sharp blade.

TO FIT flooring into nook, outline the shape on the vinyl; cut along line.

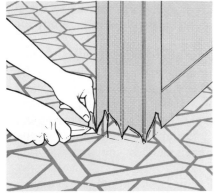

TO FIT around door jamb, make vertical slits at inside and outside angles.

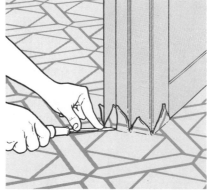

HOLDING screwdriver flat, press vinyl into the angle of the floor and doorway.

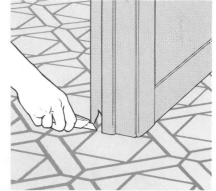

WITH a sharp knife at a 45° angle, carefully trim off excess flooring.

■ IF YOU CAN TAKE accurate measurements and handle a utility knife, you can cover a floor in your home with cushioned sheet vinyl and get professional-looking results. With the new 15-ft.-wide sheet flooring, you can do almost any floor without having to seam pieces. The finished floor on the opposite page was done in Congoleum's Colony Square pattern.

Take along your floor measurements when you shop for flooring. To do the job, you'll need a metal straightedge, utility knife, carpenter square, metal tape measure and push broom. A crowbar and hammer help remove molding; a screwdriver fits flooring around trim. Metal trim at doorways protects flooring edges.

Good-quality cushioned vinyl can be laid over most types of flooring, provided the floor is clean and smooth. Old cushioned vinyl should be

ON HALF of the subfloor apply adhesive 2 in. from the perimeter and in bands 1 ft. apart.

ROLL THE FLOORING into place and expel air with a push broom; work from the center to the walls.

stripped off. Carefully remove floor moldings and grilles so they can be used again. Clean any wax buildup and fill any large cracks in the old floor.

measure and cut the flooring

After the floor covering has been rolled out to relax it, butt one edge against a long straight wall. If you butt the store-cut edge, use a carpenter's square to check that it is true. Measure the flooring in a larger room than that being covered, or work on half the floor at a time.

Using a soft pencil, mark off measurements for the butting wall on the butting edge of the flooring. Then mark off the exact outline of the three other room sides. Cut the flooring about 3 in. outside the line.

position and fit the flooring

Position the butting edge against the appropriate wall. The extra material will overlap the other walls, so make diagonal relief (safety) cuts at corners—or at inside corners trim off crescent-shaped pieces from the corner points. Do exact fitting later. Gradually trim excess flooring along adjacent walls until the flooring is snug at the baseboard.

You may have to cut flooring to fit around built-in cabinets or appliances. Mark exact outline of the object on the flooring and carefully cut along the line.

To fit flooring at a doorway, trim it at the walls on both sides within a foot of the jamb, bend the excess material through the opening and follow the steps shown above. If you cut a corner wrong, hold it together with strong tape on the underside while installing. Later, seal it with a seam-sealer recommended by the flooring maker.

When the flooring is fitted, fold or roll it back so half the old floor is exposed. Apply the recommended adhesive 2 in. from the floor perimeter and in bands 1 ft. apart on the floor. Roll flooring down on the wet adhesive and flatten it with a push broom. Repeat the process on the other half.

installing without adhesive

Cushioned flooring can be installed without adhesive in rooms with quarter-round molding, but allow ⅛-in. expansion gap between flooring and wall. Shim up the quarter round and nail it through the baseboards. Next day, move the furniture carefully in place.

THE FIRST STEP to install seamless flooring is to position it in the room.

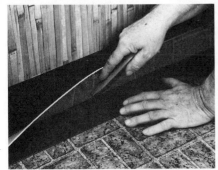

SECOND, trim the material along the room edges with a knife and straightedge.

THIRD, staple the flooring every 3 in. Quarter-round molding hides the staples.

THE BRICK design is from easy-to-install Premier Sundial group.

. . . And flooring you install with a stapler

■ HERE'S A HANDSOME flooring that's a cinch to install. And it has extra advantages: a shiny no-wax surface and a comfortable built-in cushion. The flexible flooring is Premier Sundial made by Armstrong Cork Co. It comes in 6 and 12-ft. widths in two patterns: brick and a Mediterranean design.

You can fasten Premier Sundial to wood subfloors or even to other resilient floors just by stapling it with heavy-duty staples along the border of the room. To secure it over concrete, simply apply a narrow band of special cement to its edges—no need to spread adhesive over the entire floor.

The maker claims other benefits for Premier Sundial over other flooring: 1. There's less sub-

floor preparation. The cushion eliminates the need for most subfloor sanding, patching and leveling. 2. Installation disruption to your room is briefer. Just position, cut and staple the covering in place. 3. If you install it over wood or particle-board subfloors that expand and contract from changes in humidity, Premier Sundial will move along with the subfloor to stay taut. A completely bonded floor will crack under severe stretching. 4. In most cases you can cover your subfloors with one piece of material. If two pieces are needed, Armstrong has a sealant to join them.

The covering is reported to hold a gloss longer than ordinary vinyl. A sponge mopping at regular intervals will keep it glowing.

Programmed watering—
what a way to grow!

By RUDOLF F. GRAF and GEORGE J. WHALEN

■ AN AUTOMATIC lawn-sprinkling system used to be considered a luxury. Today, with water shortages in many regions, it can be an important aid to conservation as well—an easy way to water properly but without waste. You get water only when and where you want it. With programmed controls, you can even water when you're away or asleep—they turn your sprinklers on and off at preset intervals.

The basic concept of an underground sprinkler is simple: Pipes buried below the lawn are fitted with sprinkler heads at strategic locations. The pipes have valves that are connected to the house water supply. The valves are activated by a controller that automatically directs the opening and closing of the valves. You program it, telling it when and how long to water.

Begin by drawing an accurately scaled plan of your property. (A photocopy of the survey is fine.) It should show the entire property plus the location of your house, lawn, patio, driveway, walks, garden, shrubs, trees, fences, water meter and water source. If the ground slopes significantly, note where this occurs.

You should also know the characteristics of the soil on your land. Its type and texture affect water intake rate and water-holding capacity. The agricultural extension service in your county can give you soil information.

Call your local water company and ask them what the water pressure is at your location in the summer. A pressure of 45 lbs. is about optimum for most residential watering systems. If pressure is below 30 lbs., sprinkler performance will drop and some areas may not be watered. If pressure is above 70 lbs., there may be risk of burst joints.

Also note the details of the type of water meter serving your home. You'll need to know its size, the size and type of the supply pipe and the size of the pipe that feeds the point where you will tap the supply. This information will help

EACH OF the actuator valves serves a circuit. They are hydraulically operated by tubing from the controller.

A TEE FITTING attaches to the flexible pipe with hose clamps. Next install the riser pipe and sprinkler head.

THE FILTER in this pop-up head keeps dirt from entering. The spring returns head to ground level when water flow stops.

REMOVABLE PEGS program the controller to open actuator valves at desired times on selected days in a 14-day cycle.

you determine maximum gallonage of your sprinkler system, the pressure loss along the line and what materials you will need.

Take your plan, water supply details and soil information to the local dealer where you'll be buying the parts. He can give you good advice on sprinkler head type and location, piping layout and materials needed such as automatic controller, valves, pipe fittings, risers and adapters. Flexible polyethylene pipe is used in climates that have freezing temperatures. PVC pipe is often used in warmer climates, too. Your dealer can give you advice about local code requirements.

You'll want to select sprinkler heads with discharge rates that give your land the exact amount of water it needs. Some typical heads are shown here.

Plot a tentative layout on paper by drawing the spray patterns (circle, semicircle, horizontal stream, and the like) of each head and joining them with lines that represent pipes. Try to avoid sharp bends. They reduce line pressure. Keep each line as short as possible and indicate a drain valve at the end of each line. After making the layout, add the required flow of all the sprinklers in gallons per minute (gpm) to be sure the total

flow will be available from your supply. Allow about 15 percent for friction losses in the pipes.

Your dealer can help you designate the most convenient locations for the valves. The controller that actuates the valves should be placed in a protected area—ideally in your garage. It usually comes with a transformer that is plugged into a wall outlet.

Your dealer can price the materials so you can take them with you. Residential underground sprinklers cost from $600 to $1200. The most expensive single item is the controller which costs from $60 to $250. Valves are about $15 each. Heads run from $2.50 to $20 and polyethylene pipe is about $20 per 100 ft.

Following your sketch, arrange the parts on your lawn, but don't start cutting. You can spot any materials shortages, or you may want to make a last-minute layout change. When satisfied, drive a marker stake at each sprinkler location.

Starting from the supply valve, or valves if more than one water circuit is to be used, lay out the pipe according to plan. Cut it where necessary with a fine-toothed hack-saw to install the ells and tees. Remove any burrs, being careful not to damage the pipe. Fit clamps over the pipe

TYPICAL SPRINKLER HEADS

FOR FLOWER beds, shrubs, ground cover. Water discharges in horizontal streams. Used near homes and borders. Adjusts from .9 gpm at 1 p.s.i. to 1.5 gpm at 10 p.s.i.

Stream radius 2.5-4.5 ft.

Shrub bubbler

INSTALLED at ground level. Head pops up when water pressure is applied. Patterns available are: triangle, sector, semicircle and full circle. Discharge rate is adjustable so that differing watering demands can be met in a circuit controlled by one valve. Useful in ground depressions. Delivers from .25 gpm at 25 p.s.i. to 5 gpm at 30 p.s.i.

Stream radius 11-15 ft.

Adjustable precipitation spray head

USED FOR general watering. Large-radius sprinklers deliver moderate gallonage, can be adjusted to cover 45° to 315° areas. Full circles also available. Delivers from 1.1 gpm at 30 p.s.i. to 5.8 gpm at 50 p.s.i.

Stream radius 33-45 ft.

Adjustable part-circle gear-driven head

FOR SLOPES, beds, shrubs. Discharges spray at upward angle of 10°. Gentle spray minimizes runoff and puddling. Adjustable discharge rate. Types available deliver from .5 gpm at 15 p.s.i. to 2.1 gpm at 30 p.s.i.

Stream radius 13-16 ft.

Stream spray shrub head

NUMEROUS HEAD types are available. The total output (gpm) of heads on one line can't exceed the available water supply.

at both sides of a joint then insert the ends of the fitting. Tighten clamps for a watertight seal.

Next install the riser pipes at each tee and screw on the sprinkler heads. At the end of each line, install a drain valve. The valves close when water pressure is applied, so sprinklers get full pressure. When the controller switches off, the drain valve opens so residual water in the line leaks out. This prevents freezeups.

Connect the pipe of each circuit to the main water supply through an automatic valve that can be operated by the controller. Control lines from the valves run back to the controller. Each watering circuit should also have a manual shutoff valve preceding the automatic valve. The main supply line should be able to be shut off by one master valve.

The connection to the water supply line should be at the point of entry or an accessible location in the basement or garage. An antisyphon valve may be required to protect the water supply of your home against dirt and bacteria being sucked backward through the system.

The automatic controller shown is *electrically* powered for timekeeping functions but controls the automatic supply valves *hydraulically*. This tubing runs from each automatic valve to slip-on fittings on the controller. These are water-filled when installed. Winter draining isn't required.

flushing out and testing

Before the sprinklers are connected, flush out and test this system. Open the supply valves of the first watering circuit, allowing water to push out any dirt in the pipes. Run it for several minutes and check each joint for leaks. When the circuits have been flushed, turn off the water supply and install sprinkler heads. Turn on the water again to see that each sprinkler throws water evenly over the area intended.

The finished system should be buried only 5 to 6 in. below ground—you don't have to worry about freezing. Turn on the system, circuit by circuit, and let the water thoroughly soak and soften the ground. Then turn it off and cover each sprinkler with a plastic bag held by a rubber band to keep out dirt.

Using a flat spade, dig a V-trench under the pipe. The soaked sod should lift out in easily replaced wedges. When the trench is finished, ease the pipe and control lines into it. See that riser pipes leading to sprinkler heads are at proper level—so no one will trip over the head, or it won't be buried. Dig or fill the trench as needed; remove bags.

New for your home

CATCH THE WARM GLOW from this ponderosa pine light with rough-hewn wood trim. The natural materials are designed to fit in a casual setting. Slimmer and broader designs are also available. The lamp is about $150 from Thomas Ind., Louisville, KY 40202.

SURPRISINGLY, this tailored hardwood cabinet (8½ x 13½ x 4¾-in. high) contains a burglar alarm. The alarm has a sonic filter to detect entry sounds which trigger a loud siren. The alarm shuts off automatically. Solid-state circuitry in the alarm helps insure fail-safe performance. The alarm sells for about $250 and includes a three-year warranty. Manufactured by Sentron Manufacturing, Box 312, Barrington, IL 60010.

THE PAD PAINTER covers more area per paint dip than brushes or rollers. The absorbent pad prevents dripping. The Painter sells for about $5.50 from Tip Top Brush Co., Dept. PM, 151 W. Side Ave., Jersey City, NJ 07305.

COVER ROUGH walls with Imperial Wall Cover before you wallpaper. It's about $9 per roll from Imperial, 3645 Warrensville Center Rd., Cleveland OH 44122.

THE HEIGHT of good sensation in bathing may well be reached in this fiberglass whirlpool bathing oval by Kohler. The king-size 5½ x 7-ft. oval has six adjustable whirlpool jet heads. Baths start at about $1900 and jets at $70 from Kohler Co., Kohler WI 53044.

Pitch a room outdoors

**Backyard screenhouses offer portability, protection from rain and insects
and a touch of privacy, at low-to-moderate prices**

A STEEL FRAME supports the canvas roof and fiberglass screening of this 12x12-ft. screenhouse with a 7-ft., 4-in. center height. It costs about $110 from Outdoor Venture Corp., Stearns, KY 42647. They also make a polypropylene-roofed model that sells for around $70.

■ OUTDOOR LIVING is great—but not when it includes flies and mosquitoes, showers or too much sun. A screenhouse can keep these facts of nature from forcing you indoors and give you more living space, either at a campsite or in your backyard. You can spend as little as $50 or as much as $500 for a screenhouse, basing your choice on looks, convenience and durability (in the tent type, more expensive natural fabrics may outlast synthetics). All but the 12x18-footer on the facing page can travel with you and set up quickly.

THE FANCIEST of the tent-type houses from Sears is 10x14 ft., with an aluminum frame and an unusual D-shaped door. It sells for around $200. The roof is cotton and the screening is nylon. Carrying cases for the house and screen are available.

THE CASITA screenhouse is cartop-portable. Optional privacy panels allow cabana use. General Aluminum Products, Inc., Charlotte, MI 48813, makes the $375 11-panel model, others from $250. Montgomery Ward, Sears and J.C. Penney sell similar units.

THE CENTER is 8 ft. high in this Penney 12x12-ft. screenhouse with polyester screening and woven polyethylene roof. It's priced at $100, with others offered at about $50.

SEARS' LARGEST MODEL combines a 12x12-ft. screenhouse with a 6x12-ft. storage building for $500 (floor not included). This one may require approval from your local building department.

TWO BIG PICNIC TABLES fit inside the 10x14-ft. screenhouse shown below. It's about $175 from Eureka Tent, Inc. Binghamton, NY 13902. The dining canopy shown at the lower right sells for about $25 from Sunshine Cover & Tarp, Inc., Chatsworth, CA 91311.

Energy-saving products

THE NEW WINDOW glass Solarcool, by PPG Industries, reflects solar radiation to reduce the cost of cooling your home in warm weather. It's a bronze reflective glass that has a mirror-like coating. You can use it on windows and patio doors. The cost is about 40 percent more than conventional double-strain clear window glass, but this should be made up in savings in air-conditioning costs.

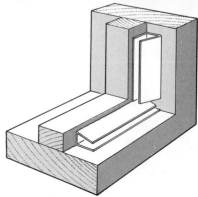

THIS DO-IT-YOURSELF sealing strip for inside and outside doors seals off heat loss, noise and weather. Measure the length needed, cut with scissors and press the adhesive backing to the jamb. The Polyflex seal comes in tan, black and white. Sealing strip for one 36-in.-wide door is about $5. It is from Schlegel, Weather Seal Group, Box 197, Rochester, NY 14601.

LATEST ALUMINUM siding from Reynolds comes with a polystyrene backing to help insulate homes. Weep holes prevent any moisture from building up. The siding comes in smooth or rough wood, or shadow-grain patterns in acrylic or vinyl finish. The cost is said to be only 10 percent more than siding without backing. This energy-saving product is made by Reynolds Metals Co., Richmond, VA 23261.

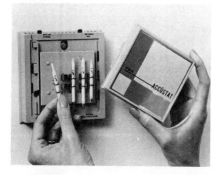

ACCUSTAT IS a solid-state thermostat with a mercury sensor that responds precisely and immediately to temperature change. The cost begins at about $20. PSG Industries, 1125 Tunnel Rd., Perkasie, PA 18944.

THE OVEN of this unique gas range operates by convection to save energy. A stream of heated air is forced back into the oven instead of being vented into the kitchen. The burners are operated by electric ignition to eliminate the need for pilot lights. This reduces gas consumption considerably. It is sold by Montgomery Ward from about $540.

So what's new in cars?

By ED NELSON

The auto industry is in turmoil. Almost every car is on a diet—even the Cadillac Eldorado has shed 1300 pounds. Russian cars are invading Canada, and manufacturers not only are importing domestics—they're building foreign cars in the U.S.!

NEW CARS OF 1979 rolled onstage at a time of auto-industry tumult. Continuing U.S. downsizing was no surprise, but action in company boardrooms brought changes around the world. New alliances and new locations portended changes in iron and steel.

The line between "domestics" and "imports" faded. Detroit brought "captive imports" to the States and foreign makers moved to set up plants here.

GM's program to shrink cars for fuel economy—while saving inside space—reached the last of its full-size luxury cars. Cadillac Eldorado, Olds Toronado, and the front-drive Buick Riviera now shared a 114-inch wheelbase. On a rigid diet, they shed nearly 2 feet and 1300 pounds, approaching Cadillac's Seville.

Eldorado lost about 20 inches overall, from 224 to about 204. Its base engine was now a fuel-injected version of the Olds 350. A diesel option was due in mid-year.

Coming from 227.5 inches overall, Toronado lost virtually 22. The same 350, gas or diesel, was now Toronado's basic engine.

Riviera, with a 350 last year, got a turbocharged 231-CID V-8 for '79. Smallest of the three, it lost the least in the de-fatting drive, coming from 218.2 inches overall to about 205.

understated new Mustang

Ford and Chrysler brought out dramatic new '79s, while GM saved its big news for the spring. Ford's new Mustang and Capri were on a short Fairmont/Zephyr platform, but Mustang was slightly longer. Its wheelbase grew about 4 inches while Capri's came down about half an inch. Both weighed a bit less.

Nearly chromeless, Mustang's understated look appealed to more sophisticated tastes. Buffs watched to see whether it stayed clean. Lincoln-Mercury now builds Capri here rather than bringing it from Germany. Its sides were pinched slightly at the waist.

Both cars had flexible urethane bumpers, dual rectangular headlights, and wraparound taillights. And both boasted rack-and-pinion steering.

Bigger Ford cars, LTD and Mercury Marquis, shrank significantly outside, although interior dimensions lost little. Each got a squared-off shell. A mini spare saved luggage space.

Lincoln Continental, Mark V, and Versailles got minimal changes for '79. Continental and Mark V body styles were scheduled to fade out after this year, so the corporation plans special "collectors' models" in the fall.

This was also the last year for the intermediate body shared by LTD II, Cougar and T-Bird. Pinto's and Bobcat's subcompact shell is due for replacement with front-drive models for 1981.

Chrysler broadened its Dodge Omni/Plymouth Horizon lines with new two-door, 2+2 hatchbacks high-lighted by a large, triangular rear-quarter window behind a heavy C-pillar. Wheelbases were 2½ inches shorter.

The two-doors were to be called Dodge Solo and Plymouth Mirada, but Chrysler finally settled on Omni O 24 and Horizon TC3. The names' future seemed cloudy. Dodge public relations, for example, noted that "an O 24 decal" was available—but kept calling the Omni "the 2+2."

The new Dodge St. Regis, Chrysler Newport and New Yorker were on 118.5-inch wheelbases. Newport and New Yorker lost 7 to 11 inches overall.

a new day at AMC

American Motors began 1979 with the newest look in Detroit. Its cars were little changed, but its marketing position was "all new." AMC and Renault began formal work toward "a definitive and legally binding pact."

Sneak preview of the 1980 models—is your next car shown here?

Automotive News photo

SURREPTITIOUS PHOTO shows the prototype of 1980 Buick Skylark four-door notchback. It will share its body with the '80 Olds Omega.

Automotive News photo

THIS IS BELIEVED to be a lightweight, two-door front-wheel-drive van that Ford is considering for introduction sometime in the mid-'80s.

Ron Lieberson photo

UNOFFICIAL PHOTO of the 1980 Chevy Nova (without windshield trim) shows new grille, single rectangular headlight, wide hatchback.

Ron Lieberson photo

1980 PONTIAC PHOENIX will be available in two-door notchback, four-door hatchback. Hatchbacks are particularly wide, perhaps influenced by AMC Pacer.

As 1979 began, more AMC dealers were to be selling Renault's R-5, recently rechristened "Le Car." Renault provided credits to hard-pressed American Motors, but had "no plans" to buy any part of it. Late in 1979 or early in 1980 AMC was scheduled to start assembling Renault's R-18 at Kenosha, WI. Later, it may stamp out body panels.

R-18, a 1-ton, five-passenger four-door, bowed last April in Paris. One report called it "a fine little family car," but said it had sudden, radical changes in understeer with changing throttle loads. Drivers were told to reach cruising speed before changing up to 4th gear, since it had little punch. That fit AMC's image.

The agreement stood to benefit both Renault and AMC. AMC faced stiff impending federal mpg demands under the CAFE (Corporate Average Fuel Economy) program. A European economy car in the product line could help.

And Renault could realize helpful economics of scale by hiking component production—even if cars were assembled elsewhere. It had no more than 300 U.S. dealers. AMC had about 1600, with 30 to 35 (including about half of its biggest 10) already selling Renaults, too.

For '79, AMC built the Spirit—a renamed and facelifted Gremlin. A sporty two-door hatchback GT got a 304 V-8 option. That model was once to be called Javelin, later Aurora or Avenger. AMC was to put a 2.4-liter Pontiac Four in some Spirits, probably for 1980. Its entire Jeep line was to be redesigned and lightened for '80 and '81.

to build Volvos here?

Other foreign firms were also active. Volvo and Saab edged toward a link of some kind—until the Norwegian government picked up an interest in Saab. Volvo continued seeking some way to make good use of a Chesapeake, VA, assembly plant acquired in the mid-70's. Weakening U.S. dollars made the move appealing: Since U.S. sales of Volvos bring less valuable currency, it's smart to use that currency building cars here.

U.S. assembly of Volvos still looked four or five years off, however. U.S. introduction of Volvo's little 343—a take-off from the Daf—was likely to take another couple of years. Safety and emissions standards were thorny problems.

The world auto industry seemed to follow VW, which finally put its Westmoreland, PA, plant into action. VW said it would build 800 Rabbits a day there.

Honda, too, sought a U.S. assembly facility. Industry specialists doubted one could be in preparation before 1981. But if, as expected, Honda introduced its sporty Action 2—a short-rear-deck 2+2—in 1979, the lack of new assembly capacity was forecast to build corporate strain. Production of both Civic and Accord was already using full capability and some said a new car would have to wait until '81. However, some capacity overlap might be possible.

As '79 began, lines between the communist and noncommunist auto worlds also blurred. Canadian Peter Dennis began importing a little U.S.S.R. car close to the Fiat 125. Punsters enjoyed its name; despite its size, they said, "It's a Lada car." Dennis said it might be the world's only car meant for terrain rougher than Canada's. In Russia, he said, "They have potholes in their potholes." Lada's $3495 Canadian price included both a 15 percent duty and a 12 percent sales tax.

top GM news is coming

Top '79 product news wasn't the cars introduced last fall, but the front-drive GM subcompacts due out in mid-year. Corporate gymnastics continued up to the last minute on whether to call them late '79s or early '80s. When they do bow, they'll bring a new, 60° cast iron V-6. Its 160 inches of piston displacement should give the little cars plenty of dash.

During its early development, Pontiac reportedly planned an aluminum block. Now such a block is expected for 1982 models. And Pontiac has been eyeing diesel and turbo-diesel possibilities.

Rumors built toward a crescendo around John Z. DeLorean, the maverick GM exec who jumped the corporate ladder as he neared its top. DeLorean quit as a GM vice-president and Chevy general manager and set out to build his own car. He formed DeLorean Motors and proposed the DMC-12, a sleek, radically styled luxury sport.

As '79 approached, DeLorean hadn't yet stumbled. He'd decided to set up in Puerto Rico. The Securities and Exchange Commission, watchdog for investors, gave him a clean bill of health. He signed up scores of dealers. And Renault agreed to provide differentials, manual and automatic transmissions, and engines—2.6-liter V-6s. Whether DeLorean would add turbochargers was unclear.

But there was no doubt that the field of cars generally was more and more supercharged.

FOR GROUP CAMPING, the peaked blizzard-shedding four-man tents offer warm shelter in the worst weather.

New ways to camp in the cold

By JIM ELDER

A BACKPACK two-man tent with fly, sleeping bags, small stove, freeze-dried food, cook gear, spare clothes, parts and tools are the essentials for a couple.

■ DO CROWDED SUMMER campsites get you down? Biting bugs keep you in? Short summer seasons freeze you out? Many campers are finding a fine new time of year out in the snow and are taking to snowshoes, cross-country skis, backpacks and snowmobiles to try out the new sport.

Heavy old-fashioned summer gear loaded on weighty cargo sleds originally bogged us down. These "trailers" for snowmobiles increased fuel consumption, decreased mobility and radius of action, and compromised fun. One ridiculous rig might have buried snow-camping forever. It was fittingly shaped like a coffin and had skis that were too long to follow a trail turn. It would open out to sleep four—if you ever got it to your destination.

But now the trend is to light gear and efficient insulated clothing that can retain the warmth. We've learned from backpackers that small tents

NO SNOWMOBILE cargo sled is needed over a weekend. A Pak Rak on the rear can carry all this equipment.

WEIGHT OF CAMPERS inside, along with long snow pegs and guy lines to snowmobiles, holds tent in place.

are easier to pack along and keep warm in than big ones when only two are on the trail. There's no need, it has been found, to build huge melt-into-a-pit bonfires. With supplies from any backpacking or ski-touring shop and perhaps a side visit to a cycle dealer, you can outfit two snowmobilers, on two machines, for a weekend in the woods in the snow and not load them down so that a cargo sled is needed. Easier still are trips where fuel is available along the way or has been cached in advance.

what to leave behind

What else do you need? Let's start with what you can leave behind: A big, heavy canvas tent, an ax, a big campstove, catalytic heater, gas lantern, weighty air mattress, cast-iron skillets and expedition-size down sleeping bags. The big tent and lantern make sense at an extended-stay base camp, and the catalytic is a luxury there for drying and warming. But folding saws work as well as axes and are safer. By switching to these types of compact items, we've eliminated a cargo-sled load of gear and a lot of weight and "hassles."

A tent does not warm you—it simply keeps your own warmth in and the snow out, so a small backpacking tent is fine. It should be strong, have a waterproof floor, be double-roofed with a rain fly. Self-supporting designs require fewer pegs and save the time required to bury deadman sticks. Short pegs won't hold in snow, so special stakes or branches must be buried securely to anchor guy lines. Unless you want to wake up with a frosted face from your own breathing,

moisture must escape. Rain-fly designs allow this. Pick a good "mountain" tent.

Inside, and on top of a compact closed-cell foam pad, you don't need 20 blankets or a fortune in goose down. Though down still offers best insulation, it absorbs moisture and can be difficult to air-dry on gray winter days. Many campers have switched to synthetics. Your bag should have good shoulder and head hooding, adjustable to your metabolism and the weather.

If your present bag isn't quite warm enough, consider adding an inexpensive liner or outside cover. And what do you wear inside? Ideally nothing. The best is dry underwear, dry socks and a stocking cap. Do *not* sleep in your snow-suit; you'll be colder during the night and all the next day. Dry out damp clothes on your warm snowmobile engine underneath the hood.

Cook with light nesting backpackers' pots rather than the familiar iron skillet. Serve in large soft plastic bowls, like those for feeding the cat. Plastic cups, too. They hold heat longer than metal plates and cups. Keep menus simple with freeze-dried items, but remember to bring enough stove fuel to melt a lot of snow for them. Small one-burner stoves cut weight and bulk; carry two of them. A Pak Rak, from Haines, OR, will hold cargo on the back of your machine. Camera, binoculars and portable CB can get a softer ride in front of you in a motorcycle "tank bag" from Eclipse, Ann Arbor, MI. It anchors on with riveted D-rings and Velcro straps.

Ralph Plaisted's North Pole snowmobile expedition proved you can now camp anywhere in the cold with the great new gear available.

Import outboards join the big leagues

By BILL McKEOWN

Tests show they're good, but have the little imports got what it takes to stand up to the American brands? Here's a look at a couple of outboards that have Japanese innards but American names

ARE OUTBOARD OWNERS, like photographers, swinging toward gear with foreign names? Already, brands like Volvo-Penta from Sweden; Honda, Suzuki and Yamaha from Japan; Seagull from Great Britain, and Carnitti from Italy are mixed in along the waterfront with Evinrude, Eska, Johnson, Mercury, Clinton, Chrysler and others.

It's no secret that some of these little mills from overseas are made with dependable craftsmanship and can push a light hull right along with good fuel economy. Often they offer moderate-speed action at a slight price advantage, though at present no import goes enough above 100 hp to compete with our big muscle machines.

For our spot checks, we tested two with Japanese innards and American names—the Mariner, a line like Mercury that is a division of Brunswick Corp., and Spirit, marketed by Arctic Enterprises. Both are available in many parts of the United States. Both, like other imports we have tested in the past, proved to be good performers with emphasis on rugged workhorse qualities and lower rpm and speed.

But performance may not be the payoff. Overseas builders have been used to selling to the commercial fisherman or back-country boatman who does his own maintenance and repairs. Americans expect corner service station service for their cars and boats. Outboard importers in the past have failed when they set up no parts and service network. Shop the imports—if they offer what you want, from a dealer you can trust.

MARINER

PLENTY OF PERFORMANCE is packed into the Mariner-14 outboard line that runs from 2 up to 140 hp. At Brunswick's test base, we pushed a little Fletcher runabout to 41.4 mph with a Mariner 60-hp motor.

SPIRIT

SPIRIT PROVIDES a pick of nine horsepower ratings, plus accessories ranging from a backpack motor cover-toter (right) to a Heavy Hauler trailer for your boat as well. The 4.5-hp unit (above) conveniently mounts extra shear pins inside a flip-down door in the cowl enclosure. A camouflage-color protective cover is also available. Horsepower range includes 2, 4.5, 5, 9.9, 16, 20, 25, 50 and 65. The larger motors provide the options of electric start, long and short shaft lengths and CD ignition with surface-gap plugs.

PICK A PRAM or dinghy, bass or johnboat, runabout or utility—a Mariner power range is designed to fit it.

UNDER A HOOD with American styling, Japanese motor shows good engineering from both sides of Pacific.

TWO OF THE models proving popular in the Mariner line are the 28-hp workhorse (at left) and the little 2-hp (right) for small craft.

TOPPING OUT at 65 horses, the newest and biggest of the Spirits offers a long shaft, electric starting, emergency stop switch and lively performance from the Suzuki mill installed under the hood. Providing power for Coleman's slick new canoe (above, right) a Spirit 2-hp mill has enough push to speed the canoe along or even flip it. Midrange models in 15-inch and 20-inch shaft lengths showed good acceleration during runabout performance tests (right). For the larger engines, a rubber slip clutch replaces shear pin holding the prop choice.

FROM LEFT: Grumman canoe model, $26; Cypress Gardens Ski-Pro, $33; Stearns Sans-Souci Sportsvest, $35; Cypress

New styles for staying afloat

By BILL MCKEOWN

THROWABLE $10 buoyant cushion is safe only when worn across the chest (as shown by a Cypress Gardens, FL, water skier) to float the swimmer in a face-up position.

■ TWO GIANT STEPS have been taken recently to keep us alive on the water.

One is a new law making it illegal to go out on any kind of boat without a life preserver along.

The second development improves the looks and fit of preservers so much that a boatman is tempted to wear one instead of stowing it out of reach and sight.

Any boat—and that now means rafts, rowboats, canoes, kayaks, sailboats, skiffs, anything you can paddle or power or sail away from land—must carry the right preserver for each person aboard if the waterway is under Coast Guard jurisdiction. You don't even have to be aboard; if you're out on water skis, a preserver for you must be carried aboard the towboat. The rules apply just about anywhere you might go boating. State laws have been passed to cover waters that don't come under Federal regulations, and sometimes are more strict than the Coast Guard requirements.

During 1971, a Federal Boat Safety Act was passed to update a number of recreational watercraft laws, and since then additional changes have been made. For a while, exceptions were allowed for canoeists who claimed they needed to wear more flexible nonapproved

Gardens vinyl jacket, $35; Stearns Pee Wee Sans Souci, $20; Cypress Gardens Tech-1, $37; and Stearns Windjammer Jacket.

vests in order to paddle easily. Now, however, light loosely fitting vests have received Coast Guard okay and all boatmen must follow the rules.

Latest requirements are quite straightforward. Life preservers are called Personal Flotation Devices (PFDs), and must be labeled "Coast Guard Approved Equipment" which shows they have been examined and comply with CG specifications as to materials used, construction and performance. Some preservers, such as ski belts and Mae West types that are inflated by CO_2 cartridge or mouth are not approved because they might not keep a wearer upright or do not inflate automatically if he is unconscious. They are useful to have along, but will not count as legal equipment if you are stopped by a Coast Guard or state mobile boarding team.

PFDs are now classified by type. The length of your boat plus the number of passengers determines the number and type of PFDs needed.

• **Type 1.** This is a large bulky vest intended for use aboard commercial vessels, but is also legal for pleasure craft use.

• **Type 2.** These buoyant vests, in various models, have a "Positive Righting Moment" intended to turn you face up in the water. For children who weigh less than 30 pounds, only this type (in a suitable size) is acceptable.

• **Type 3.** Buoyant devices in this category are designed for active water sport without restricting the wearer. While they won't necessarily turn you face up in the water, they are designed to support you in a stable upright position, also to be comfortable and good-looking, and are worth wearing all the time you are afloat. Some look like attractive fishing vests with lots of pockets and are made in many colors (in an emergency brighter colors might be easier to see). Others are full-sleeved jackets that can help ward off that other overboard danger—hypothermia—death from water-chill. Type 3 PFDs are legal for any size recreational boat.

• **Type 4.** This "throwable device" category includes the old familiar buoyant cushion and ring life buoy. If worn, the cushion must be across the *chest* (it's better to put it on in the water) with opposite arm and leg or head and leg through the grab loops. It can lose buoyancy after being used as a makeshift fender or cushion, but it's still legal.

• **Type 5.** These are special-purpose PFDs where no other type is suitable. A model with

SPECIALTY JACKETS offer worthwhile extras for added costs. The Stearns Windjammer at about $70 (above, far left) has good looks plus warmth to fight submersion chill. The Skyjacket, Simpson Marine, Torrance, CA, uses an attached parachute with a ripcord. The vests on the right are from Cypress Gardens Skis and Stearns.

extra buoyancy for white-water rafting is an example.

There you have the five basic preserver categories. To be legal, each must have a USCG Approval label, be in good condition, be the right size to fit the person who might wear it and be readily available.

THOUGH NONAPPROVED, multipurpose inflatable-type PFDs like Stearns's Angler's Vest (upper left) and Boater's Jacket (lower right) take little space. Stearns Kindergärd (upper right) is approved for children under 30 pounds. The pants match hunting vest PFDs.

On recreational boats less than 16 feet long, you can get by with one Type 4 boat cushion for each person aboard, although a Type 1, 2 or 3 wearable PFD would be better. Boats 16 feet or longer must now have a suitable Type 1, 2 or 3 for each person *plus* at least one throwable Type 4 aboard.

Canoes and kayaks, of any length, can also count Type 4 cushions (or rings) as well as Types 1, 2, and 3 as the required device for each person. Any smart paddler, however, would wear one of the new light Type 3 canoe vests especially designed for active boating.

Once you are fully equipped with legal PFDs, don't overlook the supplemental nonapproved flotation devices available. Vests that inflate by mouth or CO_2 cartridge can often fit compactly under a windbreaker, foulweather jacket or even a snowmobile suit and give added protection. Inflatables may be harder to maintain in good condition and won't blow up if you are unconscious (hence no Coast Guard approval). But they can still keep you afloat until help comes. Simple water-ski belts are useful if you take a spill and get knocked breathless, although tournament skiers and jumpers usually wear the new approved free-action models.

So which PFD will be the best for you? Each person has a different buoyancy requirement, and it's best to borrow several used models and test them in shallow water. Then pick a type you find comfortable and good-looking—one you're likely to wear all the time afloat!

Best gear of the year

Whether it is for camping, fishing, photos or any other kind of outdoor activity the sporting goods manufacturers seem to come up with clever ideas and quality products year after year. Here are some of our favorites chosen from the many we have seen recently

EACH YEAR we like to look over the hundreds of outdoor products we've examined—and in many cases field-tested—and pick our favorites. Many deserve recognition as outstanding new accessories or established aids for outdoorsmen; some could make good gifts.

for fishing

The Shakespeare Wondereel 1810 looks like a closed-face spinning reel, but has no thumb button on the back. It mounts at the bottom of your Wonderod just as a fly reel would and you grip the comfortable cork handle with your full hand, the line running over your forefinger for easy control. To cast, the reel is cranked backward about an eighth of a turn. This frees the line just as you would by pushing the thumb button or flipping over the bail of conventional spinning reels. Cast with your forefinger feathering the line and stopping it when it's right on target. The ingenious system isn't new but is simplicity itself and deserves special attention. It lets you concentrate on fishing without time out for the mechanics of the reel.

Also of fishing interest is a bright orange glove from 3M called a Gotcha Mitt. A textured palm makes fish-holding a lot easier.

for outdoor photos

The Minox 35EL is probably the smallest, lightest, quality full-frame 35-mm camera around. It looks almost old-fashioned as you fold down the miniature front cover to expose the sharp f/2.8 lens. But the results are modern all right, and a built-in meter automatically adjusts for exposure. At 8 ounces including film, the tiny unit won't weigh down a pocket and fits neatly into any backpack.

For underwater breathing, our staff testers have been diving with the Poseidon Systems Cyklon 300 regulator and report it is not only easier to use but has been found to operate dependably upside down and in all other positions they have tried—something that some scuba regulators fail to do.

for camping

For a small multipurpose tool, the Skatchet, from Charter Arms, fits easily into a pack and can be used for a knife or hammer. Screw a branch into the threaded socket in the bottom and it becomes a hatchet, pruning hook or mini-ax.

Royal Red Ball has for fishermen a Lunker wading shoe that we find comes ashore to become a comfortable camp and hiking boot as well. The mesh uppers allow water to flow out easily, and the Lunkers can be worn over hip-waders, socks or just bare feet.

And for a rubber hiking boot to keep the water out, the new Red Ball Waterdog is ankle high with the popular padded collar and a traditional hobnail cleated sole. Inside any boot, a new imported slipper-shaped oversock they call a Bama Sokket is claimed to wick away sweat while making uninsulated boots warm for winter wear.

You won't rate a ground cloth as a favorite accessory until you've spent a few weekends at muddy campsites and unpacked plastic sheeting that has torn since you last saw it. But Versa Tarp, produced by Griffolyn in Houston, TX., is almost impossible to tear—even when punctured. In five sizes from 6x8 to 12x20 feet, it's plastic and waterproof, has one green side plus a white side that can double well as a photo reflector. It can keep wind, rain, snow or mud where it belongs.

Special credit is due to the Coleman Company for upgrading some of its products already standard in the camping field. Automatic shut-offs on catalytic heaters and an automatic ignition system with a blower purge cycle of 15 seconds before fire-up of their RV furnaces make safe equipment even safer.

And for an extra pocket when your hands are already full, we like L.L. Bean's Belt Pack, and its fisherman's Tackle Bags to carry extra photo gear, a rain jacket, binoculars or whatever.

Great new tools for gardeners

FOR A LITTLE or a lot of work, try pruners from Ashflash Corp. South Norwalk, CT.

WEED PROBLEMS? You'll be glad to know about this double-edge brush cutter. It's good for trimming around objects. Ames, Parkersburg, WV.

BET YOU can't break these pruners! Blades are chrome-armored for harder-than-steel durability. They are from True Friends, Teaneck, NJ.

IN GARDENING WORK from planting to weeding, you'll find the proper tools can make a world of difference in how well and how fast you do your work—not to mention how much you enjoy it. The tools below and on the next two pages not only help you do the job, but are attractive as well. With them you can perform the many small chores that keep your lawn and garden in top condition. Some are all-purpose tools that can fill other needs; you may want to carry them in your car or on camping trips. Several are used by professional gardeners and are especially strong and long-lasting.

GRASS SHEARS to keep your lawn well manicured. You can get them from Ashflash Corp., South Norwalk, CT.

GET SUPER-SERVICE from this weeder-rooter (below left). Tines do the weeding and a straight edge cuts roots. The multi-purpose Pic 'n Planter (middle) plants bulbs, furrows and more. The rounded shape of the Hoe-Down (right) reduces drag for efficient garden work. From Mark Stephens, Sherman Oaks, CA 91403.

THESE GARDEN TOOLS can take care of your outdoor jobs and look good doing it—no small feat—but they are not ordinary tools. 1. Here's a double-edged pruning saw for clean branch cuts. Give the branch underside a few upward cuts with the fine-toothed edged, then cut downward with the coarse teeth. 2. The teeth of this limbing saw are in groups of four: Two cut on the push stroke and two cut on the pull stroke for zipping through branches. 3. This five-quart English gardener's watering can has a 28-inch spout for watering hard-to-get-to plants. 4. Here's a scoop trowel with contoured plastic handle for a comfortable grip. 5. The three-point pivot system of this hand pruner enables you to make clean cuts with surprising ease. 6. They still make 'em like they used to. This garden sprayer with solid copper tank and seamless solid brass pump is proof. 7. Another trowel, but with a difference. This fine-point trowel is for delicate weeding. All from Brookstone, Peterborough, NH 03458.

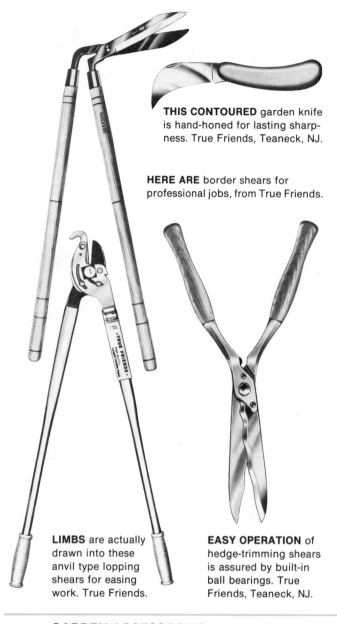

THIS CONTOURED garden knife is hand-honed for lasting sharpness. True Friends, Teaneck, NJ.

HERE ARE border shears for professional jobs, from True Friends.

GRASS SHEAR with add-on handle is powered by Disston's cordless Powerpack that snaps in the shear. It recharges from an electrical outlet.

LIMBS are actually drawn into these anvil type lopping shears for easing work. True Friends.

EASY OPERATION of hedge-trimming shears is assured by built-in ball bearings. True Friends, Teaneck, NJ.

DISSTON'S POWERPACK also snaps in to get power to the cordless electric shrub trimmer (and other tools); it's back to an outlet for recharge.

GARDEN ACCESSORIES

PUT GARDEN and kitchen waste in at the top and you collect good compost for your garden at the bottom. The unit packs flat. From Rotocrop, New Hope, PA.

INDOOR WATERING HOSE? That's right. It connects to most kitchen or bathroom faucets and extends 50 feet. Casaplanta, Van Nuys, CA.

Most versatile vise

By HARRY WICKS

■ LABELED BENCH BUDDY by its maker, the vise shown here has earned a permanent niche in my workshop. It is lightweight, easy to use and does not have to stay in one fixed spot on the workbench edge.

This tool's biggest plus is its versatility. The bench clamp is fitted on bench edge and then the vise can be affixed in one of three work positions—45°, 90° or 180°. The speed button takes some getting used to. Frequently, I found myself turning the handle when I should have been pressing the button.

Though priced a bit higher than regular vises, this tool is a dandy addition to a one-vise shop.

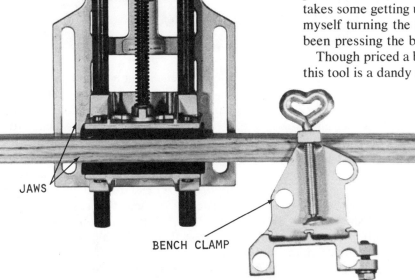

TIGHTENING HANDLE

SPEED BUTTON

JAWS

BENCH CLAMP

VERSATILE VISE is used as above when maximum workpiece support is needed.

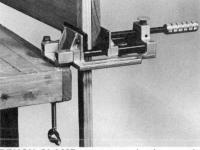

BENCH CLAMP stays put; vise is repositioned 180° from the position shown at left.

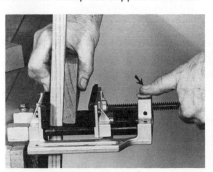

BUTTON PERMITS fast change of setup, eliminates excessive cranking of jaws.

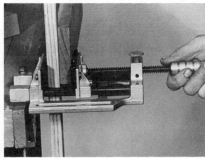

FINAL TIGHTENING to hold workpiece secure is done by turning the handle.

SPECIFICATIONS—BENCH BUDDY VISE

Jaw width: 4 in.
Jaw height: 1⅜ in.
Maximum jaw opening: 4 in.
Vise working angles: 45°, 90°, 180°.
Cast aluminum body; replaceable hardened steel jaws
Price: about $35.
Coastal Abrasive & Tool Co., Box 337, Trumbull, CT 06611. At hardware and home centers; write maker for nearest dealer.

Metalworking tools for home repairs

By PENELOPE ANGELL

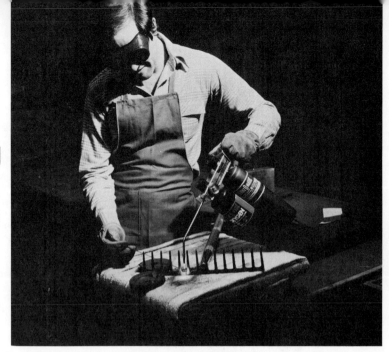

■ IF YOU'VE EVER wanted to set up a metalworking shop, but thought the cost prohibitive—here's good news. You can buy soldering, welding and other metalworking tools designed for home use at prices in line with woodworking tools. Many power tools are under $50 and make it possible to reclaim broken metal objects you would have thrown away.

Having metalworking tools can open up a whole new area of home repair and shop projects. You can make electrical repairs; fix fireplace equipment; repair play equipment from swings to bikes; mend boat propellers and shafts, fix car mufflers and tailpipes and a lot more.

Building stereo and hi-fi equipment or fixing a leaky mailbox seam are jobs where soldering tools come in handy. Use guns, irons and electric pencils to join metal wires or seam two pieces of light metal together.

Weller makes soldering guns that range from 100 to 325 watts. They have a dual-heat control for low and high temperatures, so you can use low heat on sensitive components, then switch to high heat if needed.

Disston makes a cordless soldering gun. There's no cord to get tangled in your work at the bench. It has a rechargeable power unit that also powers a screwdriver and several garden-tool attachments.

Another cordless tool, a soldering iron from Weller, makes on-site repairs possible. The handle holds a battery unit that gives enough heat for about 15 minutes of soldering before it needs recharging. You can solder wiring connections where an outlet isn't within reach or work on a yard tractor outside.

An electric pencil that heats to 700° F. comes in a Black & Decker solder and craft kit with metal tips for soldering, foil writing and wood or leather burning. Cost of the kit is about $10.

Brazing, also called silver soldering, can be done with Microflame's gas welding torch. Brazing is like soldering but done at higher temperatures (over 800° F.) and with a different solder. The Microflame torch comes with its own small gas cylinders, a butane tip for larger flames, a spark-lighter, brazing rods and flux for about $36.

The BernzOmatic OX5000 oxygen cutting/welding torch is a compact tool combining oxygen with either propane or Mapp gas. It cuts up to ¼-in. steel plate and ¾-in. bolts, besides welding, brazing and soldering.

The miniature welding and brazing kit by Victor includes a torch using oxygen and acetylene to produce a 6000° F. flame. This will fuse-weld up to 16-gauge steel. It comes with oxygen and acetylene regulators, spark-lighter, goggles and instruction booklet.

The Weldanpower 150 by Lincoln has a 4500-watt a.c. generator and a 450-volt a.c. arc welder. The auxiliary generator not only makes the welder portable and able to be used for outside repairs, but it can also provide output to operate other equipment.

Mild steel bar, tubing and channels can be bent with Di-Acro hand-operated steel benders. You can make wrought-iron* furniture and other shapes. The lightest model No. 1 bends up to $^3/_{16}$-in. round mild steel bar and $^5/_{16}$-in. 16-gauge steel tubing. Bender costs about $200; its stand, $130.

Rivets can join two pieces of metal together if

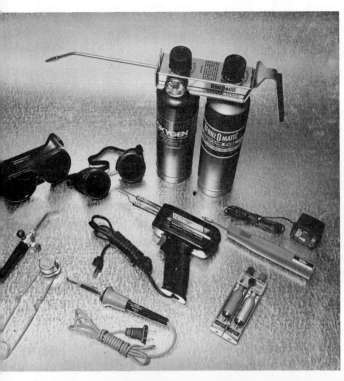

SIX METALWORKING TOOLS (left) for home repairs are (clockwise from left): Victor mini welding torch; BernzOmatic oxygen cutting and welding torch; Weller cordless soldering iron; Microflame mini torch; Black & Decker electric pencil; (center) Weller soldering gun.

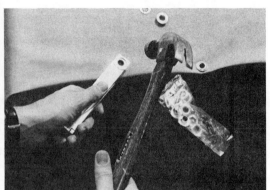

USE LUDELL'S GROMMET tool to repair canvas covers and furniture. It's about $2 with 10 grommets.

THE STIFFENER from this plow blade (left) is welded back in place with a Weldanpower 150 from Lincoln Electric, Cleveland. The arc welder has its own generator and sells for about $645.

THE FAN (right) is repaired with Disston's Powerpack Soldergun. The rechargeable Powerpack snaps into the gun to provide power. The Soldergun with Powerpack sells for about $25.

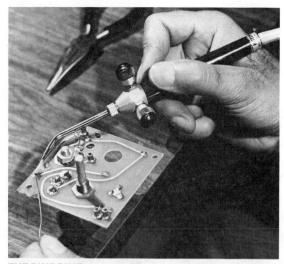

THE PINPOINT oxy-acetylene flame of this Victor torch is suited to precision work such as the circuit board shown. The unit costs about $90.

THE DI-ARCO BENDER shown above is designed to bend wrought iron and steel. You can use it in your shop to make handsome metal furniture.

THE MINI TORCH from Microflame is useful for light repairs and craft work.

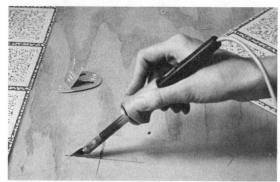

BLACK & DECKER'S electric pencil can also be used for foil writing and wood or leather burning.

THE WELLER SOLDERING GUN, about $15, has a low and high heat control. It can be used for repairing electrical parts and building stereo equipment.

THE BERNZOMATIC torch (below, left) brazes a copper pipe and fittings. It's about $40. The Wiss pipe and duct snips (middle), about $10, cuts pipe and sheet metal. Weller's cordless iron (right), about $25, makes outdoor repairs easy.

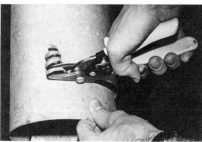

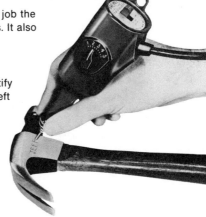

POLISHING TOOLS is one job the Dremel Moto-tool performs. It also removes rust.

YOU CAN MARK on steel to identify your valuables and discourage theft with Dremel's electric engraver. The tool sells for about $15.

RIVETING is a sure way to fasten light metals. The Swingline (left) and USM (below) riveters help with many repairs.

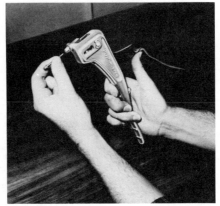

THE STANLEY TOOLS (below) shape metal and other materials. Clockwise from left: duckbill snips, $6.35; adjustable handle plane, $10.20; shaver, $2.65; round file, about $5.35. All tools should be available at your local hardware dealer.

soldering or welding aren't convenient. Rivet guns pictured on these pages are ideal for joining gutters and downspouts or securing aluminum windows.

You can probably use drills you have with a set of metalworking (high-speed steel) bits. Only a metal-cutting blade is needed for many electric saws.

Your pliers, wrenches, files, screwdrivers and ball-peen hammer can also be used on metal projects. A grinding wheel can sharpen the blades of your woodworking tools and can also be used to shape metal stock (but wear safety goggles).

If you enjoy woodworking, you might think of metalworking as an extension of your woodworking interest. When you're able to cut home repair bills, metalworking will be an interest that also pays off.

GET THE PICTURE? Suppose your camera normally uses a 50-mm lens. If the close-in view (right) made with a 24-48-mm lens is near normal, then you can zoom out to a wider angle shot (above left) to get exactly what you want in the frame.

Zoom lenses— now they're wide-angle, too

By DAVE SAGARIN

■ THESE NEW ZOOM lenses help you picture a wide, wide view. And we've tested an armload of the exciting new versions.

The blessings of zooms are well known. You pop in one lens that serves in place of three or four. You save cost and weight and don't miss

VIVITAR SERIES I
24-48 MM F/3.8

VIVITAR SERIES I
35-85 MM
VARI-FOCAL F/2.8

SOLIGOR 35-105 MM
MACRO-ZOOM F/3.5

VIVITAR 35-105 MM
MACRO-ZOOM F/3.5

SIGMA XQ
39-80 MM F/3.5

VIVITAR 70-150 MM
MACRO-ZOOM F/3.8

TAMRON 70-150 MM
ZOOM F/3.5

ZOOMING IS FUN, especially with this Soligor 100-300-mm f/5 macrozoom lens. It is good for zoom shots of sports, travelers in open country and wildlife. It has a macro range and is easy to use.

any shots by fumbling to change lenses. You frame and shoot exactly the image you want.

On the other hand, zooms usually cost more than any one lens in their range. They're heavier, bulkier and need longer exposures in dark situations. Design problems result in poorer resolution, especially at the corners.

Modern design has solved some of these problems. We're getting zooms with shorter focal lengths, wider ranges from short to long, while the overall sharpness is better and maximum apertures are getting faster. Multi-coatings reduce flair and permit *more* pieces inside for better performance, all at reasonable prices.

The 24-48-mm f/3.8 from Vivitar is wonderfully useful, covering the range from very wide to normal focal lengths. Working close-in with a wide-angle lens involves a lot of careful juggling to keep framing and perspective where you want them.

The lens has just the few large engraved numbers that you need to indicate what focal length you're set at and the focus distance.

It's quite sharp, giving an image of good contrast, and seems to hold up well from corner to corner over its range of focal lengths. The 35-85-mm f/2.8 Vari-Focal isn't a true zoom. You have to refocus at each new focal length. This allows a design of maximum sharpness, which

focuses very close. The lens has a fat collar that slides to change focal length while you twist it to focus. With practice these simultaneous operations can be done quickly. However, I find the lens bulky and nose-heavy, and the complex focus engravings aren't useful.

The Soligor 35-105-mm f/3.5 Macro-Zoom and the Vivitar of the same specs have many useful features. If you had to have just one lens to walk around with, this would be the range to choose. The lenses focus to 1½ meters. Set the zoom ring to 35 mm, snap it back into the "macro" position, and you can bring it down to 1:4.

Sigma has covered its 39-80-mm f/3:5 mini-zoom with little colored lines and numbers. It has sets of depth of field scales for minimum and maximum focal lengths in different colors.

The focus goes from infinity to 2 meters in $^1/_5$ turn, very fast. A separate macro focus brings you in to 1:3.5. The lens doesn't feel solid, a complaint I find myself making over and over.

Flimsiest of the lot is the Tamron 70-150-mm zoom, which you must buy along with the appropriate Tamron camera adapter. This is so the dealer can stock fewer lenses.

It is made to be a low-price lens, and it doesn't seem fair to compare it with, for instance, the Vivitar of the same range which sells for almost 50 percent more.

This Vivitar 70-150-mm f/3.8 macro-zoom is very good optically. It is adequately housed, compact, and has a macro range to 1:4.

The range from 70 mm to 150 mm is not very wide. It only replaces about two usual lenses.

zoom during exposure

If you have a zoom lens, one of the nifty things you can do is zoom during exposure. It's a technique that the pros use to indicate bold movement, or to salvage a dull situation by making a flashy slide.

The camera must be on a tripod, since you'll be using an exposure time of ¼ second or longer. Use a slow color film like Kodachrome 25 and get a gelatin neutral density filter like a Kodak Wrattan ND 2.00, which lowers the effective film speed by almost 7 stops. With Kodachrome 25 in bright daylight you'll be shooting around f/8 at one second.

Aim the center of the viewfinder at a simple, bright, bold object and zoom while the shutter is open. Try zooming from long toward short, short toward long, middle toward either end; and try holding still part of the exposure and then zooming.

THE 35-MM MODELS include: A. Leica CL with interchangeable, 40-mm f/2 lens, RF, manual meter, about $585. B. Minolta Hi-Matic F, EE, RF, f/2.7, about $130. C. Konica C35EF with pop-up electronic flash, EE, f/2.8, about $160. D. Voigtlander FV202, EE, RF, f/2.8, about $140. E. Minox 35 EL, folds ultra-compactly, EE, f/2.8, about $183. F. GAF Memo 35EE, RF, EE, f/2.7, about $108. G. Olympus 35 RD, RF, EE, f/1.7, about $175. H. Rollei 35S, retractable f/2.8 lens, $244.

Pocket cameras pack a punch

By **WILLIAM KANNER**

ROLLEI A110 shoots sharp. Pocket-sized cameras usually have rangefinder (RF in captions) focusing and electric-eye (EE) exposure.

POCKET 110 CAMERAS include: I. GAF 20/20, f/9.5, fixed focus, approx. $24. J. GAF 20/20S with electronic flash, around $50. K. Tiny Rollei A110, EE, f/2.8 approx. $300. L. Minolta 110 Zoom single lens reflex, 25-50-mm f/4.5 zoom lens with macro-focus to 1 foot, EE, around $265. M. Minox 110S, RF, EE, f/2.8, approx. $220. N. Fujica 350 Zoom, 25-42-mm f/5.6, EE, approx. $95.

■ THE IDEAL CAMERA would take perfect pictures every time, and be so small you'd always have it with you. So we tested 14 cameras that just about match that ideal.

As expected, the 110-cartridge models fit most pockets (and pocket-books) best, but the 35-mm models paid for their greater size and weight with sharper pictures from their bigger negatives. But the 110s—especially the Rollei—were still nice and sharp; and though the Minolta 110 is as big as a small 35, it has the features of a larger, 35-mm reflex.

For sharper focusing, all the 35-mm models (except the Rollei, Minox and Konica) and the Minox 110 have coupled rangefinders, and the Minolta 110 zoom has a reflex ground glass with a microprism focusing spot.

The others (except the fixed-focus GAF 110s) required that you estimate the distance and then set the lens. Sharp pictures still resulted, since these short lenses aren't too critical to focus; and distance scales in the finders of the Rollei 110s and Konica made it easy. A focusing camera lets you shoot in closer.

Electric eyes controlled exposure automatically in all but the Rollei 35S and Leica CL (which had manual meters) and the GAF 20/20 models (which had no adjustment).

If you wanted to alter the electric eye's setting, the Minolta 110 zoom gave you an override control, and the Olympus 35RD had manual exposure settings, too. You could out-think the meters on the other 35s by resetting their film speeds; but not on the 110 models. The Fuji had no meter, just a scale you set according to cloud conditions.

Most electric eyes are programmed to deliver a middle shutter speed and middle f-stop most of the time. But the two Minox models, the Voigt-lander, and the Minolta zoom 110 let you alter the balance by controlling its f-stop; and the Voigtlander, GAF and Minox 35s had finder scales that showed your shutter speed (the Konica showed your f-stop).

Flash was easy on most of these cameras. Nearly half (the GAF 35, Konica, Minolta 35, Minox 110, Olympus and Rollei 110) could automatically link their f-stop and focusing to compensate for light fall-off as camera and flash moved away from the subject, and the Fuji lets you do it manually. The GAF 20/20S and Konica had built-in electronic flash. All but two models could use electronic flash; the GAF 20/20 had a FlipFlash socket, and the Rollei 110 had a compact flash-cube adapter. But the Rollei's flash required manual turning (easy to forget).

AMPLIFIER AND PREAMPLIFIER KITS, from top are Ace Zero-Distortion preamplifier, $90; Ace 35x2-watt amplifier, $150; Dyna PAT-5 preamplifier, $240; Dyna ST-300, 150x2-watt amplifier, $400; Heath AA-1640, 200x2-watt amplifier, $180 (35x2-watt version, $130); Southwest Technical Products 207/B, 60-watt monophonic amplifier, $80; Schober TR-3M, 70x2-watt amplifier, $180. Far right: Heath AP-1615 preamplifier, $130; Heath AN-2016 Modulus tuner/ preamplifier, $600-770; Dyna ST-400, 200x2-watt amplifier, $585. All prices are approximate.

Amplifier kits: good sound at a savings

By ANDY SANTONI

BUILDING your own amplifier from a kit is fun, and lets you get top-dollar performance for a minimum outlay. Power amplifiers like the one shown here are easiest to build; so if you're an inexperienced kit builder, you should start with one of them.

MOST OF US would love to own the ultimate amplifier for our hi-fi systems, with knobs and switches enough for total control and enough power to drive any speakers to ear-crunching volume. What stops us is the price.

But you can get a lot more amplifier for a lot less money if you make one from a kit—and you'll make yourself a few evenings' fun in the bargain. Most amplifier kits, especially those from the major hi-fi kit companies, look good, sound right and hold up for years. (And if they do give trouble, most kit manuals—especially Heath's—tell you how to track the trouble down and cure it.)

How much do you save by building an amplifier from a kit? About one-third the cost of the same amplifier in a wired version. And since wired versions, when available, are generally competitive in price with similar units not in kit form, you can truly save yourself a bundle— several hundred dollars in the case of some top-of-the-line, high-power amplifiers.

Kit or wired, amplifiers come in two basic types: "integrated" models, with both the controls and the speaker-driving circuitry in one box, or "separates," with the preamplifier stages and controls in one box and the speaker-driving circuits in another.

Integrated amplifiers are least expensive and easiest to hook up and use, which makes them the most popular type of factory-wired amplifier. But with more circuitry in one box, they're a bit harder to build from a kit, and the build-it-yourself savings are less with less expensive components, so most amplifier kits are separates.

Separate preamplifiers and power amplifiers are usually easier to build than integrated amplifiers. In fact, power amplifiers are the simplest and easiest hi-fi kits. Preamps, though, are only a bit easier than integrated amps.

The prime advantage of separates is flexibility. You can choose a combination that most closely meets your needs and fits your wallet. Also, you can change it easily if your requirements change.

If you live in a small room and use efficient speakers, you can mate a low-cost, low-power amplifier with a complex and expensive preamp that gives you all the control features you want, such as monitoring and dubbing facilities for two or more tape decks, two turntable inputs and switching for external graphic equalizers or noise reducers. Or you can get a preamplifier with a minimum of controls and a low price. Then, if you need to drive a pair of inefficient speakers in a large room, or multiple sets of speakers in different rooms around your house, you can use the money you saved on the preamp to buy a monster power amplifier. And if your needs change, you can replace just one component, rather than the entire amplifying system.

The first steps in picking an amplifier are usually to decide how much power you need, decide what control facilities you want, see what's available in your price range, then figure how many watts and controls you're willing to do without to come within your budget. With kits, of course, you won't have to trim your list quite so much because of the money you'll save by doing your own building.

For most people, power will be the only specification really worth considering. The other specs are pretty comparable among today's kit amps. And though there are *slight* differences in sound between them (Dynaco's Stereo 150, for example, had noticeably tighter bass and slightly sharper treble than its older Stereo 120), you'd have to listen to several amplifiers a long time to really hear the difference.

Since some audiophiles feel there is a noticeable difference between the sound of tube and transistor amplifiers, Dynaco offers several power amplifiers that use tubes—their latest, in fact, is a tube model. Whether or not you hear that difference, you might appreciate the tube amplifiers' greater tolerance for such electrical abuse as shorted speaker leads. This makes tube amplifiers popular among public-address-system engineers and among audiophiles with children.

Power amplifiers need no controls at all, but most have on-off switches, quite a few have power-level meters (handy for checking channel balance and operation, but mainly to assuage your curiosity), and many have level controls for easier accommodation of a wide range of preamplifiers, or easy inter-channel balancing.

More and more amplifiers now offer plug-in speaker connections. That's handy, especially with the heavier amps, because you can wire the connector before you slide the amplifier into po-

Heath's 'Module I'; it's more than just a preamp

Heath's new AN-2016 "Modulus" is an unusual combination: A preamp with an AM-FM stereo tuner built in. That gives you the convenience of having all your controls in one place while keeping your power amplifier tucked out of the way. It also, as with any preamp, lets you choose how much amplifier power you want.

The AN-2016, "Module I" in the new Heath series, is by far the most complex—and versatile—piece of gear we tested. After about 50 hours of construction time and about $600, you'll have a preamp that can handle stereo records and four-channel tapes superbly and a digital readout tuner. The tuner's FM section performs as well as almost any FM tuner on the market, and its AM section is almost as good as most hi-fi FM tuners and a great deal better than any of the run-of-the-mill AM tuner sections now on the market.

Control features include output level meters for all four channels, signal-strength and channel center tuning meters, front-panel tape-dubbing jacks, and pushbuttons that light to show which are activated. And there's a relay that cuts the preamp's output when you turn the power on and off—this keeps amplified switch clicks from blowing out your speakers.

As the name implies, the AN-2016 has modular construction. You can build and install additional modules whenever you need them. Module IV ($40) is a noise-reduction circuit for Dolby-encoded FM broadcasts. Module V ($80) is a demodulator for CD-4 discrete four-channel records, and Module VI ($50) is a decoder for SQ four-channel discs. Total building time for the AN-2016 and these three modules is about 50 hours.

Modules II and III don't fit inside the AN-2016: They're independent stereo amplifiers of 35 and 60 watts, respectively, per channel, whose front panels match that of the Module I.

sition, while connections are still easy to see and get at. The Heath 400-watt amp uses special plugs that can only be inserted one way, to make sure your speakers are in phase with one another. The Dyna and Schober amps, on the other hand, use "double-banana" jacks whose plugs can be inserted either way, so if you've wired a plug incorrectly, you can just reverse it in its socket to correct the phasing. These jacks are combined with binding posts that also take bare wires or spade lugs. And the Ace amplifier has spring-loaded terminals that lock onto bare wire ends.

The Dynakit 400 has an additional switch, for its "Dynaguard" circuit that lets brief, high-power signals through but limits long, speaker-damaging ones. This control and circuit are omitted, though, from Dyna's stripped Model 410.

Preamps and integrated amplifiers have more elaborate controls. Make sure the one you get has enough inputs and tape monitor loops to handle all the other components you intend to hook up to it.

Dynaco's preamplifiers have exceptionally flexible inputs, including one which can be wired for a second turntable, a microphone or for a tape deck with no electronics of its own (though such decks are quite rare these days). Dyna's PAT-5 also has two tape-monitor loops and provision to control your power amplifier's output, switching it to various speakers or to a head-phone jack in the PAT-5's panel.

The Ace Model ZDP "zero-distortion" preamplifier has only selector and volume controls and a power switch—to eliminate distortion, it eliminates all circuits except the phono preamp stage.

If you need higher output levels, you can wire in the amplication circuits that turn the Ace into a Model BSP; they're included in the kit, so you can wire it either way.

how kit companies compare

All it takes to build an amplifier kit is a little manual dexterity and patience. But some kits are trickier than others (power amplifiers are easiest), so take your time. And there are differences between the ways each company designs kits, as well as in the number of kits they offer. All prices given below are approximate.

● **Ace Audio** (447 Elwood Rd., East Northport, NY 11731) provides minimal instructions. On the preamplifier kit, for example, you're told how to install components on half the board,

then just told that the other half is wired the same way. But there's so little wiring in an Ace kit that neither the preamplifier nor the 35-watt-per-channel stereo power amp ($150) should take long or be hard to build.

● **Dynaco** (Box 88, Blackwood, NJ 08012) offers more complete, step-by-step instructions, and builds most of the printed-circuit boards for you. That makes Dynakits about the fastest and easiest to build.

Dyna offers two transistor preamps one tube-type preamp, a 30x2-watt stereo integrated amp, and 10 power amps: monophonic tube amplifiers of 50 and 100 watts, solidstate stereo amplifiers of 20, 40, 60, 75, 150 and 200 watts per channel, and a 4-channel, 75x4-watt amp (the 150x2-watt amp can be converted into this).

● **Heath** (Benton Harbor, MI 49022) goes overboard in its instruction manuals to make sure that anyone, even people with absolutely no training in electronics, can build one of their kits and have it work. There are drawings to go with each step and complete troubleshooting guides if you encounter difficulties. Heath even provides solder.

Heath currently offers a stereo preamp ($130) the "Module I" tuner/preamp combination (see page 40), stereo-integrated amps of 15, 35 and 70 watts per channel, four-channel amps of 15 and 35 watts per channel, and a 3¼-watt monophonic integrated amp. Their stereo power amplifiers offer 35, 60 and 200 watts per channel.

● **Schober Organ Corp.** (413 West 61 St., New York, NY 10023) designed its amplifiers for use with electronic organs, so they're solidly built to withstand abuse. Their manuals, too, are designed for the builders of their organ kits, who are often more interested in music than in electronics, so the kits aren't hard to build.

Schober makes two amplifiers: a 70-watt monophonic model ($176) and a 70-watt-per-channel stereo model ($240).

● **Southwest Technical Products** or SWTP (219 West Rhapsody, San Antonio, TX 78216) designs kits and writes manuals for the experienced kit builder. If you've never built a kit, you may have to read each instruction a few times to get the point; but you can probably get the kit built if you're willing to take the time.

SWTP kits are exceptionally low-priced ($75 for a stereo preamp, $41 for a 15x20 and $70 for a 25x2-watt stereo amp, $78 for a 60-watt mono and $155 for a 250-watt mono amp), and their circuits are well-designed. But the low price shows in the hardware used.

Those tiny new cassette systems

By CINDY MORGAN

■ WHEN THE FIRST cassette recorders came out, everyone marveled at how small they were. Now there's a flood of far tinier recorders using tapes resembling Lilliputian versions of the original cassette. They're so light (just over half a pound) you can tote them everywhere to preserve all those spur-of-the-moment ideas.

But more than size separates the new systems from the old, standard-size cassettes: Because their tiny tapes move at a slower speed, they're not suited for taping music unless you only care about the lyrics, not the sound quality. And unlike standard cassettes, interchangeable between tape units of all makers, the new cassettes come in four different, totally incompatible forms.

If the tape runs 15 minutes on each side, it's part of the "mini-cassette" family shared by

Norelco, Unitrex, B&B Rhapsody, Radio Shack and Certron tapes. If it records on one side only, for 30 minutes, it's a DeJur Amsco tape, used only on DeJur's Stenorette 2050.

If the matchbook-size cassette records 30 minutes per side, it's probably one of the Olympus "micro-cassette" family which includes recorders by Olympus, Panasonic, Lanier, Sony and Courterport. The one exception is the Sanyko Seiki cassette, which only fits the Sankyo MTC-10.

All the small recorders except the Norelco-compatible group have capstan drive: The tape is pressed against a revolving capstan by a rubber roller and pulled across the tape recorder's heads, just as in bigger machines. Capstan drive means more constant speed and better sound quality, but it costs more.

"Mini-cassette" tapes are driven by the takeup spindle. The motor turns at fairly constant speed, but as tape builds up on the takeup hub, more tape gets pulled across the heads for each revolution of the hub and spindle. And as tape speed varies, so does sound quality.

When you purchase such a unit, make sure it's operating at the correct speed. Record a sentence on one recorder, then play the tape back on another. If the sound is okay, then so are both recorders. But if the tape sounds speeded up or slowed down, try another recorder to see which one is off.

All the tiny machines are designed for one-

WHO SHRANK the tape cassette? Thirteen recorder makers did to bring you recorders so small you can always take one with you wherever you go.

A REGULAR CASSETTE dwarfs the tiny new ones. But none of the new types can be used in the same recorders.

hand operation, but you'll find your hand fits some better than others. Most are designed for dictation, so their controls will be easy to reach when the microphone is held up to your lips—but if you're going to record others a lot, see how the controls feel when you're pointing the mike away from yourself.

The capstan units, as a group, picked up distant sounds better than the non-capstan ones. So for speeches and school lectures, the capstan units might be your best bets.

The Norelco 185 (about $135) is light and easy to hold, and its controls are handy—but none of them is marked, which could be important if you'll use it infrequently enough to forget which is which. Even in my small hands, the Unitrex Memory Recorder ($60) and Sony M-101 ($100) were very easy to work.

The DeJur Stenorette ($225), biggest of the lot, takes a stronger hand to operate, but it has some extras to justify its bulk. The tape position counter is built into the tape cassette rather than the recorder, which makes locating things on the tape easier. And you can record a beep at any point on the tape, either to alert a typist to spot where changes are to be made, or to remind yourself to pay more attention to a particular tape passage.

So you don't get carried away talking to a unit

that's run out of tape, several mini-cassette units, such as Norelco's 185 ($135) and Dictaphone's Dictamite 10 ($165) have an audible end-of-tape signal; so does Lanier's Microcassette 60 ($215), a micro-cassette (Olympus-type) unit. The Dictaphone and DeJur also signal when there's no tape in the machine.

The more expensive the unit, the more controls it has. All models have fast rewind, but none of the mini-cassette (Norelco system) recorders have fast forward except the Hermes Compur Dict ($130). A "review" feature that makes it easier to hear what you've just taped is standard on all micro-cassette (Olympus system) units and the Sankyo, but not on Grundig or mini-cassette units.

If you ever want to transcribe your tapes, you'll need at least an earphone (available for all but the Norelco 185) and a foot-pedal start-stop switch (available for all but the micro-cassette units, though one could be built to work with the a.c. adaptor socket on all of these except the Lanier).

If you do a lot of transcribing, you might want a desktop unit designed for that. Norelco, Dictaphone and Unitrex make transcribers for Norelco-type mini-cassettes. If you have a Lanier transcriber for conventional cassettes, you can get a $150 micro adapter.

FOUR TINY-TAPE
"families" of recorders and tapes include (clockwise from upper left): mini-cassette family including Unitrex, Dictaphone, Courterport and Norelco; Sankyo Seiki; micro-cassette family including Sony, Olympus Pearlcorder, Courterport and Panasonic; and Grundig Stenorette. Tapes are only compatible within families.

ONE OF THE BEST frequency counters on the market is the Heath IM-4130 shown above.

CB add-on shows your exact frequency

By J.L. GENEVICZ

■ YOU DON'T HAVE to haul your CB to a radio repair shop anymore to pay a technician to use his $2000 tester to check whether your rig is putting out signal correctly at the center of each channel.

Prices have tumbled on superaccurate digital frequency counters so you can buy your own. Just a few years ago they were in the thousands. Now they start well under $100.

Here's what you get for the money:
• An extremely accurate reading of the frequency at which you are transmitting. For instance, if you are using CB Channel 1, the red LEDs in your counter will read 26.965 MHz. The frequency of the popular trucker's Channel 19 is 27.185 MHz.
• An indication that your radio is putting out power. These new counters work by sampling a tiny bit of the actual energy radiated from your transmitter.
• An excellent shop tool if you plan to make extra income on the side repairing CBs. Get a second-class FCC ticket and you'll find that a frequency counter will be the first test gear you'll need.

Lowest priced is the $90 kit from Digitrex, 4412 Fernlee, Royal Oak, MI 48073.

Popular is the wired-and-tested CT-40, about $100, from Telco, 44 Sea Cliff Ave., Glen Cove, NY 11542.

Good for a lifetime is the IM-4130, around $530, from Heath Co., Benton Harbor, MI 49022. It will test any kind of radio or TV.

To use one of these CB add-ons, hold it near your transmitter, coax or antenna. It will pick up signals from the air and flash the frequency. Or use a special coupler to hook it into the coax line.

SOME UNITS require a physical connection for proper testing, while others need only be placed near the radio.

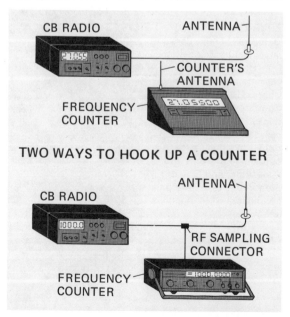

SECTION 2

GREAT PROJECTS OF THE YEAR

On the following pages you'll find the finest of the famous Popular Mechanics projects:

Projects to improve your home

Projects to challenge your craftsmanship

Photo projects

Electronics know-how

Projects just for fun

You'll also find how-to information in related fields:

Shop know-how

Tool techniques

How-to tips for the great outdoors

Turn the page to find the first article on home improvement—and go on from there!

Build an 'everything' shed

This easy-to-build garden shed has a roll-away door with a built-in potting bench and shelves. Add a bamboo screen and it does double-duty as a good-looking deck for lounging on a summer afternoon. Here's how to build it

■ THE REASON for it is simple—you need more storage space. The design is unique—a bulk storage section plus a swing-away, 2-ft.-deep door with a built-in potting bench and shelves, all on a raised 2x4 deck.

Looks expensive? Materials will run about $600, a little steep for a storage box, but not bad when you add the gardening door and the deck which give you an attractive and protected area for soaking up the sun.

Turn the slatted redwood potting bench in the door into a serving bar, roll down the bamboo shade to hide storage and you have an attractive setting for summer parties; you won't get this with many prefab sheds.

keeping it simple

If you can handle repair and renovation jobs but haven't tackled a building from start to finish, this is your chance. If you had to pick a step-by-step project to illustrate the real basics of house construction, you'd pick a project like our shed.

It's small, detailing is simple, no fancy joints or special tools are needed, and the framing pattern is standard, solid and flexible. If you add another set of piers you can extend the storage section and even extend the rafters to a post and girder setup to make a small carport. Once you've got the system clear you'll see the amazing number of alterations you can make in our plan to suit your needs and building site.

Four concrete piers support the deck. Check local building codes for all construction, but in general our 12x22x36-in.-deep piers will be enough to anchor the weight of the shed. Simply dig four holes to accommodate ½-in.-plywood forms, check carefully to be sure they're all level with each other by laying a straight 2x4 between them and reading a level on the 2x4.

When piers are level, pack dirt around the outside of the forms to keep them in place, then fill with concrete mix. Tie the girders to the piers with anchor bolts set in the concrete while it's still wet.

If your local lumberyard can get pressure-treated timbers, check the price against unsealed wood. Treated wood could be best, especially if your site is damp or collects ground water. Fir timbers should be thoroughly creosoted.

Fir 2x6 joists are toenailed to the girders 16 in. on center. Buy 10-footers for the door end of the platform where you get about a 22-in. cantilever past each girder. This floating platform (close to your lawn because the girder is partially buried) is very strong when you tie the joists with the 2x4

ROLL DOWN the bamboo shade to hide the storage section and provide a good-looking backdrop for a summer afternoon spent sunbathing on the deck.

THE SHED has three main components: the storage shed, the gardening door and the deck. Below is the view from the inside of the shed.

THE DOOR opens easily on heavy-duty casters. Inside the door is a redwood potting bench which could double as a bar and entertainment center.

LAY OUT YOUR SITE carefully, then dig girder trenches about 12 in. deep and spread a few inches of gravel in them to increase drainage. At right you can see that the full platform is built only on one side. The back of the shed is flush with the deck, but a cantilevered section of joists is necessary at one end.

NAIL THE DECK (two 10d galvanized common nails at each joist) and seal it with two coats of Woodlife. Make up your walls (complete with 2x4 shoe and one plate) on the deck and tip in place. Note the temporary angle brace.

MAIN SHED DETAILS

YOU CAN lay rafters fully across the two 2x4 plates, or 2 in. in and add a full-length 2x6.

RUN T-11 siding panels about 2 in. down the joist and nail to joist, deck, 2x4 shoe and stud.

LEAVE ¼-IN. between front panels and deck, and seal end grain to prevent water penetration.

COVER PLYWOOD ROOF with double-layer tarpaper, roll roofing, drip edge. Seal seams.

MAKE WALLS as square and plumb as you can. When you've got the frame just right, nail 2x4 angle braces on the *inside*. A true frame means minimal trimming and generally an easier, better-looking siding job.

decking. Under the main shed, 8-footers are enough for a floating platform along one side.

Coat all sides of the decking (use full 18-footers) with a preservative like Woodlife. Then make a ⅛-in. spacer and start nailing off the deck with two 10d galvanized common nails at each joist. Check actual sizes of your lumber before you begin. Frequently, long lengths like 18s are really an inch or so longer. If they are, put them on as is, allowing for a small overhang at each end.

When the deck is finished, snap a chalkline at the overhang line and trim off the color-coded lumber ends with one continuous saw cut.

TOTAL DOOR HEIGHT (including the casters) should be 3 in. less than the shed for clearance.

MAKE UP the door frame on the deck. Doubled 2x4s are tied together with doubled plates and 2x6s.

BENCH SUPPORT 2x6 across door front is notched into studs and lagbolted through the end.

USE A CLAMP to hold the 2x6 flush when turning the lags. Add 2x4 nailers for the shelves.

LIGHTEN the weight of the shed by the use of 2x2 shelf nailers across the back.

NAIL THE SIDING to all framing pieces to stiffen the unit. Match groove patterns at the joint.

SHED DOOR DETAILS

COMPLETE THE DOOR by running 2x4 nailers from the back wall studs to the front 2x6 to support 1x2 redwood slats (on edge with ¼-in. spacing). Clamp door to shed and attach hinges. Lag on a 2x4 doorstop.

Instead of nailing one wall stud at a time, cut the 2x4 base (shoe) and one 2x4 top (plate) to length, mark them for a 16-in. center layout; nail through them into ends of the studs.

Each wall is light enough to tip up in place. Spike through the shoe into the decking, then plumb the wall carefully with a level and secure it with angled braces on the *inside* so they can stay in place while you nail the siding. Sandwich the doubled 2x4 plates at the corners and spike through them to lock up the walls. Rafters can run to the outside of the plate or 2 in. across with a 2x6 ribbon on edge to tie them together. Nail the exterior-grade plywood roofing with the 8-ft.

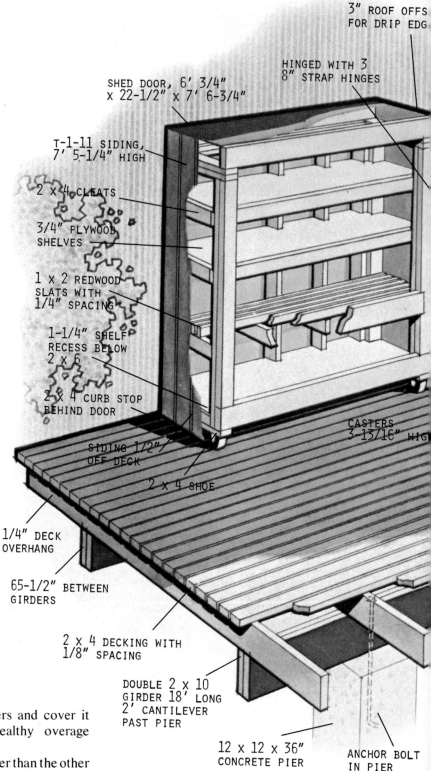

3" ROOF OFFS
FOR DRIP EDG

HINGED WITH 3
8" STRAP HINGES

SHED DOOR, 6' 3/4"
x 22-1/2" x 7' 6-3/4"

T-1-11 SIDING,
7' 5-1/4" HIGH

2 x 4 CLEATS

3/4" PLYWOOD
SHELVES

1 x 2 REDWOOD
SLATS WITH
1/4" SPACING

1-1/4" SHELF
RECESS BELOW
2 x 6

2 x 4 CURB STOP
BEHIND DOOR

SIDING 1/2"
OFF DECK

2 x 4 SHOE

CASTERS
3-13/16" HIG

1/4" DECK
OVERHANG

65-1/2" BETWEEN
GIRDERS

2 x 4 DECKING WITH
1/8" SPACING

DOUBLE 2 x 10
GIRDER 18' LONG
2' CANTILEVER
PAST PIER

12 x 12 x 36"
CONCRETE PIER

ANCHOR BOLT
IN PIER
THROUGH GIRD

HERE'S THE PLAN: Two full-length girders are supported by four piers; 2x6 joists, 16 in. on center across the girders, support a 2x4 deck. The main shed is locked onto the deck. The full-width gardening door, hinged to the shed, glides open on casters.

length running across the rafters and cover it with tarpaper, allowing a healthy overage (double-covered area).

You could make one wall higher than the other and angle-cut rafters to provide drainage. But for a roof this small you can get by with double-cover roll roofing; apply roof coating liberally to each layer and seal nailheads and seams with roof cement.

Siding panels are run from ¼ in. off the deck where the platform extends beyond the shed and

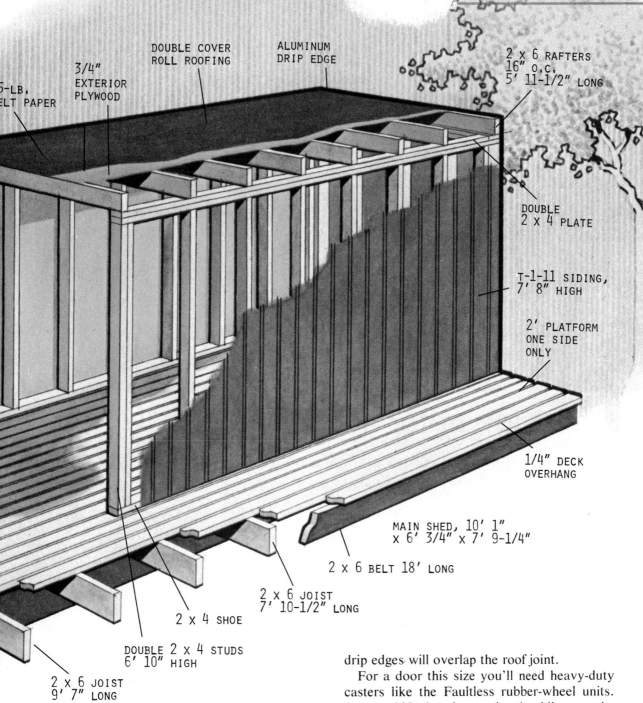

.5-LB, ELT PAPER

3/4" EXTERIOR PLYWOOD

DOUBLE COVER ROLL ROOFING

ALUMINUM DRIP EDGE

2 x 6 RAFTERS 16" O.C. 5' 11-1/2" LONG

DOUBLE 2 x 4 PLATE

T-1-11 SIDING, 7' 8" HIGH

2' PLATFORM ONE SIDE ONLY

1/4" DECK OVERHANG

MAIN SHED, 10' 1" x 6' 3/4" x 7' 9-1/4"

2 x 6 BELT 18' LONG

2 x 6 JOIST 7' 10-1/2" LONG

2 x 4 SHOE

DOUBLE 2 x 4 STUDS 6' 10" HIGH

2 x 6 JOIST 9' 7" LONG

from 2 in. below the top of the joist where the shed wall is flush with the deck. Test-fit panels before nailing and allow for the siding thickness at corners. Tack sheets with box nails and when you're sure they're right, nail along studs, shoe, plates and rafters.

To cover the roof joint between the main shed and the door add a 1x2 nailer to the edge of the shed roof to extend the drop edge over the door. Then take about 3 in. (including the casters) off the door height. This way the aluminum

drip edges will overlap the roof joint.

For a door this size you'll need heavy-duty casters like the Faultless rubber-wheel units. You can hide them by running the siding past the 2x4 shoe to within ¼ in. of the deck. To support the potting bench inside, notch the 2x6 flush with the front corner 2x4s. Then run 2x4s on edge from back wall studs to the 2x6, including nailers at each end. Cut slats to length, lay them on edge and predrill holes for galvanized box nails down into the frame.

You can stain the siding after adding the strap hinges and handle. A hasp and padlock or sliding-door locking hardware provide security. Lag on a short length of 2x4 to back edge of the deck. Without it, you could roll the door off the deck.

Great ideas for a hobby room

**This room provides plenty of workspace for your hobbies
and crafts, but also hides them when they're not needed**

■ THE GROWING INTEREST in family-oriented hobbies and crafts has created a need for extra work space in many homes. This version more than satisfies the space needs in handsome fashion. It provides a place for working on any number of projects, yet when the work is completed or interrupted, you can store materials handily out of sight. Thus the space is transformed, ready for use in other ways.

Plywood paneling applied diagonally with battens hiding the joints creates a dynamic wall pattern. For graphic interest, that pattern is picked up and repeated in bold colors on the window shades made by Joanna Western Mills. The areas to be painted on the shades are masked off with tape, then covered with acrylic paints. All the surfaces in the room are finished with hardy, easy-care materials, including the rugged indoor-outdoor carpeting by Trend.

The key elements that make this hobby center a cut above average are the colonial storage chest, the cantilevered desk and the shades that pull upward. The storage chest can hold a quantity of supplies—from model-building equipment to sewing materials—behind its clever flip-up

doors. Projects in process can also be stored in the chest. The cantilevered desk is perfect for light-duty work such as assembling and gluing parts, decoupage and other craft activities. The desk is off to the side, out of the path of traffic; it's a place where glued assemblies or small pieces can be left undisturbed. The shades serve several functions: The pull-down shades hide a storage shelf niche, as well as their usual function of blocking the sun and offering privacy at the two windows. The pull-up shades are used to hide an airconditioner and a mini-storage space under the desk. Plans for the storage chest, desk and pull-up shades on these pages can start you on your way to creating a hobby center for your family and making fuller use of your living space.

The chest is designed to organize the small equipment and materials needed for hobby work. The 24 separate compartments will provide everyone in the family a place for his supplies.

Make the case of ¾-in. pine with a ¼-in. plywood back. The dividers are grooved to accept shelves and are bored for the dowel pins that hold the door fronts.

COLONIAL STORAGE CHEST

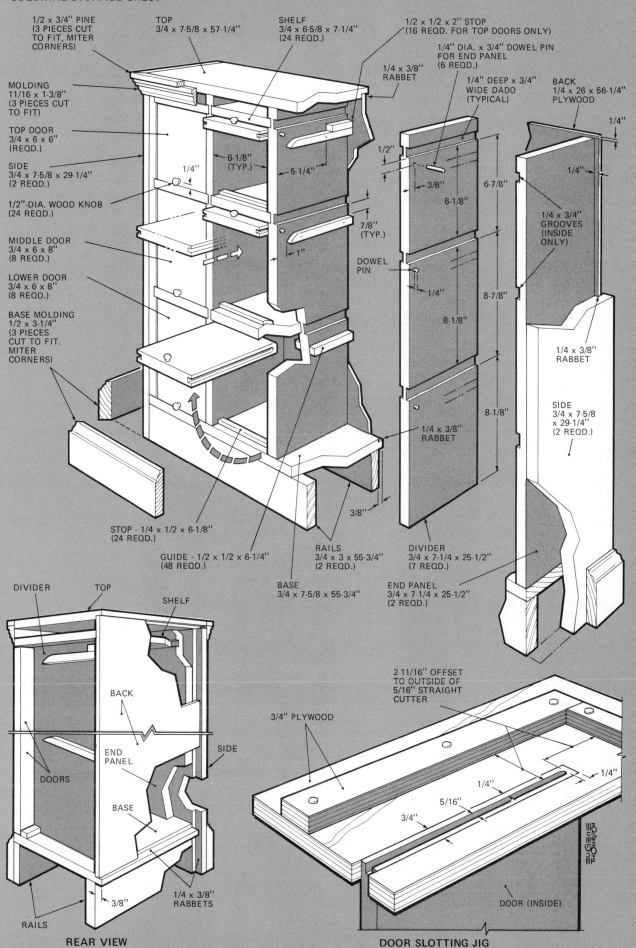

1/2 x 3/4" PINE (3 PIECES CUT TO FIT, MITER CORNERS)

TOP 3/4 x 7-5/8 x 57-1/4"

SHELF 3/4 x 6-5/8 x 7-1/4" (24 REQD.)

1/2 x 1/2 x 2" STOP (16 REQD. FOR TOP DOORS ONLY)

1/4 x 3/8" RABBET

1/4" DIA. x 3/4" DOWEL PIN FOR END PANEL (6 REQD.)

1/4" DEEP x 3/4" WIDE DADO (TYPICAL)

BACK 1/4 x 26 x 56-1/4" PLYWOOD

1/4"

MOLDING 11/16 x 1-3/8" (3 PIECES CUT TO FIT)

TOP DOOR 3/4 x 6 x 6" (REQD.)

SIDE 3/4 x 7-5/8 x 29-1/4" (2 REQD.)

1/2"-DIA. WOOD KNOB (24 REQD.)

MIDDLE DOOR 3/4 x 6 x 8" (8 REQD.)

LOWER DOOR 3/4 x 6 x 8" (8 REQD.)

BASE MOLDING 1/2 x 3-1/4" (3 PIECES CUT TO FIT, MITER CORNERS)

6-1/8" (TYP.)

5-1/4"

1/4"

7/8" (TYP.)

1"

1/2"

3/8"

DOWEL PIN

1/4"

6-7/8"

6-1/8"

8-7/8"

8-1/8"

8-1/8"

1/4"

1/4"

1/4 x 3/4" GROOVES (INSIDE ONLY)

1/4 x 3/8" RABBET

SIDE 3/4 x 7-5/8 x 29-1/4" (2 REQD.)

1/4 x 3/8" RABBET

3/8"

STOP - 1/4 x 1/2 x 6-1/8" (24 REQD.)

GUIDE - 1/2 x 1/2 x 6-1/4" (48 REQD.)

RAILS 3/4 x 3 x 55-3/4" (2 REQD.)

BASE 3/4 x 7-5/8 x 55-3/4"

DIVIDER 3/4 x 7-1/4 x 25-1/2" (7 REQD.)

END PANEL 3/4 x 7-1/4 x 25-1/2" (2 REQD.)

DIVIDER   TOP

SHELF

BACK

END PANEL

SIDE

DOORS

BASE

3/8"

1/4 x 3/8" RABBETS

RAILS

REAR VIEW

2-11/16" OFFSET TO OUTSIDE OF 5/16" STRAIGHT CUTTER

3/4" PLYWOOD

1/4"

1/4"

5/16"

3/4"

DOOR (INSIDE)

DOOR SLOTTING JIG

EUGENE THOMPSON

The shelves are fitted with stops for the doors when they are in the closed position. The top level of compartments also has backstops for the doors. These stops are added after the doors are in position—and before the back is installed.

A jig makes slotting the doors fast and accurate work. Lay it out carefully and practice routing the grooves on scrap. Work from the back of the chest to put the doors in place. Position them with dowel pins resting in the door slots and push the doors forward to the front of the chest. Attach the wood door knobs and top. Fit the back into the rabbets in the top, sides and base panels.

To give the chest a colonial look, add stock moldings at top and bottom. To finish the unit, sand thoroughly, dust off and wipe with a tack cloth. Apply the stain of your choice, following manufacturer's directions. Allow the stain to dry overnight, rub lightly with double-0 steel wool, dust and wipe with a tack cloth.

Next, apply a coat of white shellac thinned 50 percent with alcohol. Allow the shellac to dry overnight, then repeat the steel wool and dusting procedures. Finish by applying two coats of a good-quality varnish such as ZAR—following manufacturer's instructions. For an authentic look, pick the flat antique finish.

The light-duty desk cantilevered under a window makes use of space that's often wasted.

The desktop is plywood with a pine surround mitered at the joints, which gives the top a thicker more substantial appearance. The desk is anchored by a desk support and hold-down cleat. A plywood sill shelf supported by a shelf cleat and front panel finish off the top of the desk. The dimension of the sill shelf will vary, depending on the window casing, so check this dimension carefully before starting.

A corner guard notched at the bottom to fit on the baseboard covers the ends of a double thickness of paneling. The double paneling runs from the 1x4s on both sides of the window.

Finish the desk in a bright color to blend in with the room. For durability, use an enamel. A pull-up shade hides a small storage space under the desk.

The pull-up shades in this family hobby center cover equipment that would otherwise give the room a cluttered look. Installed "bottom-up" as they are, the shades offer a unique alternative to other storage units.

Two shade brackets mounted to the inside of the baseboard anchor the shade on both sides. Fasten two double-sheave pulleys to the wall or header at the highest point the shade will be pulled. Be sure that these pulleys are attached so the cords will be vertical and parallel for smooth shade action.

Bring the shade cord through a small hole drilled in the paneling to the room side and secure it by winding the cord around two cord cleats.

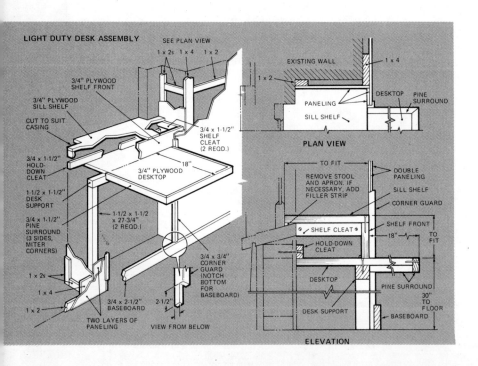

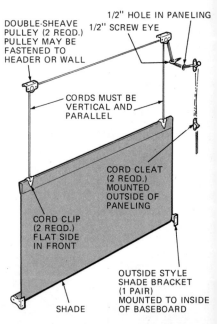

SHADES THAT PULL UP

Build a freestanding cedar closet

**Need more storage space?
Try a luxurious cedar-lined walk-in
closet made from panels of
thin red cedar flakes**

■ FROM HOME to apartment, the need for extra storage space seems to be universal. This freestanding closet holds your clothes and personal items in a luxurious, yet practical setting. The good-looking cedar panels give off a pleasant fragrance that's moth-repellent as well.

Begin construction by nailing a 2x4 frame to your dimensions. Next nail ⅝-in. plywood to the exterior of the frame. You can finish the exterior with base molding.

The interior of this closet was then lined with Giles & Kendall cedar panels. They're made of large, thin flakes of red cedar compressed into sheets. The ¼-in.-thick panels come in standard 4x8-ft. sheets and can be sawed and nailed like plywood. They are butted together and nailed to the frame interior with 1¼-in. finishing nails.

After the panels are installed, you can add weather stripping around the doors.

Shelves made from cedar panel remnants are added next. A clothes rod completes the interior.

Doors can be made from plywood, but hollow-core doors with magnetic latches are less likely to warp. Line them with the cedar panels.

Stain or paint the exterior plywood, but leave the cedar interior unfinished.

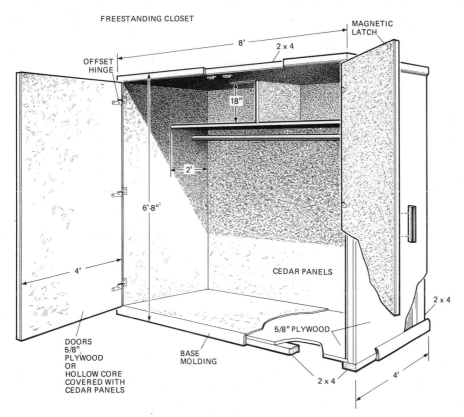

FREESTANDING CLOSET

MAGNETIC LATCH

8'

2 x 4

OFFSET HINGE

18"

2'

6'-8"

4'

CEDAR PANELS

2 x 4

DOORS 5/8" PLYWOOD OR HOLLOW CORE COVERED WITH CEDAR PANELS

BASE MOLDING

5/8" PLYWOOD

2 x 4

4'

Ceramic tile over your old countertop

This countertop, the kind that is fashionable on the West Coast, was installed right over the existing plastic laminate. Here are step-by-step instructions on how to do it yourself

■ A TILED KITCHEN countertop, the kind that's popular on the West Coast, is a real touch of luxury. It's not as hard a project as you might think, because the tile can be installed over existing high-pressure plastic laminate.

Materials used were 4¼ x 4¼-in. matte-glazed Tuscany ceramic tile in pure white (it's not advisable to use a "bright" glazed tile—it will scratch too easily), nonsanded grout in Renaissance Brown and AO 1800 adhesive—a type that's suitable for tile application over a variety of surfaces and offers prolonged resistance to water. All are products of American Olean Tile Co., Lansdale, PA 19446.

The water-cooled saw and hand cutter are specialized, expensive tools. But they can be rented by the day, and the job will go faster.

1 START by removing sink (and any other drop-in fixture) from counter.

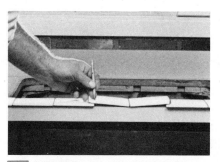
2 LAY OUT edge tiles with full pieces in corners; adjust center widths.

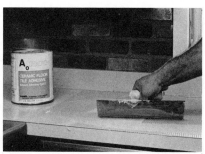
3 APPLY suitable adhesive and spread it with a notched trowel.

4 INSTALL tile along edge with ¼-in. overhang topping off edge tiles.

5 USE NIPPERS to shape tile to contours such as sink corners.

6 MAKE STRAIGHT cuts for opening edge with saw or hand cutter.

7 INSTALL additional tile, cutting to meet edge where necessary.

8 TILES on the backsplash are ¼ in. too high so edge tiles fit.

9 STRIPS for the backsplash top can be made with a hand cutter.

THIS CALIFORNIA-STYLE tile countertop has dark grout for a crisp but warm look. The technique camouflages stains.

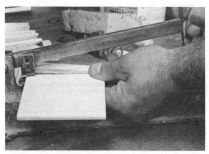

10 **SCORED TILES** break cleanly under pressure on both sides.

11 **STRIPS** butt against the backsplash to form a square corner.

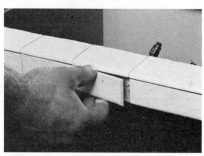

12 **TILES** adhere better if adhesive air-dries for a few minutes.

13 **NEXT DAY** is best for grouting. Mix the grout in a pail.

14 **ADD WATER** according to the manufacturer's directions.

15 **SPREAD GROUT** over all surfaces with a rubber-faced trowel.

16 **STRIKE JOINTS**—press grout into them—with a striking tool.

17 **AFTER SHORT WAIT,** wipe excess grout off with a sponge.

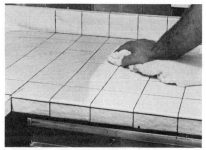

18 **POLISH THE TILE** with a clean, dry cloth and reinstall the sink.

BY BUILDING the bed/wall unit in middle of the room, each child now has privacy, a desk, and extra bunk.

Split a room in two

By HARRY WICKS

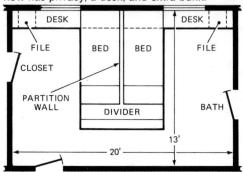

TWO DISTINCT areas were created by dividing the room. Each child then has his own part of the house.

BEFORE: Large windows in one wall made efficient furniture placement almost impossible.

■ ONE SURE WAY to keep the peace in a bedroom shared by two active boys is to split the room in two. To do it by installing a wall can prove prohibitively expensive as well as unrealistic from a space point of view. Here, the breaking up of a large bedroom was accomplished through the clever use and placement of built-in furniture.

To do it, interior decorator Abbey Darer created a bed-wall unit that serves a number of purposes:

● It physically divides the room down the middle. Now, hassles about whose whatsit belongs where are a thing of the past.

• Each youngster now has a bunk bed—with storage to spare—as well as a guest bunk overhead.

• Since homework and a quiet place to study were at the top of the list as far as the parents were concerned, each boy was also given a desk/study area of his own. Besides providing quiet spots for homework and reading, these areas also serve as hobby centers.

For beauty and rugged durability the walls are clad with prefinished ¼-in.-thick paneling—Weldwood Wayfarer Birch from Champion Building Products. For looks, the beds and bookcase unit were finished with the same paneling that is used on the walls.

Each youngster's half of the room was then decorated with touches that suit his own tastes and interests. Careful decorating keeps the room together as a whole visually—it doesn't look like two rooms shoe-horned into one.

The windows in both areas are treated with custom-decorated Bolero shades from the Graber Co. Each shade sports its own graphics, as well as the occupant's name. You will find instructions for decorating shades—including an alphabet on squares—with this article. Since the shades provide decorative relief, no other materials are used at the windows.

Since the T-shaped wall does not support any weight from above, it can be framed using 2x3 lumber. Start by laying out the wall where you want it, indicating its location on the floor by a chalkline. In the room shown, ceiling height is 8 ft. and the bed wall is built 7 ft. high. This leaves a 1-ft. space between wall and ceiling for air (and heat) flow. Erect the two wall sections and stand them in place. Once the bookcase back wall is nailed to the bed wall, the assembly will be free-standing. Since the beds and bookcase unit will ultimately be tied into the wall unit there is no need to fasten its sole plates to the floor.

When you're satisfied with wall dimensions and location, install prefinished paneling on all wall elevations—including the surface that will be the back of the bookcase unit. For a superior panel installation use adhesive on studs as well as 1¼-in. color-matched nails.

The chore in building the desk units is simplified because on both units the outboard end of the corner simply rests on a purchased two-drawer file cabinet. At the other end, a box-like enclosure is constructed to make up this dimension. The side facing the kneehole is left unfinished to provide handy storage for large, bulky items. Note that the storage box is completely finished (paneled) before bed construc-

THE BOOKCASE which is shared by the room occupants has the same prefinished plywood as the walls.

SEE-THROUGH section in the bookcase gives an open, airy feeling in the lower bunk and allows displays.

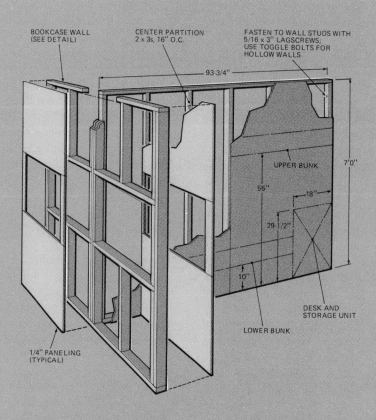

BOOKCASE WALL
(SEE DETAIL)

CENTER PARTITION
2 x 3s, 16" O.C.

FASTEN TO WALL STUDS WITH
5/16 x 3" LAGSCREWS;
USE TOGGLE BOLTS FOR
HOLLOW WALLS

93-3/4"

7'0"

UPPER BUNK

55"

18"

29-1/2"

10"

DESK AND
STORAGE UNIT

LOWER BUNK

1/4" PANELING
(TYPICAL)

NOTES
2 x 3 FRAMING JOINED
WITH 8d COMMON NAILS
1/4" PANELING FASTENED
WITH PANEL ADHESIVE
AND 1-1/4" PANEL NAILS

PARTITION ASSEMBLY

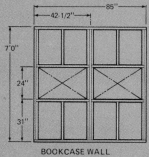

85"

42-1/2"

7'0"

24"

31"

BOOKCASE WALL

CLEAT—3/4 x 1-1/2 x 16-1/4"
FASTEN TO BOOKCASE WALL
STUDS WITH TWO 2" NO. 10
FH SCREWS

TOP—3/4 x 18-1/2" x TO FIT, PLYWOOD

FORMICA (TOP AND FRONT EDGES)

3/4 x 16-1/4 x 41"
PLYWOOD

3/4 x 3/4" x TO FIT, FRONT LIP

3/4 x 1-1/2" RAIL, TO FIT KNEEHOLE

3/4 x 3-1/2 x 14-3/4"
(2 REQD.)

3/4 x 28-7/8" x TO FIT
PLYWOOD (2 REQD.)

3/4 x 3-1/2 x 41"
(2 REQD.)

18-3/4"

SEE
SECT. DD

3/4 x 28-7/8 x 41"
PLYWOOD
(2 REQD.)

28-1/8"

29-5/8"

1/4" PANELING

18" DEEP x 15" WIDE
x 28" HIGH
FILE CABINET

3/4 x 16-1/4 x 28-7/8"
PLYWOOD

18"

NOTE:
ALL ASSEMBLY WITH
2" FINISHING NAILS
AND GLUE

SECTION VIEW

DESK AND STORAGE UNIT (2 REQD.)

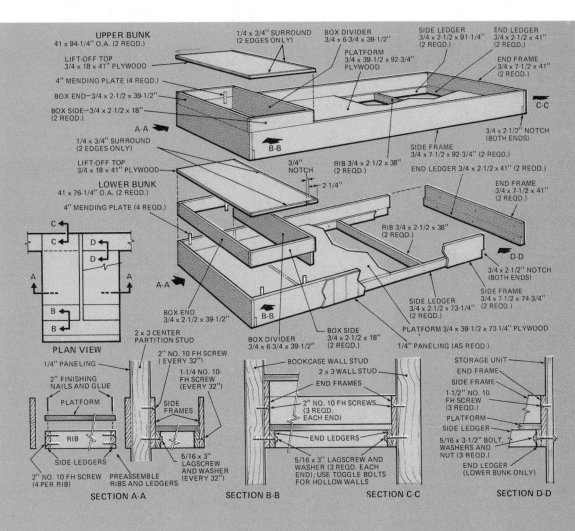

PLAN VIEW

SECTION A-A
1/4" PANELING
2" FINISHING NAILS AND GLUE
PLATFORM
RIB
SIDE LEDGERS
2" NO. 10 FH SCREW (4 PER RIB)
2 x 3 CENTER PARTITION STUD
2" NO. 10 FH SCREW (EVERY 32")
1-1/4 NO. 10 FH SCREW (EVERY 32")
SIDE FRAMES
5/16 x 3" LAGSCREW AND WASHER (EVERY 32")
PREASSEMBLE RIBS AND LEDGERS

SECTION B-B
BOOKCASE WALL STUD
2 x 3 WALL STUD
END FRAMES
2" NO. 10 FH SCREWS (3 REQD. EACH END)
END LEDGERS
5/16 x 3" LAGSCREW AND WASHER (3 REQD. EACH END); USE TOGGLE BOLTS FOR HOLLOW WALLS

SECTION C-C

SECTION D-D
STORAGE UNIT
END FRAME
SIDE FRAME
1-1/2" NO. 10 FH SCREW (3 REQD.)
PLATFORM
SIDE LEDGER
5/16 x 3-1/2" BOLT, WASHERS AND NUT (3 REQD.)
END LEDGER (LOWER BUNK ONLY)

LADDER ASSEMBLY (2 REQD.)

DETAIL E

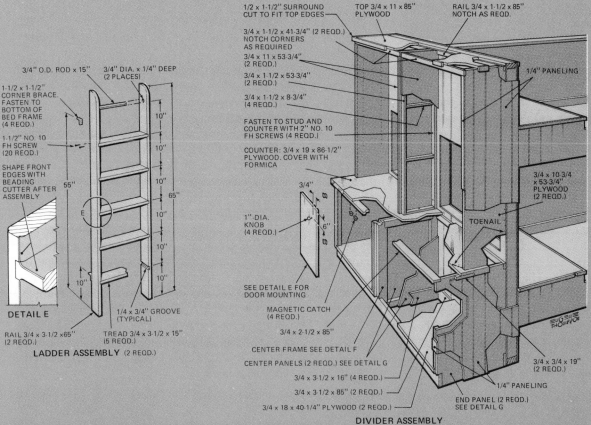

DIVIDER ASSEMBLY

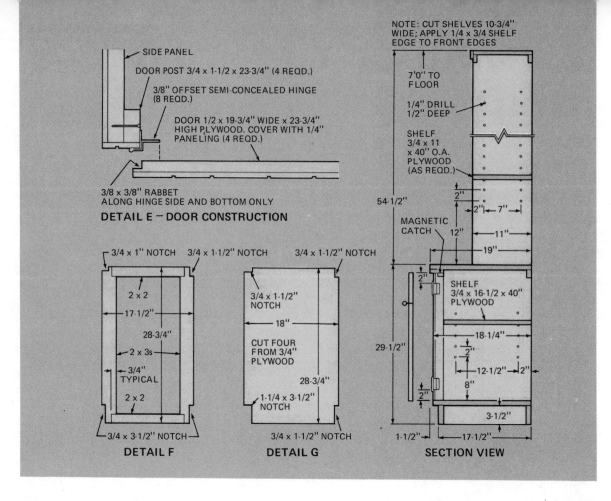

NOTE: CUT SHELVES 10-3/4" WIDE; APPLY 1/4 x 3/4 SHELF EDGE TO FRONT EDGES

DETAIL E — DOOR CONSTRUCTION

SIDE PANEL
DOOR POST 3/4 x 1-1/2 x 23-3/4" (4 REQD.)
3/8" OFFSET SEMI-CONCEALED HINGE (8 REQD.)
DOOR 1/2 x 19-3/4" WIDE x 23-3/4" HIGH PLYWOOD. COVER WITH 1/4" PANELING (4 REQD.)
3/8 x 3/8" RABBET ALONG HINGE SIDE AND BOTTOM ONLY

DETAIL F

3/4 x 1" NOTCH   3/4 x 1-1/2" NOTCH
2 x 2
17-1/2"
28-3/4"
2 x 3s
3/4" TYPICAL
2 x 2
3/4 x 3-1/2" NOTCH

DETAIL G

3/4 x 1-1/2" NOTCH
3/4 x 1-1/2" NOTCH
18"
CUT FOUR FROM 3/4" PLYWOOD
28-3/4"
1-1/4 x 3-1/2" NOTCH
3/4 x 1-1/2" NOTCH

SECTION VIEW

7'0" TO FLOOR
1/4" DRILL 1/2" DEEP
SHELF 3/4 x 11 x 40" O.A. PLYWOOD (AS REQD.)
54-1/2"
2"
2" 7"
MAGNETIC CATCH   12"   11"
19"
2"
SHELF 3/4 x 16-1/2 x 40" PLYWOOD
29-1/2"
18-1/4"
2"
12-1/2" 2"
8"
2"
3-1/2"
1-1/2"   17-1/2"

tion begins. The work counter is finished by applying a high-pressure laminate.

Start building the beds by cutting 1x8 pine to lengths required for the side and end frames. Notch each end of the side frames so that they can rest on the end ledger strips. Assemble the inside and then end frames to their respective walls using lagscrews into wall studs (see section drawings). If you must fasten between studs, use toggle bolts. Then install ledger strips on all three frame members. Finally, install outside frame and ledger strip. (Note: Install the ledger strips on all four sides using white glue and 1¼-in. ringed nails.)

Install the two rib members and cut the plywood platform to suit. If you cut the plywood neatly, it can simply float in its niche; there will be no need for fastening it.

Storage boxes at the bottoms of both upper and lower bunks are fashioned by attaching 1x3 stock to the frame members with mending plates and screws. One box end is cut from 1x7 stock so that it can be notched to rest on, and be toenailed to, the plywood platform. Their covers are simply lift-off rectangles of plywood. The upper bunk unit is built in exactly the same fashion as the lower.

Assemble the ladder as shown. After assembly, its front edges are shaped using a beading cutter in a router. If you lack a router, use a plane and sandpaper to break (round over) all sharp corners. The ladders are permanently attached to the bunks using corner braces and screws.

The bookcase has two pass-through areas which serve a dual purpose—these let light into the lower bunks to avoid a dark, gloomy look as well as providing a shelf for displaying collections.

Building the bookcase is the trickiest part of the job. Work as the professionals do by first laying out the pieces to be cut and then double checking them.

Assemble the unit using glue, nails and screws as indicated. When the bookcase unit is completed, it—as well as the beds and desk storage units—can be covered with pre-finished paneling.

Use moldings where needed but don't overdo it. You can save some money by working with unfinished pine moldings, but then you will have to mix stain to match the paneling and seal the wood with varnish. A simpler method, obviously, is to stick with the prefinished moldings.

Artist Don Mannes created the designs on the shades shown here using acrylic paints. To start, create your design on bond paper and then rub the back with a soft pencil so design elements can be transferred.

TOOLS AND MATERIALS for decorating shades include (clockwise from top) gel medium, acetone, artist's acrylic brushes, acrylic paints, various drafting supplies and X-Acto knife with No. 16 blades.

Tape the design to the shade and use a hard pencil to outline it. Lift the drawing to make certain all elements have been transferred before removing tape. Next apply a strip of wide masking tape over the design. This tape is transparent enough to permit easy cutting out. Carefully remove tape over all parts to be painted, making certain to burnish all tape edges to eliminate any chance of bleeding paint.

Apply acrylic paints as they come from the tube. If necessary, use gel medium sparingly to thin. Clean brushes with acetone.

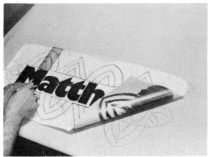

DESIGN IS transferred by rubbing back of drawing with soft pencil, taping it to shade, redrawing with a hard pencil.

WIDE MASKING tape is then affixed over design. Since it's transparent, the lines can be seen for easy cutting.

AS EACH section of design is cut, peel off the waste. Use knife tip to make certain all lines are cut cleanly.

BURNISHING of cut tape edges is very important. If poorly done, paint will bleed. Use other end of knife.

USE PAINT as it comes from tube; if it must be thinned, do so with gel medium. Clean brushes with acetone.

AFTER PAINT DRIES, peel off pattern. Carefully check all edges and touch up as necessary with artist's brush.

REPEAT pattern-and-paint operation to create designs around letters. Tape covers portion of lettering.

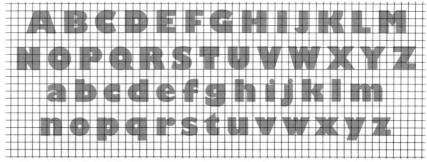

SIZE SQUARES for lettering to suit the area you are painting. On the shades shown, each square equals 1 in. Type face is Gill Kayl.

THE FORMICA-FINISHED ¾-in. plywood is sturdy, good-looking and easy to keep clean. Access to the hamper is provided through two spring-loaded door panels that always swing closed. Custom build the cabinet to fit the height of your room by adjusting the dimensions for shelf space at the top of the unit. Centered in the cabinet is a door that folds down to make a laundry sorting and folding shelf. The adjustable shelves behind the upper doors are made of ¾-in. plywood edged with a strip of pine. They are supported by recessed shelf standards and clips along the side panels.

Upgrade your utility room

Here's a handful of projects that will let you improve your utility room. Not only will you make that room more useful, but you'll also reduce the probability of fire damage. The center of focus is a hide-everything cabinet for holding, sorting and storing laundry and supplies

■ THE UTILITY ROOM is the workhorse of your house. In many home designs it holds the furnace, water heater, laundry and bulky items that can't be stored elsewhere. You can use these renovation projects to make this over-loaded room efficient, good-looking and safe.

new wall coverings

Recovering the walls and ceiling of your utility room will make it clean and attractive but, more important, if you pick the right material you can improve the fire rating of this potentially hazard-ous room. We used ⅝-in. fire-code gypsum wallboard—more expensive than standard board, but in this situation well worth it.

An average utility room has a much greater fire risk than other rooms. It holds the furnace, water heater, gas or electric lines for a dryer and, in many cases, the main fuse box. Fire code

wallboard is applied the normal way—no extra labor is involved. The material is treated with chemicals that make it fire-resistant. A three-coat taping job, plus a coat of washable latex paint, will make the walls good-looking and easy to clean. The extra margin of fire safety is built in.

custom-built laundry cabinet

This design combines several laundry opera-tions into a single, functional cabinet. Here's how it works. Dirty clothes are dropped into the hamper through two spring-loaded door panels. The hamper section below them has a center divider (light and dark washes can be separated with the two-door system) and rollers so you can pull the hamper out for easy access. You can hinge part of the face panel to get at clothes in the bottom easily.

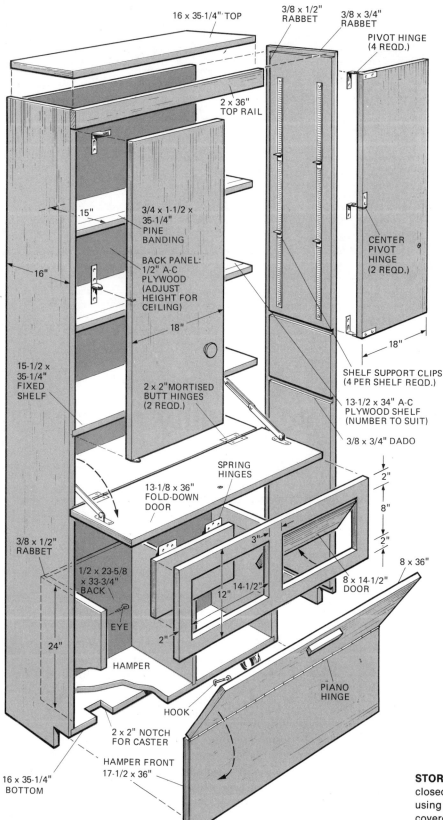

16 x 35-1/4" TOP

3/8 x 1/2" RABBET

3/8 x 3/4" RABBET

PIVOT HINGE (4 REQD.)

2 x 36" TOP RAIL

.15"

3/4 x 1-1/2 x 35-1/4" PINE BANDING

BACK PANEL: 1/2" A-C PLYWOOD (ADJUST HEIGHT FOR CEILING)

16"

18"

CENTER PIVOT HINGE (2 REQD.)

15-1/2 x 35-1/4" FIXED SHELF

2 x 2" MORTISED BUTT HINGES (2 REQD.)

18"

SHELF SUPPORT CLIPS (4 PER SHELF REQD.)

13-1/2 x 34" A-C PLYWOOD SHELF (NUMBER TO SUIT)

3/8 x 3/4" DADO

SPRING HINGES

13-1/8 x 36" FOLD-DOWN DOOR

2"

8"

2"

3/8 x 1/2" RABBET

1/2 x 23-5/8 x 33-3/4" BACK

EYE

3"

14-1/2"

12"

2"

8 x 14-1/2" DOOR

8 x 36"

24"

HAMPER

HOOK

2 x 2" NOTCH FOR CASTER

PIANO HINGE

16 x 35-1/4" BOTTOM

HAMPER FRONT 17-1/2 x 36"

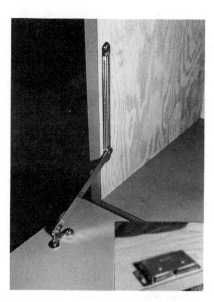

ATTACH THE SLOTTED BAR to the side of the cabinet, then brace the shelf in the down position (allow 1/8-in. for settling of the screws) and attach the other end of the slide bar. Double magnetic catches hold the doors closed. Shelf standards below are recessed to allow full-width shelves to be used.

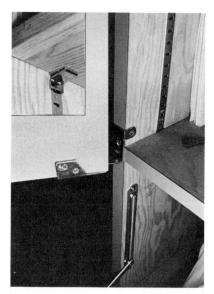

STORE CLEAN CLOTHES and supplies behind closed doors on the upper shelves; sort and fold using the drop-down door above the hamper. We covered the outside with Formica. The hardware is from Stanley, New Britain, CT 06050.

STEEL FIRE DOORS

INSTALL A 2x4 HEADER that's supported by an extra (jack) stud at each end. The sills on some doors are adjusted with washers stacked on top of each other. New

sills on the Pease doors we used can be adjusted for a perfect fit after the door is installed. This makes it easy to lock out drafts.

Above the spring-loaded panels, a full-width door folds down to make a counter for sorting and folding laundry. Behind the upper doors are adjustable shelves to hold washing supplies and clean clothes.

fire-safe doors

This renovation project has a lot going for it. Steel-skinned doors are easy to install, fire-resistant, warp-free and energy-saving. We used doors from Pease, 7100 Dixie Highway, Fairfield, OH 45023. A foam core cuts down dramatically on heat loss and a unique sill lets you make a height adjustment after the door is hung to lock out drafts and get a perfect fit. The warp-free door is a good buy ($80 and $100 for a 2-ft. 6-in. width) when you consider Class B fire-rating (1½ hours).

new washer and dryer

Installing a new, efficient laundry goes a long way to updating your utility room. The Maytag units we used are easy to install. The drain hose is provided with a siphon break and the supply hoses come with fittings to make connections between the back of the washer and cutoff faucets in your water lines.

sprinkler heads

You've seen them in commercial buildings but there's no reason why you can't use them at home. We used an upright and a pendant type

from Viking, Hastings, MI 49058. You can adapt the ½-in. male pipe threads to the nearest cold-water line.

quarry tile floors

Laying a heavy-duty quarry tile floor is a good way to start renovating your utility room. The job is somewhat involved, but you should be able to handle it by following the manufacturer's instructions provided with the tile.

There are other measures you can take to in-

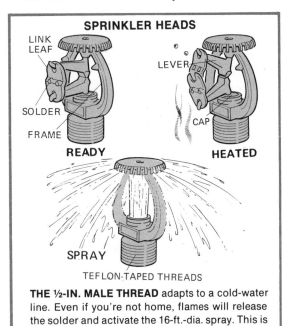

SPRINKLER HEADS

THE ½-IN. MALE THREAD adapts to a cold-water line. Even if you're not home, flames will release the solder and activate the 16-ft.-dia. spray. This is the type of unit used in commercial buildings.

crease the safety factor in your utility room. Adding a fire extinguisher has a high priority. A wall-mounted unit should be located in an obvious place. As a preventive measure you should have your heating plant inspected and cleaned at the start of every heating season. Accumulated deposits in the system can lead to puff backs which cause a mess, and could trigger a blaze.

These projects will make your utility room more efficient, and give you built-in fire protection for your peace of mind. Choose those which best meet your needs. With a little adaptation of dimensions and materials they should fit right into your plans.

WASHER AND DRYER HOOKUPS

FITTINGS ON THE WASHER supply hoses are screwed onto valves cut into the hot and cold-water lines, as shown at the right. The other ends screw into the fittings that are provided on the back of the machine, below left. The antisiphon valve, shown in the middle below, comes set up on the Maytag unit we used. To exhaust the dryer air through the wall, you'll need a vent kit like the one shown below right. Flexible duct can also be used to lead the exhaust outdoors.

PROPER DRAINAGE for your washing machine is one of the critical steps in a successful installation. To prevent siphoning action, a siphon break fitting should be used. For a suds-saving model that uses a storage tank, the drain hose should be run in a straight line with no loops. The dryer must be vented to an exhaust deflector on the outside of the house. Be sure to follow the manufacturer's installation rules. Your local dealer should be able to provide further information.

DRYER VENTING

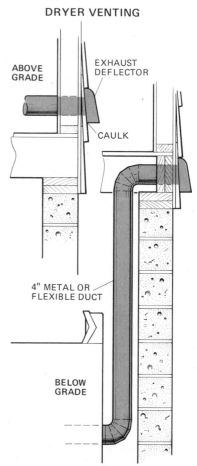

ABOVE GRADE

EXHAUST DEFLECTOR

CAULK

4" METAL OR FLEXIBLE DUCT

BELOW GRADE

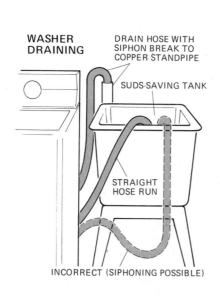

WASHER DRAINING

DRAIN HOSE WITH SIPHON BREAK TO COPPER STANDPIPE

SUDS-SAVING TANK

STRAIGHT HOSE RUN

INCORRECT (SIPHONING POSSIBLE)

Mud room makes a grand entry

maintenance, one that has plenty of storage space for all of the household's outdoor clothing and equipment.

You can build the simple shelf and bench units in this mudroom—designed by Shirley Regendahl—to provide your own family with needed storage space. The units can hold boots, skates, toys and outdoor accessories. Perforated hardboard can hold hats and coats.

Make your mudroom colorful but easy to care for by choosing durable finishes that withstand heavy foot traffic, excess moisture and outdoor elements. For example, paint the floor with floor and deck enamel and the walls with gloss or semigloss enamel, as in this mudroom which is finished with colorful Pittsburgh paints.

With a practical, welcoming mudroom, your back door may become the main entrance of your home. And the added storage and hanging space for family and guests will mean less work for you.

■ THERE'S NO NEED to bring the muddy mess of the outdoors inside your house. You can turn a small room, corner or wall area adjacent to the back door into a mudroom—a convenient storage place for hats, coats and outdoor gear.

The mudroom can be a comfortable area that entices your family to stop and shed rain or snow clothes, rather than dripping through the house. It should also be a practical area requiring little

A GOOD WAY to encourage neatness is to supply a special place for everything in an attractive, inviting room. The mudroom shown is located next to the back door, takes up minimum space, yet is equipped with easy-to-build vertical and bench storage units. Each family member can have his or her own storage place, perhaps identified by color. Plans for the shelf and bench units are shown at right.

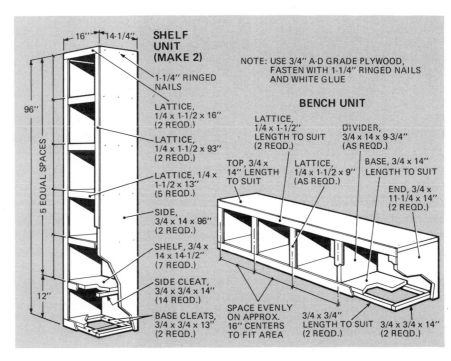

Dress up your yard with brick

By PENELOPE ANGELL

BRICK AND RAILROAD TIE WALK

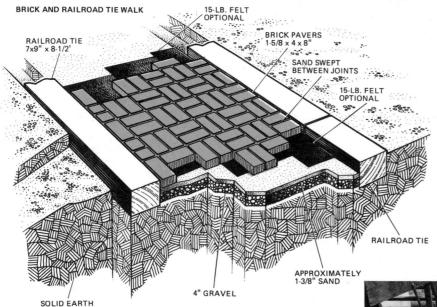

RAILROAD TIE 7x9" x 8-1/2'

15-LB. FELT OPTIONAL

BRICK PAVERS 1-5/8 x 4 x 8"

SAND SWEPT BETWEEN JOINTS

15-LB. FELT OPTIONAL

RAILROAD TIE

APPROXIMATELY 1-3/8" SAND

4" GRAVEL

SOLID EARTH

RAILROAD TIES surround this mortarless brick walk. A gravel base under a sand cushion is added. Because water drains through, bricks can be set level unless 15 lb. felt is used.

■ A SUNDAY DRIVE through almost any attractive neighborhood will prove the point that brick enhances a home. Whether it's a row of small planters or some grand steps to the door, brickwork draws attention and gives a look of permanence.

The mellow tones of brick can be a complement to your outdoor greenery and good ground cover for a large shady area where grass won't grow. Some projects, such as making stepping stones or lawn edging, are easy to do and will reward you with a functional, long-lasting product.

THE GROUND is excavated and the railroad ties are then leveled in position along the perimeter of the excavated area to form a border for the bricks.

When you plan an outdoor brick project, consider the type, color, size, shape and pattern you want to make. These factors add to the total effect. In most areas, Service Weather brick (SW grade) is best for outdoor use. Color choices include white, buff, gray, brown and, most popular, red. Brick comes in numerous sizes and shapes from rectangular to hexagonal.

You can also experiment by creating your own brick patterns. Consider a herringbone or other traditional design, or lay brick in rings around trees, planters and other stationary forms.

There are two basic ways to install brick—with mortar and without mortar. Mortarless brick has a natural look, is grouted with sand and can be placed over a gravel base. Mortared brick paving is usually laid over a concrete slab. It's more time-consuming, but it's also more permanent.

Mortarless paving such as the brick and railroad-tie walk shown here is not only attractive; it's functional. You can apply the same techniques for making this walk to other non-mortar projects, such as patios and driveways.

When you work without mortar you needn't lay mortarless brick all at one time. You can stretch the project over several weekends or when you have spare time.

You can substitute 2x4 staked redwood boards for the railroad ties. Or you can make an 8x8-in. concrete form around the paving perimeter and set the edge bricks in mortar.

Properly preparing and compacting the subgrade and base supporting the bricks will insure a paving that you can enjoy for a long time to come. If moisture accumulation might be a special problem, you can install 4-in. clay pipe drain tiles in the gravel base.

To make a brick and railroad-tie walk, first stake out the area to be paved using mason's line to define the shape. Place the railroad-ties in approximate position, then remove the topsoil beneath and set the ties.

Next add a gravel base. A 4-in. gravel layer topped by 1 or 2 in. of sand makes a good base for the brick. Add sand, rake level and tamp.

A screed board will help you control the depth of the sand. It can be made by cutting a 2½x6-in. notch in each end of a length of 2x4 that rides back and forth on guide boards. You can also make a wooden tamper from a 1-ft. length of 2x6 by nailing it to a 5 or 6-ft. length of 2x2 or 2x3. Use 10d common nails to join the boards.

If the ground where you plan to install the brick is shaded by trees causing damp conditions, laying 15-lb. felt beneath the brick reduces the amount of subsurface ground water drawn into the brick. The brick will then be relatively free of algae. If felt is added, however, the paving *must* be pitched to provide positive water runoff.

Lay the brick close together in the pattern you want, then sweep sand over the surface and into the joints. A more permanent mixture of three

POUR IN A LAYER OF GRAVEL, then mason's sand and tamp. Felt can help prevent weeds, but then the patio must be pitched. Lay the bricks close together and sweep sand between the joints. Then wet the sand down to compact it. A brick and railroad-tie walk can give many years of use and will be an attractive accent for your home.

parts sand to one part portland cement can be used in place of 100-percent sand. After sand or mixture is swept in cracks, use a fine water spray to compact it. Repeat the sweeping and spraying until all bricks are firmly locked in place. Once bricks are secure, the patio can be swept clean and used.

You can build a low wall to set off bricked paving, or make a barbecue grill or planter, once you know bricklaying basics.

Some brick should be laid completely dry and others should be dampened. The Brick Institute of America suggests this simple test to determine whether or not you should predampen the bricks.

Draw a 1-in.-diameter circle on a brick, then apply 20 drops of water from a medicine dropper inside the circle. Wait 1½ minutes. If the

HOW TO LAY UP BRICK WALLS

FIRST, WITH A TROWEL, spread the mortar evenly, adding slightly more than needed. Use a mason's line to ensure accuracy for this operation.

SECOND, BUTTER the brick end with mortar and tap it into the mortar bed so it seats in line and is level in both horizontal planes.

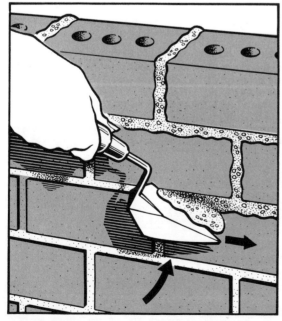

THIRD, REMOVE the mortar squeeze-out with your trowel. This can be returned to your mortar tub to be used in other sections of the work.

FOURTH, AFTER the mortar sets slightly, use a joint tool (or a bent ¾-in. pipe) to indent and compact the joints between the bricks.

BRICK PAVING WITH MORTAR

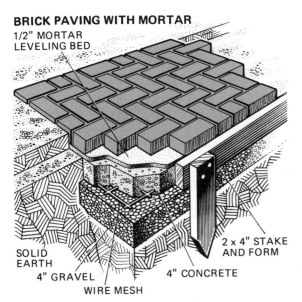

1/2" MORTAR LEVELING BED

SOLID EARTH

4" GRAVEL

WIRE MESH

2 x 4" STAKE AND FORM

4" CONCRETE

IT'S BEST to lay mortared brick paving on a concrete slab. The slab should be cured with controlled hydration for 10 days to two weeks.

water is still visible, the brick should be laid dry. If the water is absorbed, it indicates that the brick needs to be dampened. Hose down the brick pile for about 15 minutes before construction. The brick should be damp, not wet, when laid.

You can rent a mixer if you plan a large project. Begin by mixing only the amount of mortar you expect to use up in an hour or two of work. From here on, you will mix in two-hour batches. The mortar should have a consistency of soft mud. Keep it that way by adding a little water if it begins to stiffen.

Mortared joints between bricks on most projects should be about ⅜-in. thick. With a trowel, spread mortar on no more than three bricks of the preceding course, leaving a little more than the needed thickness. Texture the mortar surface by making a shallow furrow with the trowel point. A mason's line along the brick course can help check the thickness.

Next, butter one end of a brick with mortar and lay it into the mortar bed so the top of the brick is level with the mason's string. Butt the brick tightly against adjoining bricks to assure a lasting, water-tight joint. Then scrape off the squeezed-out mortar and return it to the mortar tub.

After the brick has been mortared in place and the mortar has hardened slightly, use a mason's joint tool, or short length of ¾-in. pipe, to tool each horizontal joint, then the vertical ones, pressing each to make the mortar dense, water-tight and concave.

If any bricks need to be cut at the end of the course, you can score them on two surfaces by tapping them with a broad-blade mason's chisel and a hammer. Then break the bricks by giving the chisel a sharp blow with the hammer. *Safety tips:* Be sure to wear safety goggles to protect your eyes and waterproof gloves to protect your hands from painful blisters.

Patios can be made with bricks set in mortar. The regularity of mortared brick placement gives a more formal look than brick-in-sand.

Brick with mortar joints is best laid over a very stable base like a concrete slab. An existing concrete patio in good condition will do. If you pour the slab, premixed concrete is convenient, especially for small projects. As with all mortared brick paving, be sure you have about ¼-in. pitch per foot for positive water drainage.

Use 2x4s with stakes to make the form for the slab. Be sure the stakes are sturdy, at least ¾x2½x24-in., space them every 18 to 24 in. so the wet concrete won't push the form outward. Install the 2x4 formwork with the slope of the slab you want. You can determine the pitch using a 2 or, preferably, 4-ft. spirit level and straightedge.

Smooth the concrete with a wood float that gives a coarse texture. The roughness assures a better bond between slab and following mortar bed.

Let the concrete cure for two weeks or more. For best results, cover it with burlap, canvas or salt hay. Spray it with water, then dampen it daily to control hydration.

laying mortared brick

Before you lay the brick, double-check the pitch of the concrete. Use a string and line level to establish slope with positive drainage.

Try a dry run of laying the bricks without mortar to get an idea of how many bricks you'll need per course. Be sure to consider the width of the mortar joints. If necessary, use a cut brick at the end of each course to equalize joint variation.

When you've dampened the brick (if needed) and mixed the mortar, begin by laying the brick in a ½-in. mortar bed. When the bricks are in place and the mortar has hardened slightly, press each joint with a pipe or mason's joint tool as when laying brick vertically.

After all brick is laid, sprinkle lightly with a garden hose, taking care not to disturb the joints. When dry, clean off mortar by sprinkling sand on it and sweeping.

Make your walls do double duty

Use these ideas to make your walls come alive. Some involve new products and others are novel uses for old products. Besides making your walls more attractive, they also provide easy ways for you to hang art, put away coats and tools and leave messages for the family

By PENELOPE ANGELL

■ THE DAZZLING COLORS and patterns you get in wall coverings today should be encouragement enough for updating your walls. But they can be more than just attractive. Many can provide safety and utility benefits as well.

One wall panel that's having widespread use in Europe and receiving notice here is Whyte-Board, a porcelain-on-steel material laminated to a variety of backings to make the panels. It also comes completely framed as bulletin

1. CORK WALLS
YOU CAN HANG ART or important messages directly on this cork wall covering.

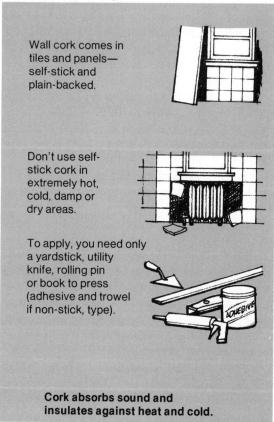

Wall cork comes in tiles and panels—self-stick and plain-backed.

Don't use self-stick cork in extremely hot, cold, damp or dry areas.

To apply, you need only a yardstick, utility knife, rolling pin or book to press (adhesive and trowel if non-stick, type).

Cork absorbs sound and insulates against heat and cold.

boards. Special markers can write or make doodles on the WhyteBoard. When erased, the writing leaves no residue on the eraser or cloth used. The hard-as-glass surface is scratchproof and comes in several pastel colors.

Another wall covering with added attraction is Formco, a waterproof Formica laminate panel that can be applied directly over old tile or other smooth wall surfaces. It comes in a number of patterns and colors, many that resemble marble. Formco panels make a good do-it-yourself project for your bathroom because they're easy to install. They're also practically maintenance-free.

A new wall covering that you can write on with chalk is Chalk-Talk. It's a flexible material, green in color, that can be glued to the wall with contact adhesive. It comes in 30-in.-wide rolls from 4 to 40 ft. long and can be cut with scissors. Chalk-Talk makes a colorful surface to write or sketch on in children's rooms, kitchens or dens.

Safety can be an important consideration in the wall coverings you choose. Some new panels made of ½-in.-thick brick bonded to wire mesh and stitched to aluminum-covered building board are fireproof. Called Brikpanels, by Ridgerock, Dover, Ohio, they measure 32 x 15¼-in. They can be used over many new and existing interior and exterior walls.

A helpful fire and sound barrier is the new RC-1 Sheetrock Resilient Channel by U.S. Gypsum. The channel is made of 25-gauge galvanized steel. It is attached with screws through prepunched holes to studs or joists. The channel can be used with plasterboard walls to give extra fire and sound control, especially helpful in homes with small children.

new twist to an old favorite

Velcro is a widely used fastening device for attaching two pieces of material together. A patch or strip of the loop-type Velcro is sewn to a fabric and a piece of the hook-type Velcro is sewn to another fabric. The loops and hooks join to form a tight bond when pressed together.

Velcro can also be used on your walls. The ¾-in. strips make a decorative pattern when not in use. Placed next to an outside door, they're a handy way to hang coats having a Velcro patch under the collar.

The strips come in black, white, olive, navy blue and beige. They can be purchased at marine suppliers and notions departments.

The most popular home wall coverings are vinyls, largely because of their easy-care traits.

2. WHYTEBOARD

WHYTEBOARD is a new type of writing system combining porcelain-on-steel panels and special dry markers. The writing is erased with a felt eraser or dry cloth, leaving no residue on the cloth. It's expensive to panel an entire wall in a home, but a framed board like the one shown is ideal in a child's room for doodles or messages. Alliance Wall, Alliance, Ohio 44601.

3. VELCRO

A SUPER GRAPHIC of Velcro becomes a coat rack. Attach the hooks to the wall and the loops to clothing.

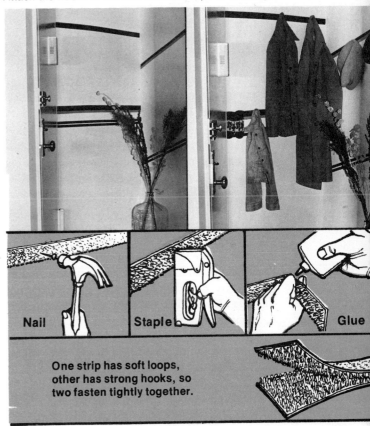

Nail   Staple   Glue

One strip has soft loops, other has strong hooks, so two fasten tightly together.

4. PERFORATED HARDBOARD

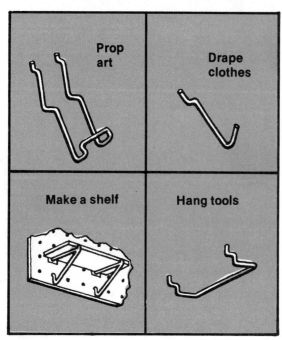

Prop art	Drape clothes
Make a shelf	Hang tools

PERFORATED HARDBOARD can help you get organized from family room to workshop. Games and play equipment can be stored in the open for easy access (right) or you can hang shop tools (below) within reach. The panels come ⅛-in., thick or ¼-in. thick for heavy-duty use such as hanging bicycles or garden equipment. Another plus: They can be kept clean with a damp cloth. The panels are available in several colors. They fasten directly to existing studs and joists.

They're washable and many are prepasted for easy hanging and dry-strippable for easy changing when you tire of the pattern.

Heavily embossed vinyl coverings called "Textures Unlimited" meet federal flammability tests and are scrubbable as well as being attractive. Made by the B.F. Goodrich Co., Marietta, Ohio, they have a rough surface that gives a three-dimensional effect. Some of the surfaces look like burlap, cane, stucco, suede, leather, corrugations and sandstone.

Several vinyl wall coverings have a fabric backing, usually of cotton knit, which makes them extra durable. An example is the Malaya line by Gilford, New York, N.Y., which can also be used as upholstery.

Some multipurpose wall coverings have been around a long time but continue to be widely used for their many advantages.

The newcomer to this group of old-timers is shiny Mylar. Shinier than the regular foil coverings, Mylar reflects almost as well as a mirror.

It's a good choice to lighten rooms because it reflects any available light.

A cork wall makes a great changing picture gallery. You can pin art and photos directly to it and easily remove them. With cork, your entire wall can be a bulletin board for messages and clippings. It also absorbs sound and acts as a room insulator.

Perforated hardboard like Peg-Board can be used for storage and display in virtually every room of your home. The panels fasten directly to studs and joists, or can be fastened to a solid wall allowing room between the wall and panel for inserting hangers in the perforations.

OTHER EXTRA PURPOSE WALLS

5. PREFINISHED HARDBOARD PANELS

Besides being decorative, they help control sound and are fireproof.

APPLYING TONGUE-AND-GROOVE PANELS OVER PLASTER

1. Lay out from the center. For best appearance, plan panels from center of wall and work out. The two end panels will probably need to be trimmed to fit, while center ones are whole.

CENTER LINE

2. Cut first panel. The left panel will be attached first. Make a plumb line from the ceiling as a guide for cutting and joining the first panel and next one. This will insure a plumb line at the joint, even if the walls are not vertical at the corners. Since the panels are tongue-and-groove, the first panel should be the width planned, plus $1/8$ in. for the tongue. Nail temporary 1x2-in. leveling strips at floor where the panels rest.

3. Apply adhesive to the back of the panel and then press the panel in place so that it is flush with the corner.

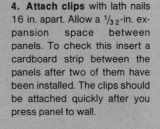

4. Attach clips with lath nails 16 in. apart. Allow a $1/32$-in. expansion space between panels. To check this insert a cardboard strip between the panels after two of them have been installed. The clips should be attached quickly after you press panel to wall.

CLIP ON PANEL

5. Attach next panel after applying adhesive and insert its tongue into the groove of the first. Press firmly together. Add other panels in the same way. The last must be cemented in place. Cut panels to fit snugly around window trim.

6. Remove starter strips, add base molding backed with scrap panel and nail to wall. Don't nail through the wall panel. Molding covers the bottom edge of the panel.

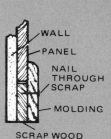

WALL
PANEL
NAIL THROUGH SCRAP
MOLDING
SCRAP WOOD

6. CERAMIC TILE
It's smooth to the touch and always looks clean and cool, besides being available in many colors with designs.

Highly durable and long lasting.
Needs very little maintenance.
Soil and water-resistant.

7. FORMCO PANEL
This is a Formica laminate with foam-core backing from Formco, Cincinnati. It comes in sheets or in tub and shower kits.

No grout lines to collect debris.
Can be applied over old tile.
Waterproof and easy to care for.

8. CHALK-TALK PANEL
Flexible, polyester laminate colored green from Conolite, Carpentersville, Ill.; applied with contact adhesive.

For writing chalk messages.
30-in.-wide rolls; 4, 8 or 40 ft.
Easy to cut with scissors.

9. RC-1 CHANNELS
Steel channels are screw-attached through prepunched holes to studs for use with plasterboard walls; from U.S. Gypsum.

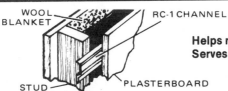

WOOL BLANKET
RC-1 CHANNEL
STUD
PLASTERBOARD

Helps reduce sound transmission.
Serves as a fire barrier.

Three versatile sawhorses you can make

ALL-PURPOSE SAWHORSES are built of redwood and finished with two coats of spar varnish. Here they are being converted to an outdoor buffet by adding a plywood top.

There have been many different and useful designs through the years for this most basic of all tools. Here are three sturdy and handsome ones that are unique

DESPITE FRAGILE looks, this design produces a rigid sawhorse that's great for heavy sawing. Strength is assured by out-of-sight shelf brackets.

INSPIRATION FOR these light-duty sawhorses came from Shaker-style clothes rack.

■ ONE OF THE FIRST tools that every home handyman needs is one he can build himself—a sturdy pair of sawhorses. There is an almost endless variety of types of sawhorses you can build. But we've narrowed our selection to three designs that are easy to build, nice to look at and rugged. The carpenter's sawhorse (above, lower left) was designed by Stephen Peterson; the other two concepts were created in our workshop by Harry Wicks.

All three sawhorses are built using standard construction techniques and stock materials available at the lumberyard. All can be built using hand tools only, but a table saw makes it a lot easier. Shaped brackets on the colonial-style horses are made by cutting with band or sabre saw and then shaping with a beading cutter in the router. If you do not own a router, simply cut brackets in triangular shape and round-over the exposed edges using either block or Surform plane.

The all-purpose horses can also double as legs for an outdoor buffet table. The top shown above is simply a 36x60-in. piece of ¾-in. exterior-grade plywood that is reinforced with furring-strip framing below.

No matter which design you decide to build, test-assemble the horse without glue after all parts have been cut. When satisfied with fit, disassemble the horses and sand all parts smooth before final assembly.

For looks, the all-purpose sawhorses shown were constructed of redwood. Start by cutting four legs for each horse. Make the two angle cuts at top end of each leg, then set the saw blade at 23° and make the leg bottom cuts. To assure that all legs will be exactly the same length, clamp a stop to your miter gauge when making leg cuts. To assure accuracy, hold the workpiece securely as it is fed into the spinning blade and use a slow feed rate. Next, lay out and cut notches for the leg spreaders.

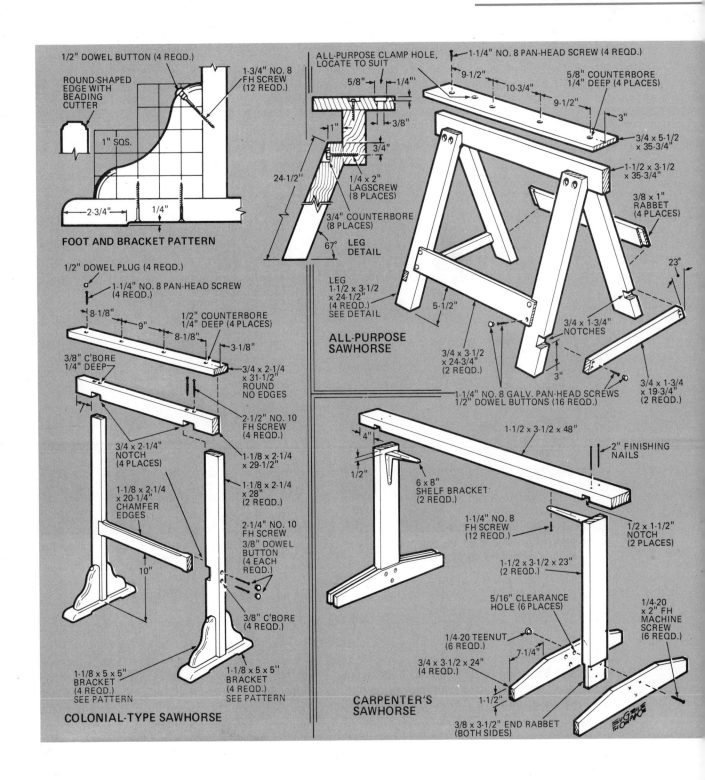

FOOT AND BRACKET PATTERN

1/2" DOWEL BUTTON (4 REQD.)

ROUND-SHAPED EDGE WITH BEADING CUTTER

1" SQS.

1-3/4" NO. 8 FH SCREW (12 REQD.)

2-3/4"   1/4"

COLONIAL-TYPE SAWHORSE

1/2" DOWEL PLUG (4 REQD.)

1-1/4" NO. 8 PAN-HEAD SCREW (4 REQD.)

8-1/8"   9"   8-1/8"   3-1/8"

1/2" COUNTERBORE 1/4" DEEP (4 PLACES)

3/8" C'BORE 1/4" DEEP

3/4 x 2-1/4 x 31-1/2" ROUND NO EDGES

2-1/2" NO. 10 FH SCREW (4 REQD.)

3/4 x 2-1/4 NOTCH (4 PLACES)

1-1/8 x 2-1/4 x 29-1/2"

1-1/8 x 2-1/4 x 28" (2 REQD.)

1-1/8 x 2-1/4 x 20-1/4" CHAMFER EDGES

2-1/4" NO. 10 FH SCREW 3/8" DOWEL BUTTON (4 EACH REQD.)

10"

3/8" C'BORE (4 REQD.)

1-1/8 x 5 x 5" BRACKET (4 REQD.) SEE PATTERN

1-1/8 x 5 x 5" BRACKET (4 REQD.) SEE PATTERN

ALL-PURPOSE SAWHORSE

ALL-PURPOSE CLAMP HOLE, LOCATE TO SUIT

1-1/4" NO. 8 PAN-HEAD SCREW (4 REQD.)

5/8"   1/4"

9-1/2"   10-3/4"   9-1/2"

5/8" COUNTERBORE 1/4" DEEP (4 PLACES)

3"

3/4 x 5-1/2 x 35-3/4"

1-1/2 x 3-1/2 x 35-3/4"

3/8 x 1" RABBET (4 PLACES)

1"   3/8"

3/4"

24-1/2"

1/4 x 2" LAGSCREW (8 PLACES)

3/4" COUNTERBORE (8 PLACES)

67°   **LEG DETAIL**

LEG 1-1/2 x 3-1/2 x 24-1/2" (4 REQD.) SEE DETAIL

5-1/2"

3/4 x 3-1/2 x 24-3/4" (2 REQD.)

1-1/4" NO. 8 GALV. PAN-HEAD SCREWS 1/2" DOWEL BUTTONS (16 REQD.)

3"

23°

3/4 x 1-3/4" NOTCHES

3/4 x 1-3/4 x 19-3/4" (2 REQD.)

CARPENTER'S SAWHORSE

4"   1/2"

6 x 8" SHELF BRACKET (2 REQD.)

1-1/2 x 3-1/2 x 48"

2" FINISHING NAILS

1/2 x 1-1/2" NOTCH (2 PLACES)

1-1/4" NO. 8 FH SCREW (12 REQD.)

1-1/2 x 3-1/2 x 23" (2 REQD.)

5/16" CLEARANCE HOLE (6 PLACES)

1/4-20 TEENUT (6 REQD.)

3/4 x 3-1/2 x 24" (4 REQD.)

7-1/4"

1-1/2"

1/4-20 x 2" FH MACHINE SCREW (6 REQD.)

3/8 x 3-1/2" END RABBET (BOTH SIDES)

Use clamps when assembling legs to the top rail; legs must be held in a fixed position while holes are bored for lagscrews. After legs are attached, install the 1x4 rails to keep legs immobile. Then add the spreaders at both ends using resorcinol glue and 4d galvanized nails.

Finally, attach the 1x6 top piece which makes it easier to handle work on the horse. The hold-down clamps are optional but welcome when you need a third hand. The redwood horses shown were finished with two coats of spar varnish.

The carpenter's sawhorses we made in the shop are of kiln-dried 2x4 fir. Start by cutting the legs and top rail to length. Install the dado head on your table or radial saw and cut the rabbets in

OPTIONAL hold-down clamp, Model 16 from Jorgensen, features easy adjustment and a secure hold.

WITH BOTTOM NUT loosened, the bolt head can be raised and the base of the clamp positioned.

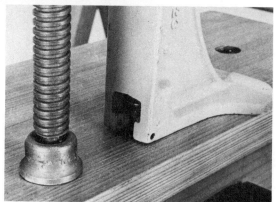

NUT IS TIGHTENED to hold the clamp. A cotter pin can be inserted to keep the clamp in place.

both sides of leg bottoms as shown. Then make the dadoes in the underside of the top rail to receive the legs with a snug fit. Assemble the legs in the dadoes using weather-proof glue and 8d galvanized finishing nails. Then install shelf brackets.

Next cut the 1x4 to length; you need four per horse. Clamp feet to legs and bore three $5/16$-in.-dia. holes per leg to receive the machine screws. Remove feet, apply glue and permanently fasten feet with machine screws and Teenuts. Note length of screws (2 in.) which will just grab Teenut and not protrude from the other side.

Since these horses are intended for carpentry, you needn't apply a finish. If desired, however, you can rub in several coats of boiled linseed oil.

The colonial sawhorses are great for light chores. Constructed entirely of clear pine, the fragile-looking horses get their strength from the joinery used (i.e., notches). Cut all parts and test-assemble them using 4d finishing nails only. When satisfied with fit and squareness, permanently assemble horse with glue and screws.

Foot brackets are made on the bandsaw and then shaped with router and beading cutter. The best way to install them is with the horse clamped in your bench vise. First bore and install the screws from beneath, then rotate the piece 180° and install the diagonal screw and dowel button. Repeat for all legs. Finish the horse with stain and two coats of semigloss varnish.

Sometimes you can't seem to find that odd-size dowel you need. You can make your own with this jig that uses a clamp-held chisel

By COLLIN BAKER

Turn dowels on your drill press

■ RIGHT-SIZE DOWELS for some jobs, especially furniture repairs, can be hard to find. This jig can be used instead of a lathe to turn any odd-size dowel you may need.

Bore a hole slightly larger than the size desired (⅛ in. larger if working from rough stock) halfway through a hardwood block. Then bore all the way through with a bit of desired size, or use a smaller bit and rasp to size. Make radial cut A, then make cut B ³/₁₆ in. inside and parallel to a line tangent to the larger hole, providing a surface for the chisel flat. Parallel notch in block's opposite side is clamp seat. Coat hole with silicone lubricant. Clamp chisel in place, chuck dowel stock, and turn, using low drillpress speed and feeding slowly.

If commercial dowel is not used, rough out blanks with octagonal bevel cuts on the table saw or by planing square stock. If stock diameter exceeds chuck capacity, reduce size of one end. To turn long pieces, swing table or head aside, hold jig by hand. For short lengths, you can hold jig in a vise and chuck the dowel in a brace or portable drill.

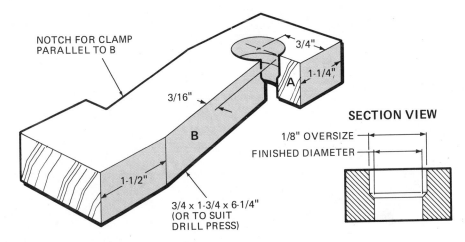

NOTCH FOR CLAMP
PARALLEL TO B

3/4"

1-1/4"

A

3/16"

B

1-1/2"

3/4 x 1-3/4 x 6-1/4"
(OR TO SUIT
DRILL PRESS)

SECTION VIEW

1/8" OVERSIZE

FINISHED DIAMETER

How to use a jointer

By HARRY WICKS

■ IN SIMPLEST TERMS, a jointer is really nothing more than a motorized plane. The difference is that a hand-plane job which might take 15 arm-wearying minutes can be accomplished on a jointer in a minute or so—and, in all likelihood, with a far smoother finish.

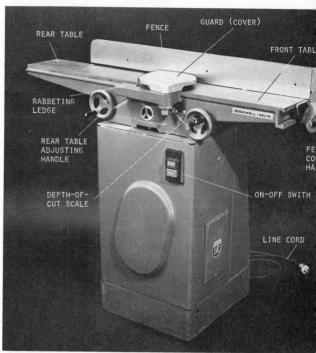

JOINTER, with its principal parts named above, can save hours for furniture builders. It will do quality work if used safely and kept in adjustment.

ACCURATE WORK is assured when the rear table is level with the knives.

DEPTH-OF-CUT scale should be checked periodically for accuracy.

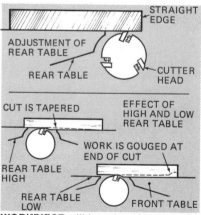

WORKPIECE will be ruined if rear table and knives are not aligned.

FENCE SHOULD be locked at exactly 90° to table, and pointer set to 0°.

FENCE ON this jointer has stop screws which permit a fast change to 45°.

WITH PLUG pulled, blades can be honed as shown; belt must be clamped to stand.

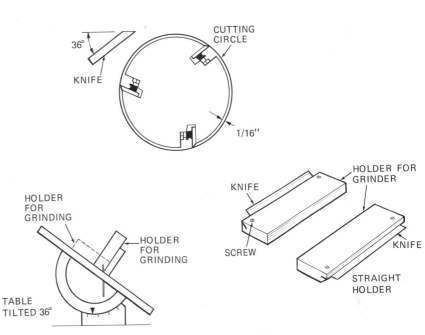

TO GRIND blades at 36° angle, run a saw kerf in a block of wood as shown above. Knife can be held snugly with screws through the jig's side.

BLADES ARE JOINTED with cutterhead revolving; stop block is a must.

AT START of cut, hands should be over front table pushing board forward.

AFTER STOCK passes cutters, left hand is repositioned over rear table.

RIGHT HAND should be kept at rear of board to prevent kickback.

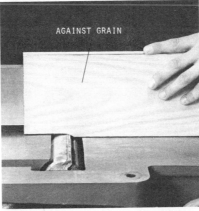

BOARD FED against grain will result in uneven, often splintered, edge.

DETERMINE BOARD'S grain before jointing.

Your degree of success with a jointer will depend mostly on two important points:
• Whether you keep the tool in adjustment and cutters sharp.
• Whether you use it properly, observing all safety rules when you do. As with all power tools, failure to do either may well result in damage to the operator or workpiece or both.

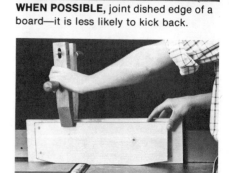

DISHED EDGE

WHEN POSSIBLE, joint dished edge of a board—it is less likely to kick back.

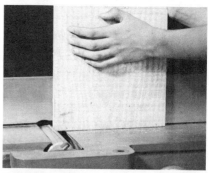

BOARD WITH uneven edge can be jointed by clamping it to a straight board.

AFTER SEVERAL PASSES, the uneven edge will be straight and square.

WHEN YOU have a wide board or an end grain to joint, add an auxiliary fence.

TO ASSURE even pass on end grain, make a short cut into the first corner.

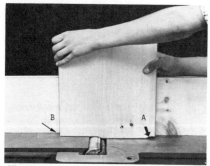

ROTATE BOARD and feed corner B into cutters and complete cut through A.

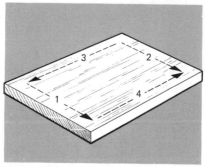

THIS IS THE proper sequence when all four edges are to be jointed.

BEVEL EDGE is jointed by tilting the fence in or out, then locking it.

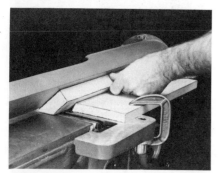

SAFE WAY is to align board for jointing, then clamp-fasten a stop board.

A BOARD jointed with fence tilted out has tendency to pull away from fence.

HERE it's better to clamp stop block to table so board can't move laterally.

ADVANCED CUTS ON A JOINTER

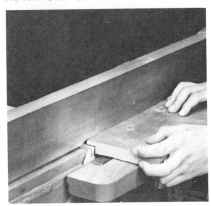

TO CUT A RABBET, fence is moved and front table is lowered.

ROUND STOCK can be rabbeted using holddown after fence and cutter are set.

TENON IS created by rotating round stock against cutterhead; *use safety devices.*

Be advised that for photographic clarity—so that readers will be able to see clearly the cutter-workpiece relationship for the various cuts—we have removed the cutterhead safety cover. In actual use, however, *never use a jointer without its safety devices in place.* The cover, in fact, is spring-loaded to assure its

snapping against the workpiece to keep the cutter knives covered.

Jointers for use in conjunction with the table-saw motor are available, but many woodworkers opt for a free-standing jointer with its own motor. Jointers are sold by the size of stock they will handle—that is, a 4-in. jointer will plane a piece of wood up to 4 in. wide. Though a 4-in. jointer will be adequate in many home shops, most woodworkers prefer laying out a few more bucks initially and pick a 6-incher. The 50-percent increase in capacity usually means that you also get a machine with more power as well as the ability to make deeper cuts.

There are, basically, two methods of feeding work into a jointer's spinning cutterhead. The first is to start the board in with both hands over the infeed table and in front of the cutters. As

PLANING THIN STOCK SAFELY

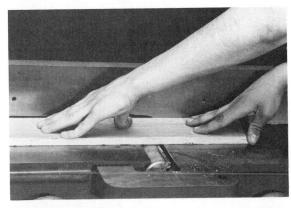

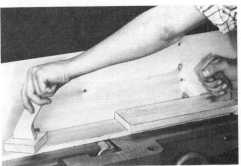

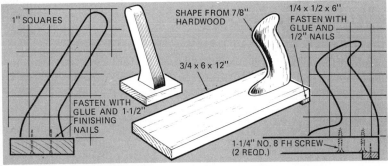

NEVER push thin stock through as in upper photo. Use pushers or move hands to the rear. The use of pusher boards is a good habit to practice. Good-sized board is of nominal 1-in. pine. Handle is hand-shaped of oak.

soon as a sufficient length of board passes over the cutters, the left hand is also moved to the leading edge of the board over the outfeed table. When the board nears its end, the right hand is also moved to the rear of the cutterhead. The important point to remember is that the hand over the outfeed table is the one that should exert the downward pressure. The other hand (in front of the blade) is used to push the board forward not down. Both hands should be used to keep a constant pressure against the fence.

The second method is to place both hands at the front of the board to start the cut—one hand slightly in front of the other—and keep the hands in this position through the cut. Some may have mental reservations about passing the hands directly over the cutterhead, but as long as the board is wide enough—and all safety guards are in place—there really isn't any danger. Keeping the hands set in this manner is the most positive way of preventing a kickback—the biggest danger on a jointer. I also prefer using this method whenever possible because it is considerably faster.

Before the jointer can be expected to turn out 100-percent-accurate work, all adjustments should be checked and corrected if necessary. The rear (or outfeed) table must be precisely aligned with the cutterhead knives or serious mistakes will be made on the workpiece (see photos and sketches on page 82).

With the power cord removed from the wall outlet, rotate the cutterhead until one of the cutters reaches the highest point of its cutting circle. Then, using a metal straightedge, align the rear table with the cutter. Check the cutter-table relationship at both ends and center of the cutter knife. This will reveal whether the knife is improperly mounted in the cutterhead. Repeat the alignment check with the other two cutters. If a knife is discovered to be out of alignment, loosen the setscrews holding it and realign the cutter knife.

check depth-of-cut scale

The depth-of-cut scale should also be checked periodically for accuracy. To do it, mark a board for a ⅛-in. cut and adjust the front table to make an exact cut. Make the cut and then check the board with a ruler to assure that the cut was exactly ⅛ in. Then set the pointer on the depth-of-cut scale to read ⅛ in. and lock it in place. Repeat the test after setting the pointer to make certain it didn't slip during the screw-tightening process. Generally speaking, the depth-of-cut

scale will require a realignment each time that the cutters are sharpened.

The fence-angle scale should also be checked for accuracy. How to do it varies from one brand to another because of different features offered by various manufacturers. A manufacturer's booklet of adjustments (as well as use instructions) comes packed with every jointer; do take the time to read and understand the one that comes with yours.

Occasionally, your cutter knives may require grinding. Because the knives are so narrow, it is necessary that you make a holder such as the one shown in the drawing on page 83. To make it, set your saw arbor to cut at 36° and saw-kerf a board as shown. The knife can then be inserted in this slot for grinding. If the knife is not held snugly, use screws through the jig's side to hold it so.

To grind the knife, adjust your grinder's toolrest to the required angle and clamp on a stop block to serve as a guide. This guide assures a straight pass across the knife blade. Work each knife in turn using a light cut for each pass. Do not make heavy cuts on steel or it will burn and render the blade useless.

Since grinding is only necessary when the cutters are in rough shape (nicked or chipped), honing at regular intervals will generally maintain the sharpness required for home shop activities. To do it, partially cover a fine carborundum stone with paper (to save the table surface) and position it on the front table as shown in the photograph on page 82.

After disconnecting power, rotate the cutterhead until the stone rests flat on a knife's bevel. Clamp the belt to the stand so the head cannot turn and hone cutter by stroking the stone lengthwise along the cutter. *Do the same number of strokes on each knife.*

To sharpen and joint knives to a true cutting circle, the edges must be jointed while the head is revolving. To do this, the stone is placed on the rear table and the jointer is turned on. A stop block securely clamped to the front table is a must or the stone will be drawn forward by the spinning cutterhead (see photo on page 83).

jointer basics

Remember to cut boards oversize to equal the amount to be removed on the jointer. For example, if you want a board exactly 4 in. wide and plan to joint *both edges,* rip the board 4¼ in. wide and set the jointer to cut to a depth of ⅛ in. One pass on each edge knocks off ⅛ in. and you will finish with a perfect 4-in-wide board.

How to crack 'impossible' nuts

By DOUG RICHMOND

■ MOST SERVICE MANUALS start out: "To remove the head (or manifold or valve cover or whatever) remove the nuts securing it. . . ." The problem is these manuals never say one word about what you are supposed to do if the nuts or screws are rusted, galled or seized!

When you encounter these "tough nuts," first apply penetrating oil liberally to the nuts and any projecting threads. Lacking penetrating oil, any thin oil will do. Even hydraulic transmission fluid will help. Allow the oil as much time as possible to work its way down through the rust and along the threads before you reach for the wrenches.

The next thing, of course, is to apply sufficient torque to the nuts to unwind them, using the right tool.

The common open-end wrench is the poorest wrench to use on hard-to-turn nuts inasmuch as it is designed solely to be convenient and fast in light-duty use. It contacts a nut or hex-head screw on only two corners and under severe stress the jaws have a tendency to give just enough to allow them to ride over the corners, rounding them off in the process.

For this reason the most popular tool in the mechanic's box is the combination wrench, the kind with an open end and a box end at opposite ends of the same tool. The box part may be either hexagon or "6-point," or double-hexagon or "12-point." The sole advantage of the 12-point is that a new "bite" only requires 30° of handle movement, whereas the 6-point takes 60°.

But for applying maximum torque to stubborn fastenings the hex wrench wins hands down. On badly rounded, soft or extremely rusted fastenings, it contacts a larger area and has much less tendency to ride over and round the corners than a 12-point.

Most combination wrenches are too short to get enough leverage to loosen really tough nuts. But this is easy to overcome by "cheating": hooking the box end of another combination of about the same size in the open end of the wrench that is actually doing the work.

Another method of cheating on a combination wrench is to strike the open end with a fairly heavy hammer. Use a heavy hammer because a light one simply wastes its energy by bouncing back.

If there's room, use a socket wrench, not a combination, because it is usually stronger and designed to exert more torque than an equivalent combination wrench. As with combination wrenches, sockets come in 6 and 12-point con-

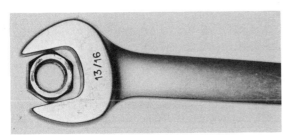

OPEN-END wrench must fit perfectly or it will slip and round the nut as shown here.

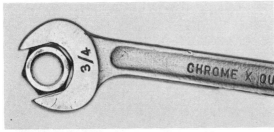

CORRECT-FITTING open-end wrench grips only two sides so it may not loosen a tight nut.

ONE WAY to "cheat" is by hooking the box end of a cheater wrench over the open end of the work wrench.

figurations. For heavy-duty work the 6-point is by far the best.

Sockets are most conveniently turned with a ratchet, especially in restricted places. Most manufacturers supply ratchets with several handle lengths. Most of the time a short-to-medium handle is perfectly adequate. But for the occasional nasties the modern professional mechanic carries a "cheater pipe" that at the very least doubles the length of the ratchet handle.

A good cheater pipe has a snug fit over the handle and is long enough so that it can slide down to the head of the ratchet, leaving adequate length for the task at hand. If the cheater bears only on the grip of the ratchet there is much greater risk of damaging the tool.

If it is possible to reach the other end of the fastening you are working on, it often helps to rap it smartly while applying torque. But *do not* hammer on a stressed socket or the box end of a combination wrench itself. This is a good way to break the tool and doesn't aid the task at hand in the least.

Occasionally the bolt or stud will twist before the nut moves. If the bolt is easy to replace, as in an exhaust-pipe clamp, then it may be easier to go ahead and twist it off than to take the trouble to salvage the parts.

You will find that some nuts simply won't budge, no matter how hard you try to turn them. This is where hammer and chisel come into play.

A nut may be "busted" from the end or side. Many times only a shallow cut will be needed at the middle of the flat to expand the nut enough to allow it to be wrenched off with ease, so the trick here is to cut into the nut a little bit and then try the wrench again.

Cutting down into the nut parallel to the threads will accomplish the same thing now and

WHEN chisel-bursting nuts from the top, be careful not to damage threads of bolt.

then, but mostly the nut will have to be opened up almost all the way to the bottom. If care is used, the bolt or stud threads will be undamaged.

Tubing fittings can be a particular pain. Usually it is impossible to use a conventional box wrench, and an open-end wrench will either collapse the fitting or round its corners. Actually, the average tubing fitting really isn't seized; it's just tight, except for hydraulic brake fittings, and it is here that the tubing wrench pays for itself. This is a heavy box wrench with a section cut out to permit it to slip over the tubing which is always smaller than the fittings themselves. As these are quite expensive and entirely too fragile for ordinary nut-turning only buy the ones you actually need.

Much of the time tubing wrenches are used in pairs on parts that won't stand a lot of stress, such as the union that connects the gas line to the

A "CHEATER PIPE" is the best way to get additional leverage. It's important for the pipe to slide all the way over the handle to the ratchet.

STRIKING SHARP blows with a heavy hammer is another way to cheat. The combination wrench here is being used on the generator nut of a VW.

TUBING WRENCHES are used in pairs and are squeezed together to loosen nuts.

TAPPING screwdriver while turning often will loosen slot-head screws.

IMPACT DRIVER will work when twisting and tapping won't loosen tight screws.

carb. Rather than pull on one wrench while holding with the other, try to use the wrenches like scissors, squeezing the ends together with one or both hands.

It is vital that the wrench fit the nut or fitting. An oversize wrench rides over the corners with the greatest of ease, in some cases rounding the corners to the point where the correct wrench will be unable to get a grip. Badly rusted fastening nuts often will not allow the proper size wrench to slip over them with ease, and there is a temptation to go to the next larger size. Don't! Instead tap the correct wrench over the fastening or fitting with a hammer.

Screws, both slotted-head and Phillips, are used from one end of a car to the other for trim, striker plates and carburetors, and most of the time they present no problem. Slotted-head screws are easily damaged by a dull screwdriver

SINGLE BLOW of sharp cold chisel often will expand a nut when torque alone is not enough. Hold the chisel against flat of the nut parallel to both sides.

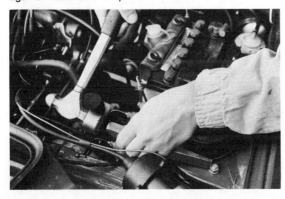

when it slips out of the slot. For tight slotted-head screws, especially the small ones such as hold the top of the carburetor to the body, the trick is to take a sharp-cornered screwdriver and catch the corner of the screw slot. Then tap the handle lightly with a small hammer and the screw can usually be "walked" around until it's loose enough to permit removing it conventionally.

The Phillips-head screws that hold the striker plates on most cars are intended to be tight. At the factory they are installed with power equipment; removing them with a hand screwdriver may be impossible.

This is where an impact driver will pay for itself. They usually include a few heavy-duty screwdriver bits. They are available to take either ⅜-inch or ½-inch drive attachments, and most mechanics prefer the ⅜-inch drive size. To use the impact driver, install the correct size bit, insert it in the screw and rotate the tool in the direction you wish to turn the screw. Strike it sharply with a medium-weight hammer—about 16 or 20 ounces. The force of the hammer blow not only causes the handle of the driver to rotate due to the cam action but also forces the bit into the slot. After each hammer blow rotate the driver in the direction of desired rotation as the handle will often rotate enough to cause it to reverse.

In reassembly, use petroleum jelly to prevent rusting and galling and seizing. A good grease may be used, or even oil. But put *something* on the threads; later, you won't have much trouble getting them apart!

THE BADLY WORN chair above gets years of extra life with a covering of new upholstery.

THE FRESH SUEDE-LOOK fabric in beige gives the chair a contemporary, trim look.

Secrets of reupholstering

By JOSHUA MARK

■ YOU MAY THINK reupholstering is a job that takes a professional, but with the right tools, patience and a steady hand, you can reupholster your favorite living-room chair in several weekends.

The old fabric, although stretched from use, is a good clue to the approximate amount of new fabric you'll need. If you use a print design, you'll need to purchase more material than you'll actually use since the print must be

1 **START** by removing the old fabric with mallet and ripping chisel.

2 **STRIP** the old fabric on the outside of the arms.

3 **PLIERS** help remove the burlap covering springs and webbing.

4 **CUT** weak twine and begin by retying the springs.

5 **WEAVE** jute webbing on the bottom. Pull taut with a stretcher.

6 **WITH** a tack hammer attach webbing to the bottom of the frame.

7 **WEAVE** the webbing from front to back and side to side.

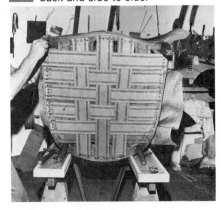

8 **TACK** burlap over seat springs, then sew it to top of seat.

9 **FOX EDGE** sewed to the burlap is used to cushion seat edge.

10 **IF THE FRAME** needs repair, glue and clamp for a strong bond.

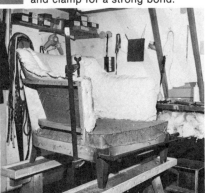

11 **MEASURE** the final fabric, then cut it larger than needed.

12 **SEW** inexpensive scrap to fabric for pull-strip handholds.

13 **PULL STRIPS** help to position fabric to produce a tight fit.

14 **SMOOTH** the new fabric over the chair seat and into position.

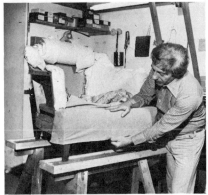

15 **THE FRONT** edge of seat fabric attaches to frame with tacks.

16 **SEW** the back side of the new fabric to front edge of seat.

17 **POSITION** seat fabric by the pull strips at chair back.

18 **FIT** fabric over inside of arms. Note extra fabric at top.

**Reupholstering is
easy when you learn
the secrets of
a real pro**

19 CUT the fabric up to the frame at stress points.

20 CAREFULLY TACK inside arm fabric so no wrinkles occur.

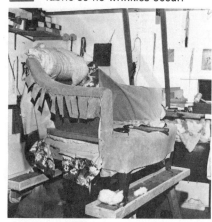

24 POSITION fabric for outside of arm. Chalk the contour inside.

25 TACK cotton topped with burlap to outside of arms and back.

26 TACK cardboard strip to back side of arm fabric for roll effect.

matched. The store where you buy the fabric can help determine the quantity needed. Here are some helpful tips from professional upholsterers at Carlin Decorators, Wantagh, NY.

Your first step is to remove the existing upholstery. Use a mallet and ripping chisel to strip away the material. Remove the burlap underneath the material with pliers.

It will help to take notes as you work, listing the materials to be replaced and the order that they are stripped. Materials will be replaced in reverse order.

A sewing machine is the only large piece of equipment you need to reupholster a chair. It's helpful for sewing pull strips to position the material and for sewing fabric around welt cord, but in a pinch you can hand-sew them.

Sources for specialized tools and materials are in the classified directory under "Upholsterers'

Supplies." Tools include a ripping chisel and mallet, pliers for removing the old upholstery, webbing stretcher, tack hammer, and a curved upholstery needle.

The materials you'll need depend somewhat on the chair you reupholster. In many cases, you can use the stuffing already in the chair, particularly if it is hair or a resilient fiber that doesn't pack down. Other supplies include: Italian spring twine, webbing, burlap, cotton padding, heavy nylon sewing thread, tacks, fox edge, welting, cardboard tacking strip and the final fabric. A muslin cover may attach to the frame of your chair before the final fabric is applied.

Upholstery kits containing tools and some materials are available from Albert Constantine and Son, 2050 Eastchester Rd., Bronx, NY 10461 and Craftsman Wood Service Co., 2727 South Mary St., Chicago, IL 60608.

21 POSITION padding on inside chair back to cushion fabric.

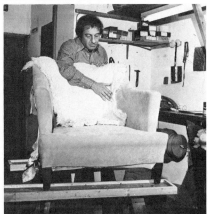

22 TACK top of the fabric to chair frame. Smooth all sides.

23 FOLLOWING chair contour, tack welting on outside of arm.

27 STRETCH fabric tacked at top over back and sides, and tack.

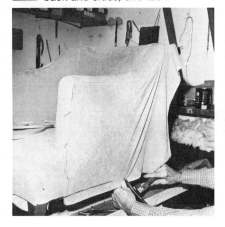

28 SEW outside arm fabric by hand using an upholstery needle.

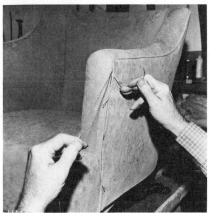

29 IF YOU want to add a kick pleat, sew it to bottom of fabric.

Before you apply new materials, make any needed repairs on the wood finish. Also make structural repairs that can't be made later.

Begin by retying the springs with twine in the same way they were tied previously. Next tack the new webbing in a pattern similar to that of the old webbing. The webbing stretcher will help you pull the webbing taut (Photo 5) before it's tacked and cut.

You can upholster the chair in sections. Work on this chair was done in seven parts: seat (Photos 8-17); inside of arms (Photos 18-20); inside of back (Photos 21-22); outside of arms (Photos 23-28); outside of back; kick pleat skirt (Photo 29); and cushions.

Allow about a 6-in. overhang when cutting material for each section except the cushions. Cut the fabric, then position it section by section. Be sure that each layer of material is securely and smoothly attached before proceeding.

After the final covering is in place, take measurements for fitted cushions such as the seat cushion on the chair shown. The covering on these cushions must fit smoothly—excess material can't be pulled under the chair frame.

Cushions are made up of a top, bottom and middle panel called boxing. Panels are joined together with welt.

It's safe to make a paper pattern of the cushion, then transfer the pattern outline to the fabric, leaving a seam allowance. Be sure to align and center the fabric grain and pattern before cutting.

Here it is also advantageous to make a trial run with a muslin case which doesn't require welt. With time, patience and care you should achieve professional results.

Tricks of the saw sharpener's trade

By ROSARIO CAPOTOSTO

■ OBVIOUSLY, A SHARP handsaw makes cutting easier and gives cleaner cuts. Besides making good cuts, a sharp power saw blade is a must for maximum safety. Feeding a board into a dull table-saw blade can cause kickback, and cutting with a dull blade can burn out a saw's motor.

Saw sharpening is an inexpensive and money-saving do-it-yourself operation that requires some basic knowledge and a little practice.

basic steps

Before you begin to sharpen any saw, you must remove all accumulated resin, pitch and gum. Use kerosene or a commercial solvent sold for the purpose.

The essential steps in sharpening both handsaws and power-saw blades are: *jointing* to standardize teeth height; *shaping* to restore correct tooth shapes; *setting* to prevent binding (so the saw kerf will be greater than blade thickness); and *filing*, the actual sharpening of the edges or points of teeth.

Not every operation will be necessary every time you sharpen a saw blade. For touch-ups, a thorough cleaning and filing may be enough.

Mill files (single cut) should be used for sharpening because they leave smooth, finished surfaces. Keep file strokes level, and always lift the file off the tooth before drawing it back for the next stroke.

sharpening handsaws

The file used on a handsaw depends on the fineness of the saw, as measured by its "points" or teeth per inch. This information, usually stamped on the blade, can be readily checked with a ruler. Use the chart on the facing page to find the file of the right size and taper for the saw you're working on.

A simple-to-make plywood clamp will hold the blade while you work on it. Or you may be able to locate one of the old commercial clamps.

If the saw teeth have been worn unevenly, joint by stroking an 8-in. mill bastard (single-cut, medium-coarse) file over their tips. A file-hold-ing jig or easy-to-make jointing block will assure even, square filing. Don't overdo it. Check your work frequently and stop when a spot of bright metal shows on each tooth.

For shaping, clamp the saw so the gullets are not more than ⅛ in. from clamp jaws. Hold the file level at 90° to the blade and all the way down into the gullet. File the forward slope of each tooth until exactly half the flat spot left by jointing has disappeared. Then file the rear slope of each tooth until the rest of the flat has disappeared. The result is sharply pointed teeth.

To set the teeth, raise the saw in the clamp. The tool, called a saw set, is adjustable. You want a set of about one-third blade thickness on rip saws, one-fourth on crosscut saws and even less on hollow-ground handsaws.

First set every other tooth—those set toward you—then reverse the blade in the clamp and set alternate teeth. To set evenly, use the same pressure for each tooth.

filing crosscut saws

To file a crosscut saw, clamp the blade with the saw toe pointing left, handle to the right (reverse if you're left-handed). Start at the toe and file the teeth that are set toward you. Place the file into the left side of the first tooth's gullet, holding it horizontally and at the same side angle as the original bevel (usually about 65°). The file should touch both sides of the gullet with each stroke (remember to file with forward strokes only). When every other tooth has been filed, reverse the saw in the clamp, start at the toe again, and file the alternate teeth.

To file a rip saw (jointing, shaping and setting are the same), stand directly in front of the clamp and hold the file straight across the saw at a right angle to the blade. File so that tooth points, not edges, are sharpened. After every other tooth is brought sharp and square, with the file to the left of the tooth set toward you, reverse the saw and file the remaining teeth.

For a finishing touch, many craftsmen like to add an operation known as side-jointing. It's performed by stroking each side of the blade two

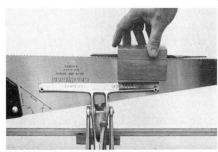

JOINTING to reduce all teeth to uniform height is the first step. It's done by passing a file lightly but squarely over the top of teeth. The jointing block assures a level pass.

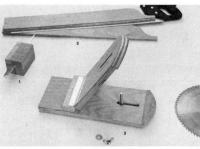

EASILY MADE sharpening aids are: 1. jointing block; 2. circular-blade clamp; 3. handsaw clamp. Plans are shown below.

File guide for sharpening handsaws	
Blade points per inch	**Taper (triangular) files recommended**
5, 5½	7″ taper regular
6	7″ or 8″ slim
7	6″ or 7″ slim
8	6″ slim
	7″ extra slim
	8″ double extra slim
9	6″ extra slim
	7″ extra double slim
10	5″ or 6″ extra slim
11	5″ extra slim
	6″ extra double slim
12	5″ extra slim
13, 15, 16	5″ double extra slim

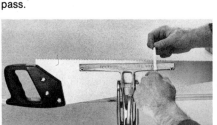

SHAPING is done with a taper file in the gullet used at 90° to the blade. File forward tooth slope until half jointing flat disappears; then file rear slope.

SETTING or bending the saw teeth is done here with a Stanley pistol-grip saw set. You can adjust it to give the amount of tooth set you want (see text).

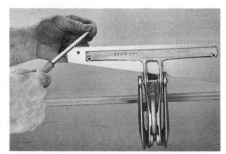

FILING a crosscut saw begins at the saw toe. Hold file at a 65° angle to blade and file teeth that are set toward you on push stroke. File both gullet slopes. Reverse saw, file alternate teeth.

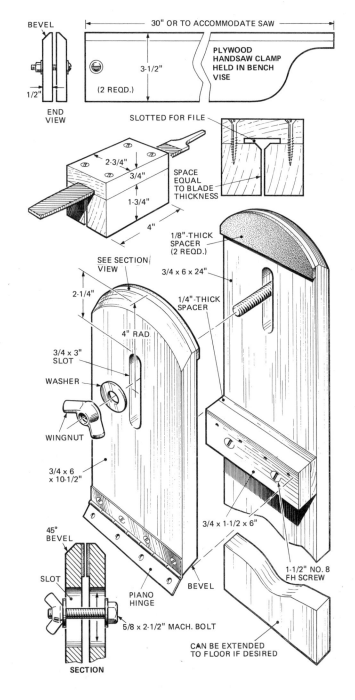

BEVEL

30" OR TO ACCOMMODATE SAW

PLYWOOD HANDSAW CLAMP HELD IN BENCH VISE

3-1/2"

1/2"

(2 REQD.)

END VIEW

SLOTTED FOR FILE

2-3/4"

3/4"

1-3/4"

4"

SPACE EQUAL TO BLADE THICKNESS

SEE SECTION VIEW

1/8"-THICK SPACER (2 REQD.)

3/4 x 6 x 24"

2-1/4"

1/4"-THICK SPACER

4" RAD.

3/4 x 3" SLOT

WASHER

WINGNUT

3/4 x 6 x 10-1/2"

3/4 x 1-1/2 x 6"

45° BEVEL

SLOT

PIANO HINGE

BEVEL

1-1/2" NO. 8 FH SCREW

5/8 x 2-1/2" MACH. BOLT

CAN BE EXTENDED TO FLOOR IF DESIRED

SECTION

or three times—*lightly*—with the fine side of an oilstone. (Wrap cloth or thin cardboard around one side of the stone to keep from scratching the blade.) Side-jointing removes filing burr and dresses tooth alignment to uniform set. It will help you get the smoothest cuts your saw can make.

circular-saw blades

The principles of sharpening circular-saw blades are the same as those of sharpening handsaws, but the techniques are different. Proper set and tooth uniformity are particularly important to assure a smooth-running blade. Extra strain on a tooth left larger than its fellow teeth can lead to breakage or a cracked gullet.

You can restore steel saw blades, but for carbide-tipped blades, see a professional saw sharpener.

The first step in keeping a blade sharp is taken when it's brand new: Make a close tracing of its outline on paper. This pattern will be a vital reference after several sharpenings.

A blade should be sharpened as soon as it

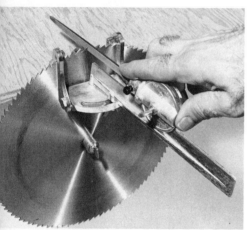

THIS CIRCULAR SAW sharpener lets you sharpen blades by hand with almost foolproof accuracy. You just set the scales to the pitch and angle you want, and file. It handles 6 to 12-in.-dia. blades and is about $17.25 from Brookstone Company, 350 Vose Farm Rd., Peterborough, NH 03458

SOME SAW-SHARPENING aids: Attachment (left) to use with a bench grinder, about $60; blade-setting tool designed for circular blades (right foreground), about $60, and blade sharpener attachment for radial or table saws (right background), about $30. All are from Sears.

FILING CHAIN-SAW TEETH

Your chain saw needs sharpening when the sawdust turns from chips to fine powder. The best way to file teeth is with the chain locked in a chain filing vise, but you can do a satisfactory job "on the bar" if the chain is tensioned so that it doesn't wobble.

Be sure to maintain the correct filing angle and height relative to each cutter's top plate (tooth's top surface). Bevel angles and the proper file are usually specified by the manufacturer. Round-hooded, chipper-type chains are simplest to sharpen—the right file and good technique will give the proper angles. Get a file holder if available for the chain—it will insure accuracy.

Strictly as an example, here are filing data for a 37 Series Chain according to Homelite:

Use a 5/32-in.-dia. round file held 30° from a line straight across the chain. Hold the file level and stroke toward the front corner of the tooth. Keep 1/10th of the file diameter above the top plate.

Use light pressure and press more toward the pack of the tooth. Lift the file away for the return stroke. Avoid a rocking motion.

The result should be proper top and side plate angles and a 60° hollow-ground under-edge. Now file the depth gauges (forward points of cutters) to specified level below top plates—use a gauge-jointing guide for this.

Teeth damaged by nails must be filed down—and then all other teeth must be filed back to the lengths of the shorter ones. Have this done commercially.

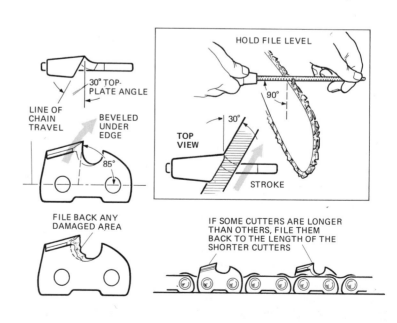

A CANTSAW FILE bevels the teeth of this combination blade, while blade is held by the circular clamp. File is available with a "safe-back"—a smooth side. It will fit in angles of less than 60°.

shows symptoms of dullness—increased feed effort, rougher cuts and burning. Start by jointing, with the blade in place on the arbor of the table or radial-arm saw, and the saw *unplugged*.

Place an oilstone on blocks so it straddles the blade. (Since the blade will groove the stone, don't use an expensive oilstone for this.) Adjust the blade so the teeth just barely scrape the stone. Then slowly rotate the blade backward by hand until every tooth has contacted the stone. To joint on a radial-arm saw, rest the stone on the table and bring the blade down to it. *Never joint with the saw under power.* For a portable circular saw, you'll have to jury-rig a way to hold the stone in a fixed position in contact with the blade.

Combination and planer blades with rakers—teeth that don't cut but clear chips—present a special problem. These teeth must be filed individually about $1/64$ in. below the cutting teeth. Block the blade so it remains stationary and file squarely across the top of each raker with a 6 or 8-in. mill bastard file. With a table saw, you can block up the file for uniform height, sliding the block to cut. It's good practice to

count strokes, too, and give each raker the same number.

Use a wooden clamp to hold the blade firmly for shaping and filing. To shape crosscut and combination blades, file the teeth straight across (no beveling) until the jointing flats vanish and the teeth have received their correct outline shapes.

Because tooth sizes vary widely, no specific file sizes can be given here. In general, you can probably use one of these files for most crosscut teeth: 4 to 8-in. slim taper, extra slim taper or double extra slim taper. For combination teeth, which usually have less than a 60° face rake angle, a 6 or 8-in. cantsaw file must be used because a slim taper would misshape the cutting edges of the teeth.

For a rip blade (and some large-tooth combination blades), use an 8 or 10-in., two-round-edges mill bastard file—its round edges can shape gullets and teeth—and, again, file straight across. For extra-large gullets you can use a 10-in. round gulleting file.

setting, filing, dressing

Use a circular-saw blade setter or secure the blade in your clamp for use of a hand set. Set all teeth exactly alike, first setting alternating teeth, then reversing the blade and working in the opposite direction to set the remaining teeth. You can increase or decrease set, but don't exceed half-tooth thickness, and *never* increase the depth of set. The depth should be limited to one-third the tooth height. The hollow-ground blades and rakers on combination and planer blades are never set.

File with the same files used for shaping. File as closely as possible to the original outline until you get a sharp point. Don't file sharp corners into gullets—they can make the blade crack.

Maintain original bevel and angle of teeth when filing crosscut blades. File one slope of one tooth at a time. File the teeth set toward you, then reverse the blade to finish. File rip-blade teeth straight across. Count strokes to equalize filing of the front and back of each tooth.

Cutting teeth of combination blades with rakers are usually filed with a 10° face bevel. Those without rakers are filed straight across the face and with a bevel across the back, generally about 5°.

You can dress or side-joint a circular blade like a handsaw, with the same benefits, merely by passing an oilstone over the sides of the teeth—*lightly*.

ROLLTOP DESKS are regaining popularity. This one was finished with a quality penetrating resin.

Complete guide to furniture refinishing

By PENELOPE ANGELL

As wood prices skyrocket, the purchasing of raw furniture to finish at home is becoming more and more popular. Or maybe you have a favorite antique that needs some revitalizing. Here's everything you need to know to do the job like a professional

■ IT MAKES GOOD SENSE to learn how to finish furniture. That skill can often be the key to filling your house with valuable antiques at bargain prices. You can also acquire new furniture less expensively if it's unfinished. With a little patience and a moderate bit of work, you can put a professional finishing touch on all types of furniture.

Finishing is a step-by-step process; along the way you must make a few decisions. When working with older furniture, you must first decide whether to restore or remove the old finish. If it is removed, you can bleach the bare surface to make it lighter. After that, the surface can be treated in much the same way as new, unfinished furniture. Sanding, staining, sealing and filling are all possible steps that lead to applying the final finish.

While most of us don't have to worry about devaluing a precious antique by removing the original finish, sometimes it simply isn't necessary to remove a slightly damaged one.

Original transparent finishes can be considered sound if they are clear so the wood pattern can be seen, and a coin or fingernail doesn't scrape down to the bare wood when run across the surface. Merely clean the finish with a cloth slightly dampened in mild soap and lukewarm water, dry, then rewax or polish.

You can restore dull, transparent finishes with

FINAL FINISH CHART

Types	What they do	How to use them
Shellac	A past hero, shellac is not used much today because it isn't very water-resistant and is soluble in alcohol. But it *is* easy to apply and dries quickly. Since shellac has such a short shelf life, it's best to buy shellac flakes and dissolve them in denatured alcohol as needed. A 3-lb. cut (3 lbs. of flakes per gallon of alcohol) is a good ratio.	Thin first two shellac coats to 2 parts denatured alcohol and 5 parts 3-lb. cut shellac. Apply final coat full strength. Rub with 3/0 steel wool and clean with a tack rag after first coat has dried fully—at least 3 hours. Finishing takes patience. Apply 3 more coats, rubbing between coats with steel wool; then clean and wax. Note: Shellac clouds in high humidity, so work in a dry place.
Lacquer	Lacquer is a fast-drying, very clear finish. It wears longer than shellac and is more water-resistant. However, it can crack if exposed to extreme temperature changes.	Since lacquer is so quick drying, you'll be wise to use spray equipment. Some lacquers, such as Deft, come in a spray can. You can also buy brush-on lacquers with drying retardants for a better chance at a smooth finish. When lacquering bare wood, thin the first coat to seal the wood and apply generously until wood has had time to soak it up. After it dries, rub with 3/0 steel wool and clean. Apply full strength and let dry 2 hours or more before using steel wool. Recoat, let dry 24 hours and rub.
Varnish and poly-urethane	Super polyurethanes give wood a very hard finish that withstands water, alcohol and mild scratches. Regular oil-based varnish, not quite as hearty, is longer-drying. Neither is easy to apply; both pick up dust while drying—which takes fairly long. Polyurethane finish comes in satin or gloss (Gloss Zar or Satin Zar, Minwax satin or gloss).	Polyurethane takes time to dry (at least 6 to 8 hours) and varnish takes longer, so plan to apply a coat daily for 3 days. But don't exceed 24-hour dry time between coats or urethane will harden completely, making other coats hard to apply. When brushing on urethane, thin first coat to seal the wood pores according to directions. Use 3/0 steel wool or fine sandpaper between coats. Polish final finish to the sheen you want.
Pene-trating resins	Easiest of finishes to apply, among most durable. Most are actually oil and resin mixture. As the name implies, they impregnate wood, fortify fibers. (Wood should not be sealed when this is used.) Some types have stain in finish (Flecto oil sealer). Another plus for penetrating resins: If wood is burned or scratched, rubbing with steel wool can repair it.	To apply, just pour it on the surface and smooth with a natural-fiber rag (purists often use a hand) to let wood absorb the moisture. Wipe up excess with a natural-fiber, lint-free cloth. Apply a second coat almost immediately if the wood soaks up the first. Let second coat dry—at least 36 hours to be sure—then cut the gloss with 3/0 steel wool. Apply more coats; dry and degloss each until the wood has an even tone.
Oil	A craftsman's finish for a special piece of furniture, a true oil finish is often preferred by professional finishers. Many have their own favorite recipes. One formula is *boiled* linseed oil and turpentine in a 3:1 down to a 1:1 ratio. Some antique finishers use refined beeswax dissolved in equal parts of boiled linseed oil and applied to the wood while the mixture is warm.	Saturate a natural-fiber rag in the oil mixture and rub thoroughly into one small area at a time until the whole surface is coated uniformly. When the wood will not absorb more oil, wipe off excess with hard-fiber cloth like denim. Wait two or three days, then apply another oil coat. After several weeks, apply a final coat. Oil once or twice yearly.
Wax	Paste wax can be used as a primary finisher *if* the wood has been sealed with white shellac or other sealer.	Apply a thin, even coat with steel wool or a soft cloth. After 5 to 15 minutes, buff with a clean cloth and repeat.
Paint	A fantastic range of paint colors is available—or you can brew your own. Spray lacquers are good for special pieces like wicker, wrought iron or carved furniture. Alkyd "oil base" enamels are the most durable furniture paints. Untreated wood should have a sealer coat of thinned shellac. All furniture should have a base coat.	After smoothing all surfaces, brush on an undercoat as evenly as possible. Let it dry and smooth it with fine sandpaper. Next, apply a half-and-half mixture of enamel and undercoating (made by the same manufacturer), let dry, sand and clean. Apply the final enamel coating. It should cure—this can take up to two weeks—before rubbing with a mixture of FFF pumice and water or oil.

ROCKING chair was stained, finished with polyurethane.

MIRROR FRAME is finished with a glossy lacquer.

DESK

We finished this white pine rolltop desk with Watco Danish oil, a penetrating oil and resin mixture. The finish added a slight honey color to the desk but let the character of the natural pine stand.

The first step, as with finishing all raw furniture, was to sand the wood smooth with the grain. This was done with successively finer grades of sandpaper. Some new unfinished wood is very rough and will require extra work.

Since we used a penetrating finish, a sealer coat was not necessary. However, most other types of finish (see chart) required that the wood first be sealed with a coat of final finish thinned with turpentine or a commercial lacquer-based sealer.

The finish we used was applied liberally with a brush. More was added to areas that soaked it up. After 30 minutes we wiped off the excess with a cloth, smoothed the wood with 3/0 steel wool, and applied another coat for 30 minutes. The excess was again removed and the surface was smoothed. Next day two thin coats of butcher's wax were applied on the surface, left for 15 minutes, and buffed.

1. AT THE Woodsmith's Studio, Jarrett Strawn uses a block with 150 finishing paper for the final sanding.

2. PENETRATING RESIN is applied liberally to the surface. Any spots that drink up the finish get an extra dose.

3. ANY PENETRATING resin not soaked into the wood after 30 minutes is wiped off with a clean, natural-fiber cloth.

4. THE SURFACE is rubbed with 3/0 steel wool to smooth the wood. Then another coat of finish is applied.

a single coat of the *same* finish originally used. Remove the wax with water and detergent, dry, sand lightly and apply the finish.

Here are some clues to detect the type of finish: Lacquer has been used on most *mass-produced* American furniture in recent years; shellac could well be on *old furniture* that still has its original finish; and varnish has been used most often in past years by *home craftsmen.*

If the old finish can't be preserved, you can apply a stripper to remove it, then start from scratch. The easiest type of stripper to use is in a semi-paste, jelly-like form (Zip Strip, Strip-ease, Wonder-Paste). Some wash off with water and others with mineral spirits. You'll need a natural bristle paintbrush (chemicals in the strippers can soften synthetic bristles), a paint scraper or putty knife for softwoods, 2/0 coarse steel wool, rubber gloves, a couple of coffee cans, rags and mineral spirits or water for cleanup.

First read the directions on the can. When you're ready, just brush the stripper on liberally and allow it to soften the finish. After waiting for 10 or 15 minutes, you should find it soft enough to scrape off with the putty knife or steel wool and be dumped into the coffee can. Wash off the whole piece with water or mineral spirits, whichever is called for in the directions.

On ornate pieces with intricate carvings and turnings, the stripping process can be rather time-consuming. But if you find a beautiful wood beneath the layers of paint, it can be well worth the effort.

bleaching to remove color

Commercial bleaches to reduce pigment left by strippers, or to lighten the natural wood color, are available at paint and hardware stores. Use a

ROCKING CHAIR

When we got this decorative rocking chair from a second-hand store, it was covered with countless coats of paint. We used Bix stripper, a jelly-like substance that stays on vertical surfaces better than liquid strippers. This was applied liberally with a brush, allowed to soften the paint (about 15 minutes in this case), then carefully scraped off with a putty knife so as not to damage the softened wood. A toothbrush and coarse No. 2 steel wool were also used to remove the stripper on the turnings.

We uncovered a lovely hickory chair with a pine seat and delicate carvings on the back. Hickory is a very porous wood, and the paint remained in the pores. The chair could have been bleached to remove the pigment. But since the paint in the pores was a reddish brown and the chair was an indefinable country style, we let the light paint speckling blend in to look rustic.

The next day a mahogany oil stain was applied to the chair with a rag. The carvings on the chair back were kept lighter. The third day we gave it the first of three polyurethane coats.

1. THE ROCKING CHAIR had many coats of paint, but its excellent condition otherwise made it good project.

2. STRIPPER AND PAINT are scraped off the chair with special care to avoid any damage to softened wood.

3. MAHOGANY OIL STAIN is applied with a clean, natural-fiber cloth. Any excess is wiped off the wood.

4. THE FIRST COAT of polyurethane is brushed on the chair with careful strokes to cover surface evenly.

MIRROR

When we found the handsome old walnut mirror it was painted a lackluster gold. Imperial Wonder-Paste, a jelly-like liquid, was used to strip the paint. Then we sanded the wood smooth with coarse, medium and fine grades of sandpaper.

Walnut is a porous wood, so we used a wood filler made by Mohawk to fill the pores. You add benzine to the paste until the mixture reaches a consistency of heavy cream. Then apply it with a cloth and allow to dry about five minutes (it will cloud slightly). Rub the excess filler off by working with and across the grain, and allow the wood to dry.

Next we applied "Qualasole," a padding lacquer finish with a cotton pad (hence the name "padding lacquer"). The pad is dipped in lacquer which is dispersed throughout the pad by a tap of the palm. The lacquer is padded on in short, quick strokes, working with the grain. It took 20 minutes drying time between the first three coats and two hours between the next two coats.

1. STRIPPER is applied to the frame by Kipp Gosewehr at John Harra Woodworking Studio to remove the paint.

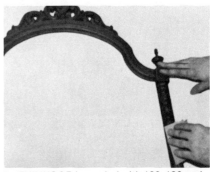

2. THE WOOD is sanded with 120, 180 and 400-grit sandpaper to smooth the raised wood caused by stripping.

3. A MIXTURE of filler paste and turpentine is applied to the mirror frame with a cloth. It clouds as it sets.

4. A PAD of cotton cloth wrapped in more cotton cloth held by rubber bands is used to apply padding lacquer.

YOU CAN steam out any gouges and dents that later occur. Simply place a medium-hot iron over a damp cloth on the indented area for a short period.

SCRATCHES that can be seen in your finished piece are easily treated with wax pencils. These are available in a wide variety of wood colors.

AFTER MANY years, the finish on a piece may need reviving. The dull finish on this desk was brought back to life with Minwax Antique Oil.

natural bristle brush to apply the bleach evenly to the clean wood surface. The bleach will raise the grain and it will be necessary to sand after the bleach has dried.

preparing the surface

After removing the old finish, you can repair surface dents, scratches and holes with wood putty or other filler. Then prepare the entire wood surface for the final finish.

Sanding: Begin sanding with smallest grit, the finest paper, capable of smoothing the wood. For rough sanding on raw wood, begin with 80 to 100-grit aluminum oxide, open-coat abrasive paper. If the raw wood is already fairly smooth,

begin with 120 to 220-grit aluminum oxide, open-coat paper. Between finish coats use 3/0 steel wool. You'll find that a tack rag to pick up the dust and wood particles is invaluable. (Note: Many refinishers feel sanding should be done on raw, unfinished furniture only. Old furniture and antiques acquire a "patina" through many years which could be destroyed by sanding.)

Staining: A matter of personal preference, staining is a cosmetic step not really necessary for protecting the wood. There are four main types of stains: oil, water, non-grain-raising and spirit.

Oil stains are most common for home use, although wood can take this stain unevenly. You can prevent uneven shading by applying a diluted sealer coat or diluted coat of the final finish (diluted by five parts of its solvent) before staining. Apply stain with a brush in even coats. Remove the excess with a cloth and be sure it's dry before proceeding.

Sealing: To prevent the final finish from being absorbed into the wood (except those penetrating finishes that should be absorbed), a sealer coat is applied to close the wood pores. Lacquer-based sealers are most commonly used. They are brushed on, allowed to dry, then lightly sanded.

Filling: Woods with coarse grain such as oak, walnut and mahogany require a filler, if you want a perfectly smooth finish. Fillers conceal pores so you can get a glass-like finish.

Now your piece is ready for the final step. Study the chart, then make your choice of final finishes.

1. DO-IT-YOURSELF with tender loving care—that's the best car wash you can get. Biggest investment is about $7 to $10 for a good chamois (or shammy). Washing is done with a sponge and the shammy is used for the all-important job of drying the car.

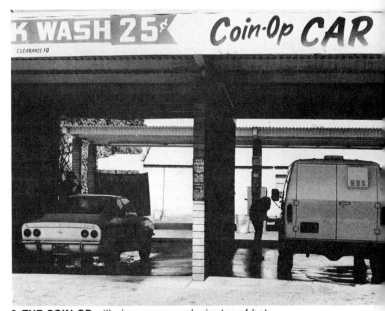

2. THE COIN-OP will give you several minutes of hot water under pressure for 25 to 50 cents. You will also get a protected area to work in. But if you dawdle, you'll wind up feeding the coin slot enough quarters to have gone to a commercial car wash.

How to wash your car

By MICHAEL LAMM

3. PROFESSIONAL CARWASH can save you time and energy, and in winter it's a must, but make sure you pick an establishment that does a conscientious job. Avoid "short-line" washes (30 to 60 feet). "Long-line" washes (120 feet or more) have more brushes. Also look for or ask for vacuuming, steam wand, whitewall scrubbers, clean brushes, as well as final touchup towelling.

■ BASICALLY, YOU'VE GOT three approaches to washing a car. You can: 1. Do it yourself with hose, sponge and shammy. 2. You can give it a lick at a coin-op carwash. 3. Or you

CAR-CLEANING TIPS

William Trevorrow, commercial car-wash consultant and founder of Gem Auto Wash in Sacramento, Calif., lists the following tips to help keep your car looking young for years.

1. Remove tree sap, bird droppings and bugs from you car's finish immediately. Although household soaps and detergents aren't recommended for ordinary hand car-wash jobs, it might be necessary to use them to remove these things. Sap, bird droppings and bugs can permanently discolor paint. Eggs, vomit and spit can cause paint to shrink and lift.

2. If you live in areas of high salt atmosphere near the ocean or where salt is used to melt snow, wash the car often, especially underneath.

3. Never put bumper stickers on painted areas of your car. Remove such stickers with rubber-cement thinner (office-supply stores).

4. Always try to park your car in shade on sunny days and indoors at night. Fabric car covers are no substitute for carports or garages.

5. When buying a car, remember that metallic colors fade and deteriorate more quickly than nonmetallic paints. Some metallics also grow dull with polishing when aluminum particles become exposed to air.

6. Remove road tar quickly with solvent or white gasoline. Be sure to rewax the area rubbed down.

7. Two-step polish and wax jobs beat all-in-one waxes, and hand application beats polish/wax machines or buffer rubouts if done correctly. A good paste-wax job should last (make water bead up) at least six months and makes hand-washing easier. Chrome trim usually needs waxing more often than paint.

---

can let a commercial five-minute car-wash clean your car for you.

Simple choices, you say. Yes, but what's really the *right* way to shammy a car? Do you use a detergent in your wash water? Are you aware that some commercial car washes put a caustic into their wheel scrubbers? How do you come out on a 25-cent coin-op if you have to keep stuffing quarters into the meter? What's the difference between a "short-line" and a "long-line" commercial car wash?

wash it by hand

Hand car washing represents almost a lost art nowadays. Very few car owners even attempt it, and many who do don't know the best way. Done right, though, hand washing beats other methods—mechanical and semi-mechanical—in all ways, especially in terms of quality and gentleness to a car's finish. But if the job is done wrong, you're better off at a long-line mechanical car wash if you can find a really good one.

For a classical hand car wash, you need the following equipment: a deerskin shammy (a variation of the word *chamois*), access to a garden hose with adjustable spray nozzle, a five-gallon plastic or metal bucket, one large sponge, one plastic-mesh-encased small bug sponge, and some paper towels. A hand wringer comes in handy but isn't absolutely necessary.

A good shammy is all-important and holds the key to the entire wash job. Get one of ample size—six feet square or so, it will cost about $7 to $10, but if properly cleaned and dried after each use will easily last you 10 years or more. Towels, rags and synthetic shammies are no substitutes for the real thing.

You have to remember there are two crucial things about a shammy:

First, when you get a new one, you have to soak out the preservative oils before you use it. You soak it in a detergent solution, but be sure you rinse all the detergent back out. You never use household detergent or soap to hand-wash a car. These merely cut waxes and speed oxidation to dull paint. (Commercial carwashes use a special mild detergent, mostly to lubricate the surface of a car.)

Second—and this is the point most often missed—you *must* wring your shammy out virtually dry before you use it. This lets it absorb water from the surface of your car. And each time your shammy starts to get soppy, you have to wring it dry again.

To hand-wash a car correctly, follow these 10 steps:

• **Park your car in complete shade.** Direct sunlight tends to make water spots. Also, water droplets on paint act as tiny magnifying lenses and can burn blotches in your car's finish.

• **Shut all windows and doors,** once your car is shaded and cool. Then hose down the exterior thoroughly. Now fill your bucket (with warm water if it's wintertime), wet your large sponge in the bucket, and sponge the entire surface of your car. Keep dipping the sponge to keep it wet and clean. Go panel by panel, but start at the roof and work your way down. That way gravity carries the dirty water the same direction as you're sponging. Leave the rocker panels, wheels and tires for last. If you don't your sponge and/or shammy might bring road oil and dirt up to the windows.

• **Once you've loosened all film and grime** by sponging, spray your car again to wash off the floating dirt. Once more, work your way down from the roof.

• **Spray a strong jet under all fenders** and under the chassis to get rid of mud and salt. Run your hand carefully up under fender beads to make sure you've flushed out all the mud and debris. Do the same behind bumpers and in body pockets where rust traditionally forms.

• **Using your bug sponge, remove stuck-on insects** from your windshield, grille, hood and front bumper. Rinse with a powerful hose spray. *Note again that at no time should you use a soap, soapy cleaner or detergent when hand-washing your car.* Even those waxes that say they're detergent-proof aren't, and besides, there's no need to use soap. If your paint is dull, polish and wax it after you wash your car. That'll make subsequent washes that much easier.

• **To drain water from inside your car doors,** swing each door back and forth on its hinges. Don't let the door hit its full-open stop, but swing it briskly. You'll see water come out of the drain hole on the bottom of each door.

• **Now shammy your car.** Wet the shammy thoroughly, then wring it out as dry as possible. If you don't have a double-roller wringer, it often helps to loop your shammy around a firm stanchion or through a door handle so you can twist harder. You want to start with a shammy that's virtually dry (never with one that's totally dry).

• **Open the shammy flat,** grip it by two corners, and flop it on top of your car's roof, pulling it toward you in big swipes. The roof will now be dry where you've shammied it. As the shammy absorbs water and gets wet, wring it out again (and again and again—it's a process you have to repeat throughout your wash job).

• **Next do all windows, inside and out.** You want to shammy your glass before your shammy picks up dirt and oil from the lower body. Use paper towels to remove any streaks that show up on window glass.

• **Finally, shammy chrome,** then hood, decklid, fenders, doors, door jambs, interior and wheelcovers, in that order. And keep wringing out your shammy. You might also wash it in your bucket once or twice during the wash, especially if there's still dirt on the car's surface. Remember, you can't wring too often or too much.

coin-op car washes

At times, coin-operated car washes make good sense, especially for apartment dwellers and RV owners.

Basically, each 25 to 50 cents in the meter gives you two to four minutes of water from an ajustable pressure wand. You also have shade. For additional quarters, you can usually rent a vacuum nozzle and, more rarely, hot water, which is nice in winter.

The question is, by the time you've fed more than four or five quarters into the coin-op meter, are you better off going to an automated commercial car wash?

commercial car washes

As in any business, you'll find good and bad commercial car washes. Few car owners know the difference. Here's how to judge them.

Note whether it's a short-line or a long-line car wash. Short-lines (30 to 60 feet) usually contain only one or two sets of brushes, have no wheel scrubbers, no steam, no water-pressure boost, and they're often adjuncts to filling stations, sometimes stuffed into what used to be a single lube bay.

Long-line washes stretch 120 feet or more and almost always do a considerably better job. They have more brushes, use more water for wash and rinse, have pumps that boost water pressure to 600 p.s.i., often heat water to around 140° F., and give more washing time.

Also look for or ask about the following:

• **Do they use a powerful vacuum** as a first step?

• **Do they have a man on a steam wand** at the entrance to their wash tunnel? Ideally, this wand puts out a jet with 400-p.s.i. pressure at 140° F. It's used to remove impacted bugs scratchlessly, from the front of your car and, on request, to spray the undercarriage to clean away road salt and dirt in winter. You *do* have to ask for a special undercarriage spray in most car washes.

• **Are there steam-emitting movable tire scrubbers** to whiten your whitewalls? The better ones do.

• **Can you see that the big, revolving brushes are clean?** Managers who take pride in their operations use light-colored brushes so their customers can judge cleanliness.

• **Does the operation have a dryer** and delinter for its towels?

use good judgment

As I say, you're still best off washing your car by hand yourself. I realize that's not always possible or practical. But if you use good judgment and know what to look for, you can get almost as good a job at a long-line car wash as you can at home. Just be sure to choose one that takes pride in its work.

Revolving table for painting

By ROBERT C. BARNES

■ UNTIL YOU'VE USED a revolving work-table, you can't imagine the many different jobs you'll be able to do faster and more easily than on a conventional stationary bench.

One of the most important uses of the rotating top is in simplifying spray painting. You can control the speed and direction of rotation with one hand while spraying with the other. The time spent on upholstering small and medium-size pieces of furniture such as chairs and ottomans is also reduced by using the revolving worktop.

THE WORKTABLE is made from scrap lumber. Top and sides are ⅝-in. particle board. Corner posts are two pieces of ¾-in. stock glued together. Drawer supports are glued and screwed into dado joints. Cleats serve as runners for the top drawer to keep it in place when you're reaching for items in the back.

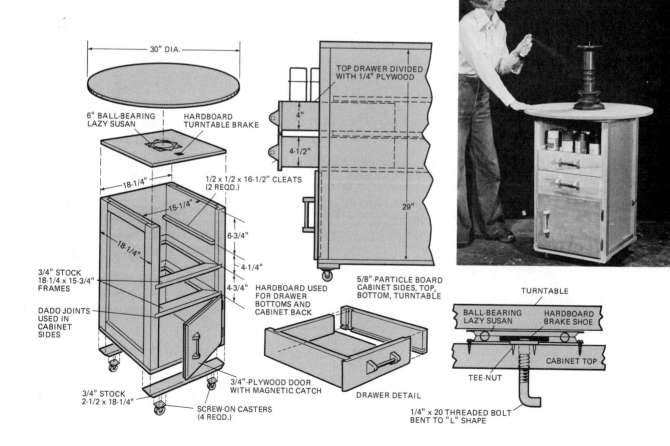

30" DIA.

6" BALL-BEARING LAZY SUSAN

HARDBOARD TURNTABLE BRAKE

18-1/4"

1/2 x 1/2 x 16-1/2" CLEATS (2 REQD.)

15-1/4"

6-3/4"

18-1/4"

4-1/4"

3/4" STOCK 18-1/4 x 15-3/4" FRAMES

4-3/4"

DADO JOINTS USED IN CABINET SIDES

HARDBOARD USED FOR DRAWER BOTTOMS AND CABINET BACK

3/4"-PLYWOOD DOOR WITH MAGNETIC CATCH

3/4" STOCK 2-1/2 x 18-1/4"

SCREW-ON CASTERS (4 REQD.)

TOP DRAWER DIVIDED WITH 1/4" PLYWOOD

4"

4-1/2"

29"

5/8"-PARTICLE BOARD CABINET SIDES, TOP, BOTTOM, TURNTABLE

DRAWER DETAIL

TURNTABLE

BALL-BEARING LAZY SUSAN

HARDBOARD BRAKE SHOE

CABINET TOP

TEE-NUT

1/4" x 20 THREADED BOLT BENT TO "L" SHAPE

At our house the biggest use of the worktable is in assembling and finishing picture frames. An easy quarter turn of the table takes you from one mitered corner to succeeding corners without moving a step. Spraying or brush painting the frame is just as easy, as each side rotates past your position—which can be on a very comfortable stool.

Even preparing large quantities of food for a family outing or decorating a cake is made easier with the table.

As an extra bonus, the materials used to build the table are leftovers from other jobs. A piece of ¼-in. hardboard is enough for the cabinet back and two drawer bottoms. The cabinet sides, top, bottom and 30-in.-diameter turntable surface are made from scrap pieces of ⅝-in. particle board. Plywood can be used, but it is much more expensive. All of the solid wood parts are ¾-in. pine. The four corner posts are glue-ups of two ¾-in. pieces of pine 29 in. long. Even the drawer pulls are fashioned from dowels and pine.

The only money spent was for a 6-in-diameter ball-bearing lazy Susan pivot, four screw-on casters and a pair of hinges for the door.

The two drawers slide on mitered corner frames that are screwed and glued into dado joints in the sides of the cabinet. The top drawer

A SMALL 1-in.-square hardboard shoe prevents the turntable from spinning too fast. It's operated by moving a bolt on the underside of the cabinet top.

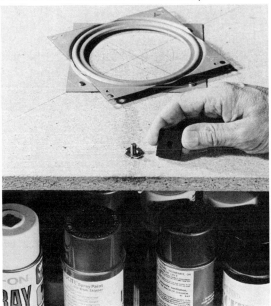

is handy for storing tall containers like spray cans. You can divide the drawer to fit your own needs with ¼-in. plywood dividers to keep the containers from tipping over when the drawer is opened. The center drawer makes a good storage area for brushes, paint rollers and sandpaper. The bottom door compartment can hold larger equipment from pressure spray attachments to power sanding tools.

The 6-in.-diameter lazy Susan is equipped with 70 ¼-in. ball bearings and has a load capacity of 500 pounds. It supports the 30-in.-diameter turntable. You can purchase the lazy Susan at hardware stores complete with installation directions for a few dollars.

The ball bearings allow you to revolve the turntable at a fast rate. In fact, you need a brake to slow it. Use a piece of hardboard 1 to 1½ in. square pressed against the underside of the turntable as a brake shoe. To install it, drill a ⁵/₁₆-in. hole and drive a ¼-in. Tee-nut into the cabinet top at the center front.

Thread a ¼-20 bolt through the Tee-nut. Drill a ¼-in. depression part way through the hardboard square and secure it on top of the bolt. If you bend the bolt at a right angle it will be easier to adjust the brake pressure.

other worktable uses

If you want to refinish or reupholster any fairly large piece of furniture, you can temporarily fasten a larger top to the 30-in turntable using a few wood screws. Reupholstering and refinishing are a snap when the work can be rotated. You can make the permanent turntable larger than 30 in., but a larger diameter won't roll through a standard-size door.

Assembling models and doing other craft work are easier with the help of the revolving worktable. You can lay out the many small parts in the order needed, placing them toward the center of the table. Revolve the table as the parts are needed. Carving or sculpturing on the worktable also has its advantages. You can rotate your project as you cut or mold each of the sides.

Before you begin building the table you might consider using perforated hardboard for the cabinet sides in place of the particle board. The perforated hardboard can hold tools and work rags on snap-in hangers within easy reach as you use the table.

Considering the countless ways it can be used and the many storage spaces it provides, the revolving worktable could well become indispensable in your workshop.

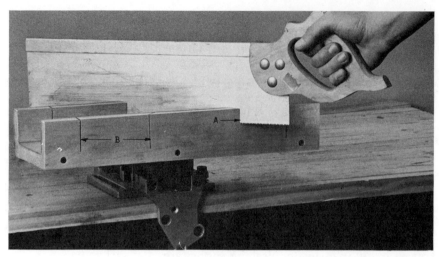

CONVENTIONAL HARD-WOOD miterbox comes with slots that are cut shallow for rigidity in shipping and storage. Slots must be deepened before use. Backsaw cuts slot A and corresponding slot on opposite side of miterbox down to base. Slots labeled B have already been deepened.

How to cut miters by hand

By RONALD E. THOMAS and STEPHEN WALTON

■ ONE OF THE SATISFACTIONS of woodworking is making a mitered cut that comes out perfectly square. It's not that difficult, if you work with care and use the right tools.

While the power miterbox is gaining in popularity among professional carpenters, it's not a reasonable purchase for most home craftsmen—not when there's a wide range of devices available to help make hand mitering fast, easy and accurate at much lower cost.

What you'll want to have will depend on how often you need to cut miters. For most do-it-yourselfers, a basic hardwood or plastic miterbox, backed up by the miter-cutting capability of the radial-arm or bench saw, will suffice. But if you're thinking of operating either a picture-framing or a custom-furniture business from

your basement, you'll probably want to invest in a high-grade miterbox, a trimmer, or both. Either will give you good service for a long time.

The essentials of cutting an accurate miter are precise measuring and marking, an accurate miterbox, a sharp saw and a firm hold on the workpiece. Your miterbox is a precision instrument and should be treated as such if you want to produce professional-looking joints.

Even if you've cut a miter well, the joint may still require adjustment for a perfect fit. Sanding is usually required (though not with a trimmer), but mitered ends may instead be planed smooth—with a length allowance for the stock removed. No matter how careful you've been to make an accurate miter, wood-putty filling may be necessary for a smooth-looking joint, but it

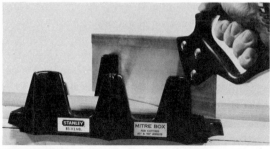

INEXPENSIVE PLASTIC miterbox gives 45° and 90° cuts with reasonable accuracy. For rigidity and best results, holes are provided for fastening box to workbench.

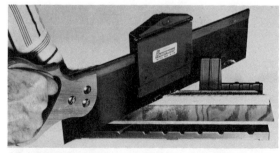

AT A REASONABLE price, this miterbox offers a depth-of-cut adjustment and locking stops for common angles. Hardwood under workpiece protects saw teeth.

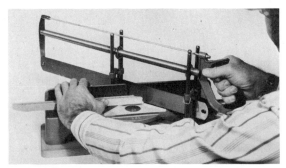

MITERBOX WITH integral saw costs about $120, but it is convenient and precise, and lasts a lifetime. Blade is fully supported; deflection is minimized.

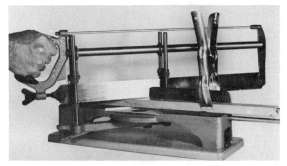

NARROW 10-point blade provided is kept stiff by tension adjustment. Clamping of the workpiece whenever possible helps to assure the most accurate cut.

DEPTH STOPS on a combination miterbox and clamp move up to contact the backsaw rib. Capacity of this unit ranges up to 2 in. wide and 1¾-in. deep.

ALTHOUGH LIMITED as a miterbox to 45° and 90° cuts, a combination unit with right-angled jaws also can be used to clamp a mitered joint for gluing.

will show if the work is stained rather than painted.

There's a trick finish carpenters use on trim that you may find helpful—undercutting (back-cutting) the mitered surface slightly with a plane

iron. When you do it this way, only two edges have to line up, not two faces.

The weakest but best-looking way to fasten a miter joint is to glue and clamp. It's fine when the glued-up pieces are attached to a backup

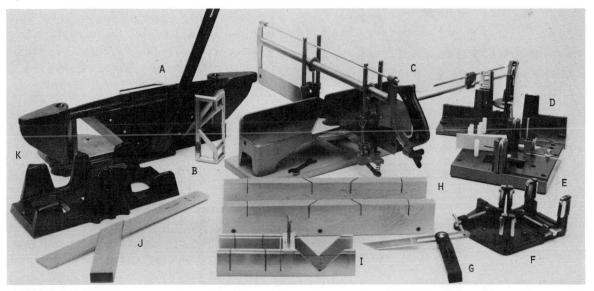

AIDS FOR hand mitering include: (A) shearing trimmer; (B) marking template; (C) Ulmia miterbox with a built-in saw; (D) Stanley Handyman miterbox; (E) Jointmaster sawing jig; (F) combination miterbox and clamp; (G) sliding bevel used for laying out odd angles; (H) rock maple miterbox; (I) miterbox used for cutting metal moldings; (J) 45° and 135° hardwood miter square; (K) Stanley plastic miterbox. Range of the devices shown here is not intended to be comprehensive; miterboxes are available from a variety of sources with prices from just over $1 (for use with modelmaker's razor saws) up.

MITERING JIG called a Jointmaster is a unique and useful device that utilizes movable nylon pegs to hold the work in exact position. It is especially suited for neat end mitering of small workpieces. From Woodcraft Supply Corp., Woburn, MA 01801.

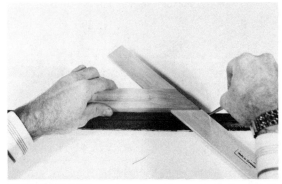

FREEHAND CUT can be extremely accurate if carefully laid out with a miter square like this. A combination square will also do the job. A sliding bevel can be used but must be set accurately. When you are cutting follow the line as closely as possible.

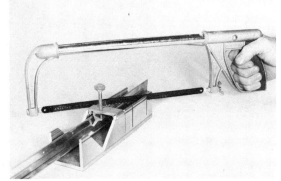

INTENDED for mitering metal moldings, this simple box for use with hacksaw has a built-in clamp that slides along beads formed in the sides of the box.

THE TEMPLATE is designed to allow marking of both 90° and 45° lines at once.

MITER TRIMMER USES a shearing (knife) action to make an extra-smooth finish cut. The work must first be cut to within ⅛ to ¼ in. of the desired size.

board—decorative moldings on a kitchen-cabinet door, for example. This joint can be strengthened with brads that are set, and the holes plugged with wood filler.

Corrugated nails will also beef up a joint; use them where the work is thick and they can be driven from the rear. One strong commercial fastener is the Skotch connector, which is also

intended for use where it won't be seen.

A purist will probably prefer to reinforce a joint with wood: glued-in keys, spline or dowel pegs. Be advised that cutting accurately for a spline, or boring for dowels, does take skill, experience and some specialized equipment.

SOURCES OF MITER DEVICES
(Letters refer to photo on page 109)

Woodcraft Supply Corp. 313 Montvale Ave., Woburn, Mass. 01801: (A) Woodcraft Miter Trimmer, (B) miter template; (C) Ulmia miterbox, (E) Jointmaster Sawing Jig; (F) combination miterbox and clamp; (J) horn-beam miter square.

The Stanley Works, 195 Lake St., New Britain, Conn. 06050: (D) H114A Handyman miterbox, (K) 85-112MB plastic miterbox with 14-in., 13-point backsaw.

Durall Tool Corp., 923 Old Nepperhan Ave., Yonkers, N.Y. 10703: (H) No. 116 rock maple miterbox.

Beno J. Gundlach Co., Box 544, Belleville, Ill. 62222: (I) No. 601 Quick-Lock Miterbox.

Pootatuck Corp., RR 2, Box 18, Windsor, Vt. 05089; (not shown) Lion Miter Trimmer.

Shop tricks from a pro

Shop professional Rosario Capotosto has designed, built and described original projects in how-to articles for more than 23 years. Here he offers some handy time and work- saving tips to help you get better use from your shop and tools

SELF-LOCKING BENCH STOP

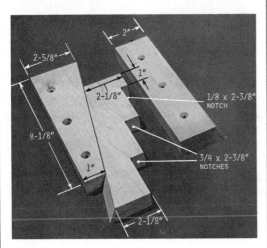

CHISEL-ROUTING JIG

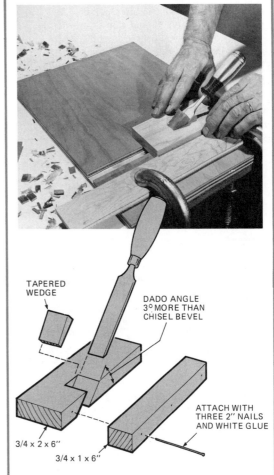

The harder you push on the work in this unique planing bench stop, the tighter its hold. Yet the work is quickly released when you pull it back lightly. The jig shown holds 1/8 to 2½-in. stock and can easily be built in your shop.

Make the stop of hardwood such as maple, oak or cherry for strength. Cut the right side of the left member and the left side of the center member with bevel angles. This helps prevent the sliding block from lifting during normal use. Use six countersunk 1¼ in. No. 8 flathead screws to secure the rig to your workbench.

You can adapt a chisel to do a router's job of making the finish passes on a hand-cut dado or groove. Cut an angled notch or dado in a block of ¾ x 2 x 6-in. hardwood to a depth that equals the chisel width. The notch angle should be 3° greater than the chisel's bevel angle. Insert the chisel in the notch and determine the size to make the wedge. Then attach the ¾ x 1 x 6-in. closure strip.

To use: Cut two saw kerfs for the borders of the dado to be finished. Working freehand, clear some waste with the chisel. Insert the chisel into the plane opening, let it project to the dado bottom and lock it into place with the wedge. Butt a guide strip against the plane, clamp it, then run the jig against the guide. Lower chisel as required.

RUSTPROOFING BOLTS

Apply a coat of shellac to bolt threads to prevent rust, and the nut won't "freeze" to the bolt. Just dip the bolt threads in shellac, remove and permit the excess to drain off slightly. Then run the nuts onto the bolts.

HIGH FENCE FOR PRECISION PLUNGE CUTTING

To make accurate internal cuts, use a high fence. Keep the saw base touching the fence and the blade will enter the work on target. Here's how: Situate and clamp the fence. Raise and tape the blade guard. Hold the saw base against the fence with

the blade clear of work. Start the saw, slowly lower it until the base is flat on the work. Maintaining contact between shoe and fence, finish the cut. Turn off the saw. When blade stops, remove the saw and use a handsaw to complete the cut to the corner.

TABLE-SAW MITERING JIG

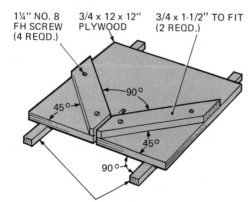

1¼" NO. 8 FH SCREW (4 REQD.)
3/4 x 12 x 12" PLYWOOD
3/4 x 1-1/2" TO FIT (2 REQD.)

90°
45°
45°
90°

TWO HARDWOOD STRIPS SIZED AND SPACED TO FIT SAW-TABLE GROOVES. FASTEN WITH 3/4" NO. 6 FH SCREWS (2 PER STRIP)

You can make perfect miters on your table saw with this jig. To the bottom of a board, fasten two strips spaced to ride in the miter gauge grooves. On top, using glue and screws, attach a pair of cleats so they form a 90° angle. Then push the jig into the spinning blade.

FITTING A PANEL INTO A TIGHT GROOVE

Often, fitting a plywood panel in a grooved rail can be hard due to slight variations in the panel's thickness. To avoid splitting the rail, run a narrow saw kerf centered in the panel edge to a depth slightly more than the groove's depth.

BAR CLAMP STANDS

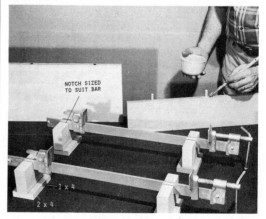

A pair of stands for a bar clamp keeps it in position and ready to go. The stands are a great help when you're gluing panels that require the use of both hands. Make them of 2 x 4 blocks notched at the top to a depth allowing ½ in. of the bar to project. Nail the blocks to their bases.

USING SHOP POWDERS

Dispense pumice, rottenstone, emery and other shop powders easily and evenly over your work surface with an oversize restaurant or barbecue-type salt shaker. Or, for greater economy, make your own shaker with a discarded glass jar and screw-on lid. Don't punch holes through the lid with an awl; instead, drill a series of 1/32-in. holes for uniform distribution of the powders.

TABLE-SAWING WIDE PANELS

When straight or angle sawing of oversize panels prevents your using a miter gauge or rip fence, you can still handle the panels easily. Cut a strip of wood to suit the saw table miter gauge groove and about 2 ft. longer than the panel. Secure the strip to the underside of the work with brads, letting it project 1 ft. at both ends. Fasten the strip so it runs in the table groove as you feed the work. Wax the strip if needed. NOTE: Blade guard is removed for photo clarity only.

PANEL RAISING WITH A CIRCULAR SAW

A rectangular opening in a panel that wraps around the base of a circular saw lets you cut concave grooves for panel raising or other decoration. A wood strip attached at an angle to the bottom does the trick. Press the guide strip firmly against the work while advancing the saw slowly. Groove is cut in stages, with the blade lowered about 1/16 in. for each pass. Angle of the guide strip relative to the blade governs the groove width. To create a raised panel, cut off the outboard waste after completing the grooves.

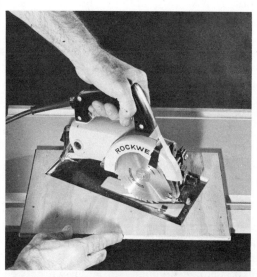

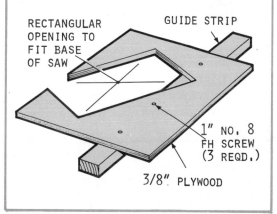

Multiply your vegetable harvest

By EDWIN F. STEFFEK

■ WITH FOOD PRICES CLIMBING higher, the home vegetable garden is taking on greater importance. A home garden will save you money and provide your family with fresh, nutritious produce without additives, preservatives or dyes.

Your first step is to decide what you want to grow and to plan the garden so that you get the most out of it with the least effort. You don't have to follow our two-plot garden completely, but keep the general idea, and substitute crops of essentially the same size and growth habits.

In Plot A we took advantage of air space by making the cucumber grow up a piece of 4 or 5-foot wire across the border. If it will block out the sunlight on your garden, run the wire down one side instead.

Loose-leaf lettuce and peas are suggested next because both are planted early and are out of the way before the space is needed for a follow-up crop of bush beans or the cucumbers do too much shading. Spinach can be grown between the peas because it can be planted in late spring or early summer. You can substitute broccoli

and kohl-rabi (which tastes like a mild cabbage) for lettuce and spinach.

In the center of Plot A is parsley. Soak it overnight before you plant it; otherwise, germination will be slow and poor. Since parsley is slow anyway, you might mix radish seeds which grow faster with the parsley to mark the row. The radishes will be out of the way before the parsley appears.

Carrot seed, like lettuce, is very tiny. Spread it sparsely so you don't have to thin too many plants, or buy seed tapes with seeds already spaced. Beets present a different problem. Each seed is really a collection of up to four seeds. Again, give them room—3 to 4 in. between seeds.

Cabbage, like all the other crops in Plot A (except cucumbers) is quite hardy and can be planted early. You can plant the cukes in flower pots and wafers which can be set out as soon as the danger of frost has passed.

Plot B is bordered with tall pole beans. Grow these on 6 or 7-foot poles spaced 2 feet apart. The tomato plants can be tied to trellises. Corn is

PLOT A

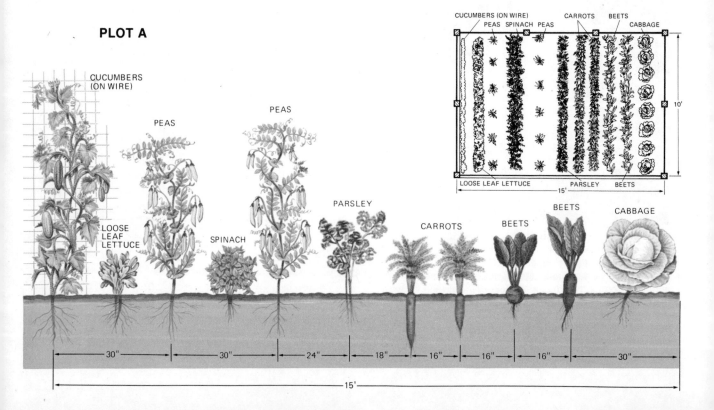

sown in hills of four or five seeds each, or 8 to 12 inches apart in single rows.

Head lettuce, onion sets or plants and cauliflower are hardy and can be planted early into Plot B.

With a fork, spade or shovel dig up and turn over the soil, breaking it up as fine as possible. Rake it smooth after it ceases to be sticky. If it is heavy and sandy or claylike, humus must be added.

Your garden will need fertilizer. Ask a garden supplier to recommend a fertilizer with the proper mixture of nutrients for the soil in your area. The amount usually used is 5 pounds per 100 square feet—7½ pounds for each plot. Work several pounds in when preparing the soil, and mix the balance in under the rows where the roots can readily reach it at planting time. Later, during the growing season, hoe in about 1½ pounds parallel to the rows and a few inches from them once a month. If the soil is acid as proven by a soil test, work in 2 to 3 pounds of ground limestone per 100 square feet yearly for several years.

When plants appear, thin them and loosen the soil every week or two to prevent crusting, watering as needed. If the season is dry, you can cover the ground with a 1 to 2-inch mulch of grass clippings, buckwheat or ground corn cobs to retain moisture. If pests appear, spray or dust as necessary, but not more than needed.

TOMATO TRELLIS

YOU CAN MAKE a tomato trellis with three 4-foot-high stakes, 2 feet apart, and three cross slats nailed to the stakes. Paint will preserve it for years.

PEA WIRE

TO MAKE permanent pea wires, staple 3 feet of chicken wire to 4-foot-high stakes 5 feet apart. You can make a continuous wire as wide as your garden. Paint the wood to preserve it; roll up at season's end.

PLOT B

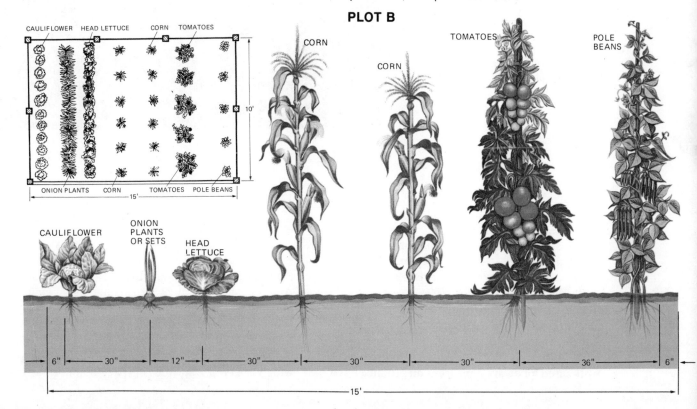

Dwarf fruit trees are big producers

By JAMES DWYER and JOHN ALBERT

THE POTTED peach tree, a Stark Starlet, is a genetic dwarf, decorative shrub for any terrace or patio garden—and will bear fruit for its owner with minimal care. Because of their compact size, the little trees literally can permit a city dweller with a tiny terrace or even a postage-stamp-size yard to have a mini-orchard that will yield a startling crop of full-sized fruit with even moderate care. Abundance of the potted trees is impressive.

■ MANY PEOPLE think of dwarf fruit trees— if they think of them at all—simply as ornamental novelties. They *are* ornamental, no doubt about it. Covered with blossoms in the spring and with fruit in late summer and fall, they bring a unique beauty to any yard or garden. But they are far more than mere novelties.

For one thing, even though a dwarf fruit tree is smaller than a standard tree, its fruit is as large or larger. And because more of its nutrients go to making fruit, its proportional yield is greater. A well-cared for dwarf apple tree can produce up to 150 pounds of fruit per season. It's one reason commercial growers are turning more and more to dwarf trees.

Another is that maintenance is so easy. All branches, fruit and leaves can be reached from the ground for spraying, pruning and harvesting. And, because the trees are smaller, they can be planted as close as 10 feet apart—except for pears, which may require slightly more separation. The benefit to a commercial grower is obvious. For the home gardener, it allows planting a wide variety of fruit trees in space that normally would be taken up by a single standard-size tree.

Finally, a dwarf may start producing the first year after planting, compared to the three to 10 years required by most standard fruit trees. And don't be put off by stories that dwarfs are short-lived. With proper staking and soil care to protect their relatively shallow root systems, they will live and produce every bit as long as their larger cousins. Before you rush to buy and plant an orchard in your back yard, however, there are a few things you should know about these interesting little trees.

Some, like peaches and nectarines, are true genetic dwarfs that always grow to midget size from seed or cuttings. But most are the result of grafting. A normal-size fruit tree is grafted or budded onto the "stock" (stump and root system) of a small species of the same family. This rootstock controls the size, while the upper grafted portion, called the scion, retains all other characteristics. Finding a compatible combination isn't always easy, however.

Sometimes a third section, called a stempiece, is used to make the transition. For example, quince is the normal dwarfing rootstock used for pears, but some varieties of pears are not compatible with quince and refuse to "take." The problem is solved by grafting a compatible pear variety onto the quince root and then grafting the fruit-bearing variety onto this.

A variation of the same principle often is employed with dwarf apples. To get around the characteristically weak root support of apple dwarfing stock, a dwarfing stempiece is grafted onto a rugged crab apple root system, and the fruit-bearing scion is grafted onto this. In this case, the length of the stempiece can make a difference in the degree of dwarfing. The Clark Dwarf Apple, for instance, is made from parts of four trees: The roots are quince, the lower stem-piece is a strong-trunked variety of apple, the upper stempiece is a winter-hardy natural dwarf apple, and the scion is a fruit-bearing variety.

Many types of fruit trees, including some apples, pears, plums and sweet cherries, will not produce fruit unless they are pollinated by another variety of the same fruit growing nearby. Peaches, nectarines, sour cherries and apricots do not have this problem, but many other dwarf fruit trees do. So, before you buy a dwarf fruit tree, find out if it must have a mate.

Another important thing to know before buying a dwarf fruit tree is whether it will survive winter where you live. All varieties need a cold period to start fruit development. Just how much cold depends on the type of fruit and the variety. The same goes for resistance to damage from cold. The U.S. Department of Agriculture has compiled a hardiness chart, in which the Continental United States is broken down into zones based on the average low temperature for each area (see map).

Differences between fruits can be considerable, and in some cases trees have been bred for unusual hardiness. Check with a reputable nurseryman in your area, or consult the USDA county extension service before you buy.

preparation for planting

First and most important consideration in planting is to make sure the tree is not too deeply seated. The bud union—that knotty portion near the base of the trunk where the scion or stempiece has been grafted onto the rootstock—must be several inches above the ground so that it will not develop its own roots, thus sabotaging the grafting process.

The time to plant is in early spring as soon as the ground is workable and before leaf buds have begun to open. Dig the hole a good deal wider,

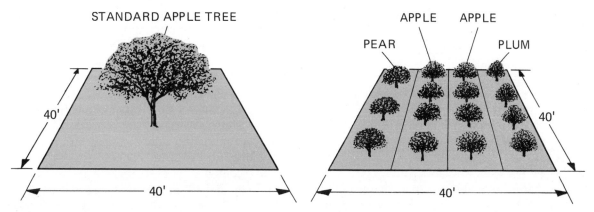

IN A 40 BY 40-FOOT plot a standard apple tree would fill, 15 dwarf fruit trees can flourish.

THE SIZE, QUALITY and abundance of fruit that dwarfs produce can exceed that of standard trees bearing the same variety. Stark Blushing Golden Delicious apples at left are a good example of the fruit dwarfs can produce. Starkrimson apples shown provide some idea of the size of the trees, easy to prune, harvest without ladders.

but not much deeper, than the root system of the tree. Put the dirt that you take out of the hole in a pile, to be mixed with organic matter—peat moss, well-rotted compost or manure—at a ratio of one part organic material to two parts soil. Do not work large amounts of organic matter into the area directly under the tree, however. To do so may cause the tree to settle too deeply. Since dwarf trees have shallow, spreading root systems, it will not benefit them anyway. If you have drainage problems, elevate the planting bed by bringing in more soil, or choose another site.

When the hole is dug, drive a stake into the center. It should be high enough to reach just above the first branches of the tree.

preparing the tree

Dwarf fruit trees usually arrive bare rooted. Let the roots stand overnight in a pail of water before planting.

If the tree is growing in a container, remove the container and gently shake the soil away so the tree can be planted bare-rooted. In addition to pruning damaged or diseased roots, trim off those that cannot be positioned to grow outward. Any root growing around the circumference of the pot will continue to do so in the ground, producing a pot-bound effect.

Place a mound of soil at the base of the hole and spread the roots over it, checking on planting depth. The previous soil level should be indicated on the trunk. Match it.

Hold the tree against the stake and fill the hole about halfway with the soil you took out—with no organic matter added. Make sure it is well crumbled to avoid air pockets, and shake the roots gently as you go to help the soil settle between and around them. Tread the soil down firmly. Fill the hole with water and let it all drain down.

Mix the rest of the soil with organic material and finish filling the hole to just above ground level. Again, tread firmly. Finally, make a shallow doughnut-shaped trough all around the tree, about a foot from the trunk. Fill this several times with water and let it settle. Tie the tree to the stake at two places, near the top, and about halfway up the trunk. Use padded ties sold for the purpose or strips of heavy cloth tied in a figure-8 to provide a buffer between the trunk and the stake.

Until the roots have established themselves, the greatest problem will probably come from cold, drying winds that often occur in spring. The best protection is to water regularly. The tree can be further protected by spraying with an antidessicant like Wilt-Pruf, and by wrapping the trunk with burlap.

care for the tree

Since root systems of dwarf trees are shallow, mulching is important. It maintains viability of the soil surface by holding moisture. It prevents overheating, inhibits weeds and protects organisms such as bacteria and earthworms that loosen the soil. It will also break down in time and supply nutrients. So, each spring, put a ¾-inch layer of bark chips, peat moss, peanut hulls, or some similar mulch around the tree. Take care that it doesn't build up around the

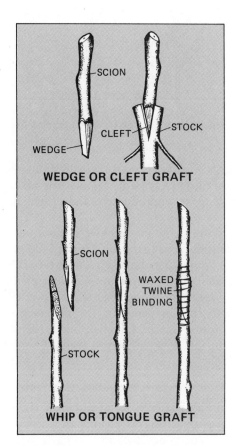

WEDGE OR CLEFT GRAFT

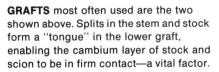

WHIP OR TONGUE GRAFT

TEMPERATURE HARDINESS CHART

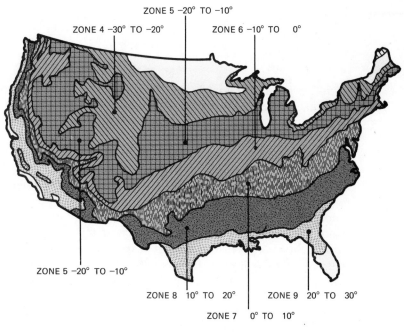

ZONE 5 −20° TO −10°

ZONE 4 −30° TO −20°

ZONE 6 −10° TO 0°

ZONE 5 −20° TO −10°

ZONE 8 10° TO 20°

ZONE 9 20° TO 30°

ZONE 7 0° TO 10°

GRAFTS most often used are the two shown above. Splits in the stem and stock form a "tongue" in the lower graft, enabling the cambium layer of stock and scion to be in firm contact—a vital factor.

RESISTANCE TO COLD WEATHER and response to temperature changes vary widely for different types of dwarf fruit trees. Care must be taken to plant the ones that do best in your zone. The U.S. Department of Agriculture map above shows zones of average annual low temperatures for the Continental United States. Apples generally grow best in Zones 4 to 8. Pears, peaches, apricots and nectarines do best in Zones 5 to 8 (but Keiffer pears prefer Zones 4 to 9). European and Damson plums, and sweet cherries, do well in Zones 5 to 7, and sour cherries like Zones 4 to 7. Japanese plums need Zones 5 to 7 for best results. To be sure before you buy, check the USDA in your county.

SPURS, PICTURED ABOVE, develop toward summer's end on all fruit trees but peaches. They are the budding twigs that will bear next season's flowers and fruit. Trimmers look for spurs to check on next year's production, and snip them judiciously. Spurs usually appear in clusters of three buds; the outer two being fruit buds, the center one a leaf bud. The diagram at right illustrates how a plant should be pruned back to the main leaders, reducing all crotches to stems. Even in the second season, the tree is pruned back to the trunk and main branches.

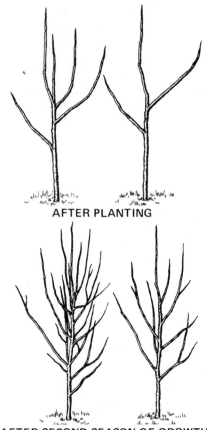

AFTER PLANTING

AFTER SECOND SEASON OF GROWTH

trunk, especially in winter. This can encourage rodents to take up residence. They will damage the roots and gnaw the bark and vital cambium layer.

In most garden soils, dwarf fruit trees will produce reasonable yields without adding any fertilizer. Yields can be increased, however, by doing so. After fruit has begun to appear, the addition of nitrogen will increase its size. Toward the end of summer, a general-purpose fertilizer (5-10-5 or 10-10-10), worked in around the base should result in a richer spring flush the following year.

Properly cared for, your dwarf fruit trees can produce a tremendous fruit set—far more than a standard tree. Flower-bud thinning should be done to increase the size and quality of fruit and to prevent "cyclical" harvest years. With apples and pears, leave about 7 inches between fruits. Peaches, nectarines, Japanese plums, and apricots should grow at 4-inch intervals. Cherries and plum types generally need no thinning.

Pruning of dwarf fruit trees is best done in winter, while the trees are dormant. The purpose is two-fold: to maintain desired height, and to encourage as much lateral growth as possible.

The inner, center portion of the tree should be kept fairly clear of growth. Shoots originating there tend to be unproductive and crowd the tree.

When pruning, either remove a shoot completely, cutting close to the branch from which it originates, or cut just above a bud that faces the way you want the shoot to grow. You can tell the difference between shoots that will be productive and those that won't by the presence of "spurs"—those sharp, spikelike buds that develop in the fall. They are where fruit grows the next season.

DWARF FRUIT-TREE SUPPLIERS
Stark Bros., Louisiana, MO 63353.
W. Atlee Burpee Co., Fordhook Farms, Doylestown, PA 18901.
Henry Leuthardt Nursery, King St., Port Chester, NY 10573.
Kelly Bros. Nurseries, Inc., Dansville, NY 14437.
Jackson & Perkins Co., Medford, OR 97501.
Stern's Nursery, Inc., Geneva, NY 14456.
Gerard Nurseries, Geneva, OH 44041.
Gurney's Nursery, Yankton, SD 57078.

CONTRAST OF BACKGROUND with area to be cleaned (above) shows what this simple mulcher add-on can do. In right photo it's held on mower deck with stovebolts. Holes are ⅜-in. dia. Homemade "power rake" (below) speeds springtime cleanup of twigs and leaves. Handle clears fender of mower to permit dumping.

Riding-mower accessories you can make

By RALPH S. WILKES

■ IF YOUR LAWN is large enough to require a riding mower, these simple attachments will save you many hours of hand labor each fall and spring.

The leaf mulcher—an accessory *not* available for most mowers—is a plate fastened over the discharge chute that keeps leaves churning against the blades until thoroughly pulverized. It makes raking unnecessary. I used ¹/₁₆-in. sheet aluminum with 1½-in. tabs bent at the ends to allow mounting with ¼ x 1-in. roundhead stovebolts, with lock washers. Perforated plates work a little better than solid ones; you might try a piece of expanded metal instead of drilling ⅜-in. holes at ¾-in. intervals as I did. Note that leaves will pulverize only when completely dry.

Rake-attachment details are at right. Use only good steel rakes with reinforced teeth, adjusted to ride at 30° to 35° to the ground. One handle is cut short; the full-length handle is lifted to apply pressure, lowered for dumping.

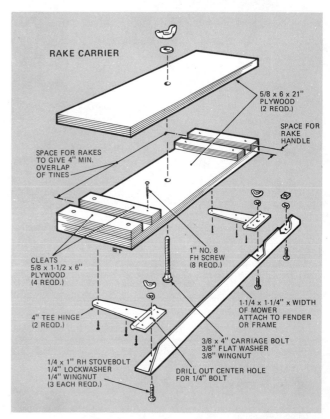

RAKE CARRIER

5/8 x 6 x 21"
PLYWOOD
(2 REQD.)

SPACE FOR
RAKE
HANDLE

SPACE FOR RAKES
TO GIVE 4" MIN.
OVERLAP
OF TINES

CLEATS
5/8 x 1-1/2 x 6"
PLYWOOD
(4 REQD.)

1" NO. 8
FH SCREW
(8 REQD.)

4" TEE HINGE
(2 REQD.)

1-1/4 x 1-1/4" x WIDTH
OF MOWER
ATTACH TO FENDER
OR FRAME

3/8 x 4" CARRIAGE BOLT
3/8" FLAT WASHER
3/8" WINGNUT

1/4 x 1" RH STOVEBOLT
1/4" LOCKWASHER
1/4" WINGNUT
(3 EACH REQD.)

DRILL OUT CENTER HOLE
FOR 1/4" BOLT

Build a loom for weaving fun

■ YOU CAN BUILD this frame loom from ¾-in. hardwood stock for a total cost of about $10. Besides wall hangings, it can be used to weave throw rugs, tote bags or whatever you can create. Experimenting is half the fun.

We call it a lap loom. With the back part resting on the table, the front end rests in your lap—quite a comfortable working position. You can use it to weave pieces up to 20-in. wide. It can be strung for tapestry-type weaving where the warp (the threads running lengthwise through which the filling threads are woven) is completely hidden as it is in our wall hanging. It can also be strung in the regular way where the warp is part of the color scheme and design.

To become familiar with the various parts of the loom see the loom frame diagram. The shuttle which carries the filling threads as they are woven through the warp can be formed to the dimensions in the diagram or purchased inexpensively. We used four shuttles to make the wall hanging.

constructing the frame

Cut all of the pieces for the loom frame from ¾-in. hardwood stock. Either birch or maple would be a good choice.

Begin by cutting the two side strips (Fig. A) to the dimensions given. Drill the dowel peg holes ½-in. deep into the bottoms of the strips as indicated. The 3-in.-long, ¼-in.-dia. dowel pegs are used for measuring the warp. To serve as support legs when weaving. Make the dado cuts as indicated to accommodate the two cross braces; then cut the latter (Fig. B). Four 2¼-in. screw hooks hold the cloth beam in front and the warp beam in back. Turn in the hooks ½ in. from the ends of the side strips as shown in the loom frame diagram.

The take-up beams (front and rear) are used to tighten and loosen the warp threads. They are moved by ratchets.

Cut the rear take-up beam and the warp lock strip (Figs. C, D). Drill ¼-in.-dia. holes ½ in. deep into the take-up beam as indicated. Use dowel centers to locate positions for matching holes in the warp lock strip, and drill these ⁵/₁₆ in. deep. Cut three pieces of ¼-in. dowel ¾ in. long. Glue them into the holes in the lock strip. Sand the protruding pegs and round the ends so they will slip in and out of the holes easily (Photo 1). The warp lock strip will press against the rear take-up beam to "lock" the warp threads.

Cut the front take-up beam and tie bar (Figs. E, F). Later, the warp threads will be brought over the tie bar and tied to it. Web strapping material ⅝ in. wide is used to connect the tie bar to the front take-up beam. You can buy it at shoe repair or canvas shops. Three pieces, each 12 in. long, are needed. Cut the slots in the tie bar to let the webbing slip through. Seal the ends of the straps with white glue to keep them from fraying, then slip the straps through the slots. Nail the ends to one edge of the front take-up beam with carpet tacks (Photo 2).

ratchets and stops

The ratchets are wheels having notched teeth fastened to the ends of the front and rear take-up beams to turn the beams and help you keep proper tension in the warp threads. Saw the ratchets and the ratchet stops from ⅜-in. hardwood stock (Figs. G, H). The center hole in each ratchet is for a free-running axle. Mount the ratchets on the take-up beams by countersinking flathead screws (Photo 3).

heddle blocks

The heddle blocks hold the heddle, which in turn holds the warp threads. Cut the two heddle blocks (Fig. I), making the dadoes indicated. Then cut the two plug pieces to fit the dadoes. Glue the larger plug into the left-hand slot, positioning it ½ in. from the top of the slot and ¼ in. from the slot bottom. Glue the smaller plug into its slot, flush with the bottom of the heddle block. Prepare the other heddle block the same way, *reversing the plug positions* so the blocks will line up with each other when on opposite sides of the frame. Secure the heddle blocks to the side strips by countersinking flathead screws (Photo 5).

assembling the frame

To assemble the loom, begin by fitting one end of each cross brace into the two dado cuts of one side strip and fasten with flathead screws countersunk from the outside of the strip. Drill holes into the center of the ends of the warp and cloth beam dowels and slip the dowels onto the heads of the screw hooks for partial assembly of the frame. Position the other side, slipping the screw hooks into the holes in the dowel ends and fitting the cross-brace ends into the dado cuts of the frame. The warp and cloth beam dowels should turn on the ends of the screw hooks (Photo 6).

Set the rear take-up beam between ends of the frame, pass a roundhead screw through the hole at the end of the frame strip and drive it into the

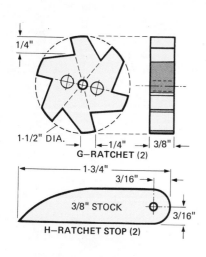

1/4"

1-1/2" DIA.   1/4"   3/8"

G—RATCHET (2)

1-3/4"

3/16"

3/8" STOCK   3/16"

H—RATCHET STOP (2)

1/8" DEEP x 3/4" DADO CUTS

1-1/2"   2-1/2"   3/4"   2-1/2"

1/2"

A—SIDE STRIPS (2) 21-1/4 x 1-1/2 x 3/4"

1/4" DIA.

22-1/4 x 1-1/2 x 3/4"

B—CROSS BRACES (2)

1"   1/4" DIA.   C   1"

21-1/2 x
1-1/2 x 3/4"   1/2"

C—REAR TAKE-UP BEAM

1"   1/4" DIA.   C   1"

21-1/2 x
1-1/2 x 3/8"

D—WARP LOCK STRIP 3/4" LONG DOWELS   3/8"
5/16"

21-1/2 x 1-1/2 x 3/4"

E—FRONT TAKE-UP BEAM

1/4"   C   3/4"

21-1/2 x
1-1/8 x 3/4"   1/4"

F—TIE BAR   SLOTS FOR WEB STRAPS

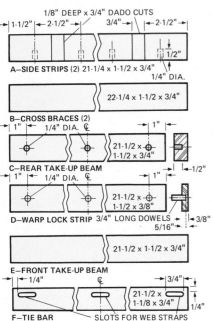

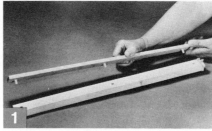

1 **THE DOWEL PEGS** in the warp lock strip fit into matching holes drilled in the rear take-up beam.

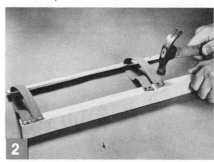

2 **THREE PIECES** of ⅝-in. web strapping are brought through the tie-bar slots and tacked to the front take-up beam.

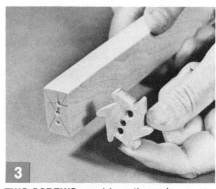

3 **TWO SCREWS** are driven through pre-drilled holes in the ratchet and into the end of the take-up beam.

4 **PLUGS** to form the warping and up-shed positions are glued and fitted into the heddle block.

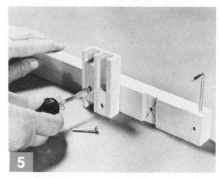

5 **A SCREW** is driven in the pilot holes running through the heddle blocks and into the side bars.

6 **A SCREW HOOK** is fitted into the warp beam. Cross braces will be attached for complete frame assembly.

(4 REQD. FOR WALL HANGING) 21 x 1-1/4 x 1/8"

SHUTTLE

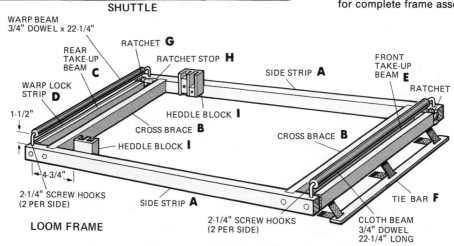

WARP BEAM
3/4" DOWEL x 22-1/4"

RATCHET **G**

REAR
TAKE-UP
BEAM **C**   RATCHET STOP **H**

SIDE STRIP **A**

FRONT
TAKE-UP
BEAM **E**

WARP LOCK
STRIP **D**

RATCHET

HEDDLE BLOCK **I**

1-1/2"

CROSS BRACE **B**

CROSS BRACE **B**

HEDDLE BLOCK **I**

4-3/4"

2-1/4" SCREW HOOKS
(2 PER SIDE)

SIDE STRIP **A**

TIE BAR **F**

LOOM FRAME

2-1/4" SCREW HOOKS
(2 PER SIDE)

CLOTH BEAM
3/4" DOWEL
22-1/4" LONG

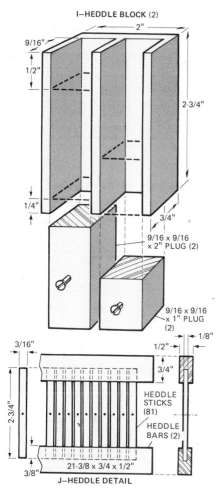

I—HEDDLE BLOCK (2)

9/16"
1/2"
2"
2-3/4"
1/4"
3/4"
9/16 x 9/16 x 2" PLUG (2)
9/16 x 9/16 x 1" PLUG (2)

3/16"
1/2"
1/8"
3/4"
2-3/4"
HEDDLE STICKS (81)
HEDDLE BARS (2)
21-3/8 x 3/4 x 1/2"
3/8"
J—HEDDLE DETAIL

K—A SET OF WARP THREADS

A JIG makes cutting heddle strips to matching lengths much easier. One can also be used for drilling.

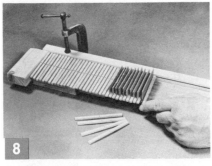

CARDBOARD STRIPS are used to space the heddle sticks evenly in the dado of the heddle bar.

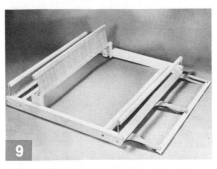

THE LOOM IS ASSEMBLED and heddle is placed in up-shed position. For warping it is placed in back slot.

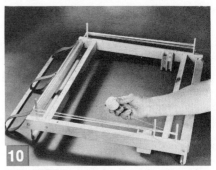

THE WARP is made by wrapping thread around pegs. This makes a 56-in. warp for over 30 in. of weaving.

BEGINNING at the center, one set of warp threads is passed through the heddle slits.

WHEN ALL slits and holes needed are threaded, warp threads are tied to the tie bar in groups of four.

pilot hole through the ratchet and into the end of the beam. Do the same with the other side strip. Screws passing through the holes at the end of the frame act as axles for turning the beam. The front take-up beam and tie bar assembly are attached in the same manner. Screw on the ratchet stops. They swing freely on the screw shanks and drop into the ratchet teeth for locking to tighten the warp. Now the loom frame is basically completed and you are ready to make the heddle.

heddle

The heddle holds the warp threads in position. To make it cut the heddle bars 21⅜ x ¾ x ½ in. (Fig. J). Make dado cuts for the heddle sticks as indicated. The sticks (there are 81) are 2¾ in. long. However, they should first be cut longer, then carefully trimmed to size. Begin by cutting strips ³/₁₆-in. wide and ⅛-in. thick, using a hollow ground blade in a circular saw for smooth edges. Use a fine blade in a jigsaw to cut the sticks to their 2¾-in. length. A jig for cutting (Photo 7) is a good automatic measuring device for accuracy. Drill a ¹/₁₆-in.-dia. hole through the center of each stick, again using a jig for accuracy.

Glue the ends of the sticks into the dado of one of the bars. Place the first strip ½ in. from the end of the bar. A number of spacer strips cut from heavy cardboard (approximately ¹/₁₆-in. thick) and slipped between the sticks as they are glued into the dado will assure even spacing and parallel sticks (Photo 8). Mark the center stick. After a few minutes the glue will be set enough that you can move the cardboard ahead in the gluing sequence. When all sticks are glued into the dado of one bar, spread glue into the dado of the other bar. Then, beginning at one end, work the free ends of the sticks into the second bar dado.

Now the loom is completed and your weaving fun begins. Photo 9 shows the assembled loom with the heddle in the "up shed" position of the heddle block. In this position, it's ready for weaving.

Weaving the wall hanging

Our wall hanging was made by the tapestry form of weaving. In tapestry weaving, the weft threads are beaten down with a tapestry fork so they completely cover the warp, making a dense, rich surface. To make the wall hanging and other patterns, yarns of different colors pass part way across the loom, meeting in a tapestry slit join. This means there will be slits wherever two colors meet.

The secrets of successful weaving are keeping an even and tight tension on your warp yarns; keeping your selvedges straight (it's easy to let them pull in by not leaving enough yarn to beat down); and beating in the yarns evenly.

To weave the wall hanging pictured you will need the following yarns (symbols noted are those found on the wall hanging pattern; your yarn supplier can help you with unfamiliar terms): 350 yards white cotton warp yarn; two lightweight weaving yarns in different shades of blue (darkest blue, ×, and next darkest blue, ▲); one lightweight weaving yarn in light blue, +; one blue/brown Irish tweed yarn, □; two mohair yarns (a royal blue, ○, and a light blue, ●); one gray rya yarn; one brown thick and thin yarn; two thick boucles (one white, one in blue ombre stripes, ■). You will also need at least four shuttles and a tapestry beater (a table fork works well).

Start by measuring your warp as follows and stringing it to the loom.

winding warp sets

Begin winding warp sets by first turning the loom upside down and inserting five pegs in the holes (Photo 10). Tie the white cotton warp yarn to Peg 1. Bring the thread from Peg 1 outside around Pegs 2 and 3, inside of Peg 4, outside and around Peg 5 in a figure eight, then outside the other pegs back and around Peg 1 for the first wrap. Continue wrapping in this way until there are 5 complete wraps—10 threads. This is a set. Wrap the free end of the thread around Peg 1 several times to keep it taut.

Use a short length of contrasting thread to tie the set at the cross over of the figure 8. Also tie the set between Pegs 2 and 3. Cut all the threads where they wrap around Peg 1. Remove the set, and hang it over the back of a chair. Make 17 more sets to warp the loom for the width of the wall hanging.

stringing the loom

Turn the loom over again to string it. Mark the center hole of the heddle. Set the heddle in the warping position of the heddle block, the slot with the 1-in. plug. The proper warping and weaving position is with the rear take-up end farthest from the weaver, the cloth beam directly in front.

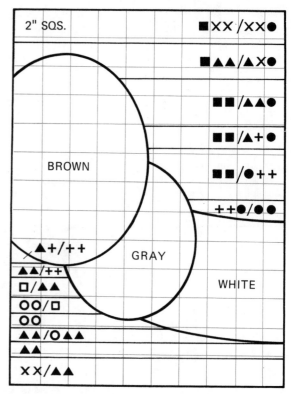

FIG. L. Fill shuttles with the number of strands and colors noted. Where there's a slash, fill two shuttles, one for each side, and weave every other row alternating shuttles. For colors, × denotes darkest blue; ▲, next darkest blue; ○, royal blue mohair; □, blue/brown tweed; +, light blue; ●, light blue mohair; ■, ombre boucle. Use one strand on others.

Slip the loop of one set of warp threads over the hand (Fig. K). Remove the contrasting tie thread. Lift the top loop off your hand and pull the double warping thread from the set. Pass the loop through the heddle slit to the left of the marked heddle stick and pull the thread through until it is about 1 in. beyond the rear warp beam (Photo 11). A steel crochet hook, size 6 or smaller, can be used to pull threads through.

Continue lifting the threads off your hand and threading through the slits to the left until the set is used. Beginning with the first one threaded, slip the loops over the lock strip which has been removed from the back take-up beam, work the loop to the center of the strip and slip on the others in sequence. This will keep the threads from slipping back out of the slits as you warp.

Place a second set of threads over your hand and continue as before, this time working to the right of the center. Continue warping, alternating the side of threading with each set until all threads are used, with an equal number of threads on each side of the center. Move to the opposite end of the loom, spread the threads evenly along the lock strip, being sure that none crosses over another. Slip the pegs of the lock strip into the corresponding holes of the take-up beam to hold the threads in place.

Have someone help wind the warp threads onto the take-up beam. Any tangles in front of the heddle can be combed out with your fingers. Separate the warp threads into two groups and grasp one with each hand, being sure the tension is even on all threads. Your helper can slowly turn the warp take-up beam to wind the threads while you maintain a firm grasp and even tension on all threads in front of the heddle. Leave enough length of thread unwound to tie to the cloth beam tie bar. You're ready to thread the holes in the heddle.

threading the heddle

Beginning at the right side, pick up two threads running through the first slit. Pull one thread back through the slit but hold onto the other to keep it in the slit. Thread the free warp thread through the hole just to the left of the slit it was in. Continue rethreading one thread of each group of two into the holes to the left of each slit until all holes and slits are filled.

Starting at the left, pick up the first four threads and bring them towards you in a straight line. Bring them over the tie bar, around and up the back, separating them into two pairs of two threads each, one pair passing to the right, the other to the left of the set of four threads. Bring them up and tie into a square knot. Continue working towards the right, tying each group of four threads to the tie bar. Photo 12 shows the warping.

Next, lift the heddle out of the warp position of the heddle block and place it in the up-shed position in the heddle block to open the other shed. (For down-shed position move heddle directly in front of block.)

'throwing' the shuttle

Wrap the colored yarn weft (filling) on the shuttle and begin to weave by passing or "throwing" the shuttle across the warp threads, and alternately placing the heddle in the up or down-shed position with each pass. The warp threads are tightened by turning the rear or front take-up beam, letting the ratchet stop fall into the ratchet teeth to lock in position. To loosen the warp when you're not weaving, turn one takeup beam just enough to allow the ratchet stop to be lifted and loosen the tension.

Begin work on your wall hanging by enlarging the pattern (Fig. L) to the full size (19½ x 26 in.) and place it underneath the loom to guide you in your weaving. Don't worry about following it precisely. Explore color combinations and shape variations as you go along and let your weaving become a one-of-a-kind creation.

You'll need a heading at the beginning of your weaving to space the warp yarns and make a surface to beat against. To do this, weave with rags for about an inch, beating them down straight and even against the bottom of the loom. Then switch to yarns.

beating down the yarn

A lot of yarn gets beaten down in a tapestry, to cover the warp ends. Be sure to leave surplus yarn in each shed so your sel-

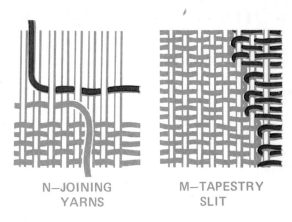

N—JOINING
YARNS

M—TAPESTRY
SLIT

Two ways yarn meets.

vedges won't draw in, but not enough surplus so that parts of your weaving buckle.

The technique is to throw the shuttle across the shed and draw the yarn through diagonally, while one hand holds the yarn firmly at the selvedge. Starting at the selvedge the yarn is coming from, you'll pass the shuttle across the width of the loom. Then, starting at the same edge, beat the yarn down against the finished weaving. Excess yarn will slide across the loom and exit at the shuttle side. Check your selvedges often for straightness, and examine the weaving to see that warp is fully covered.

Begin with yarns by winding a double thickness of the darkest blue (×) onto a shuttle and pass or "throw" it across the loom, then beat it down. Change sheds and repeat, holding onto the selvedge edge where the yarn begins. Weave this color for several inches (the first inch will be turned under as a hem), then follow the pattern or mix your own colors. The second stripe, beginning on our pattern, involves weaving a row with the darkest blue, the next with the next lighter blue.

joining yarns

You will need to join yarns whenever your shuttle runs dry, when you change colors, and when you are working tapestry slits (Fig. M). For changing colors or shuttles, leave a 5-in. tail on the old and new yarn ends. Join the new yarn so it overlaps with the old.

Continue weaving stripes straight across the loom until you get to the bottom of the white circle on your pattern. Then start using the tapestry slit technique (Fig. M), letting colors intersect in mid-loom to form the pattern.

For tapestry slits weave the first color across the shed to where you want it to stop. Weave the second color up to, but not intersecting, the first. Change sheds and turn each color around, making sure that no warp ends in the shed are uncovered. Slits are connected by moving one of the colors over an uncovered warp end. Try not to let slits get longer than half an inch before connecting them.

When you've woven 9 or 10 inches, loosen the take-up and warp beam ratchets. Cover the woven section with a sheet of wrapping paper and roll the weaving and paper forward under the take-up beam.

As you're finishing your piece, weave an extra inch of the last color for a hem. Place the heddle in warping position and keep tension tight. Cut four warp threads at the center of the loom, leaving them about 8 inches long. Pass them through the heddle and tie in an overhand knot close to the weaving surface. Do this across the loom, working alternately to left, and right of center. Unroll the weaving, remove the rags you wove in at the beginning, and repeat tying the threads.

Clip the ends to 1 or 2 inches, fold them and the extra inch of weaving under, and hem. Slip a dowel through the pocket at the top. Your tapestry is ready to hang.

Veneering: beautiful wood on a budget

By PENELOPE ANGELL

■ YOU CAN BUILD the intriguing markings and the meandering grain patterns of exotic hardwoods into your projects once you know the secrets of veneering. These wafers of wood offer an inexpensive way to give unfinished furniture and humble surfaces the rich look of hardwood. Veneers can also counter-act warpage when they're applied to both sides of a panel. Since you can select the veneer pieces that join together, you can create patterns in wood. Veneers usually come in $1/28$ to $1/36$-in. thicknesses in sheets from 4 to 12-in. wide and 3 ft. or longer. Two ways of applying veneer are explored in these projects. The first uses no clamps and the second requires presses or clamps.

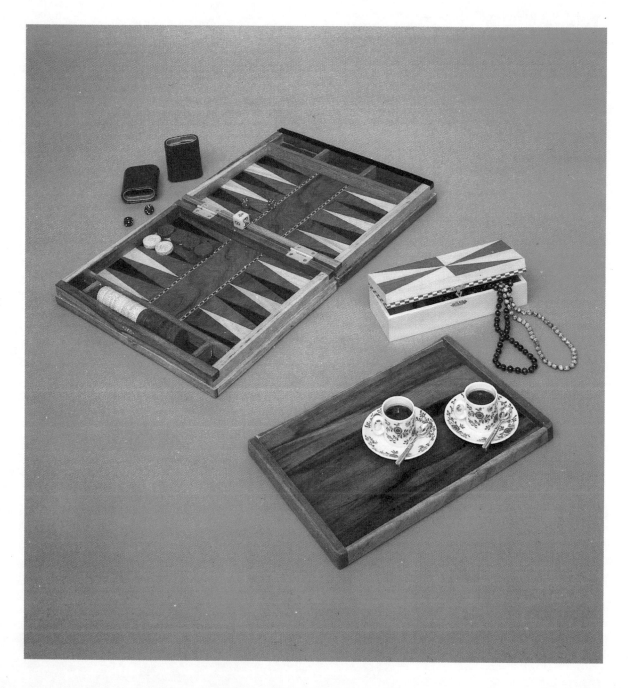

JEWELRY BOX

THE TOP VENEER is glued to the box with tape side up. Brown or wax paper between veneer and box is removed as veneer is positioned.

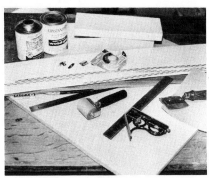

TOOLS YOU'LL NEED include a model knife equipped with fine blades, steel rule to cut against; a square; veneer roller and a veneer saw.

THE TOP of the box is pressed down with a roller immediately after the veneer has been cemented on to insure a good bond over entire glued area.

VENEERS FOR top are cut with a model knife. The light veneer is aspen and the dark is mahogany. Pieces are placed on the pattern to check fit.

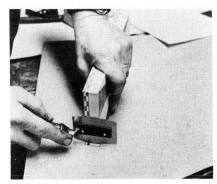

THE OVERHANGING veneer is cut off with a veneer saw. Later it's sanded smooth. The extra overhang is added at the corners to insure a smooth edge.

■ WITH A LITTLE EFFORT and *not* much money you can turn an inexpensive basswood box from a craft·shop into a unique and elegant box for jewelry or odds and ends by applying veneer. You can make the top design by cutting two light and two dark rectangles, halving them diagonally and joining the pieces together alternating wood types.

Materials include a box, light and dark veneer, fancy inlay border, hinges, lock, veneer tape, contact adhesive, No. 180 garnet paper and varnish or other finish. Begin by removing any hardware and tracing the box outline on paper—top, sides, front and back. Draw the design shown or one you've devised yourself. Cut the veneer sections for the top exactly to size with a model knife and tape them together.

Glue the assembled design (make sure joints are tight) to the box—taped side up—with contact adhesive. To assure proper veneer placement (you can't move it once it's down), put a sheet of brown wrapping paper or wax paper between the box top and the veneer, leaving a slight margin at the front. Align the front veneer and box edges, press the veneer in place, then gradually slip the sheet away. Then roll the veneer firmly and evenly.

Next mark and cut the veneer and border for the sides, lid and bottom, allowing an extra 1/16 in. to overhang at each corner. Tape the veneer and inlay together and glue them to the box using the slip-sheet method just described. Go over the veneer with a roller and trim the overhangs.

Mark, cut, tape and glue the front and back veneers in the same way, again allowing a 1/16-in. overhang that is trimmed off. To finish the box, first peel off your tape. A razor blade used carefully helps. Sand the surface smooth, then apply a finish.

If you can't locate veneers or inlay borders in your area try Constantine, 2050 Eastchester Rd., Bronx, NY 10461; or Craftsman Wood Service, 2727 South Mary St., Chicago, IL 60608.

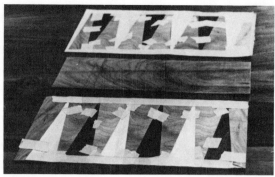

JOINING VENEERS makes it possible to create interesting patterns in the grain. Set up your patterns by first joining the veneer sections with short pieces of tape across the joint. Then add one long horizontal strip the length of the joint.

APPLY PLASTIC RESIN (left), such as Weldwood, with a thin-nap roller to be sure the glue is evenly applied. Any area not covered may cause a bump. Work quickly after you apply resin. Top and bottom veneer edges all have been taped to the plywood (left) and the tray is now prepared to be sandwiched into the press. To make the veneer press (right), use three hardwood 2x2s, birch plywood and a wax-paper sheet on each side of the tray. Hold the assembly with C-clamps.

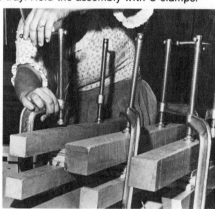

■ YOU CAN MAKE a striking grain design as on this tray top by using two pieces of veneer taped together. Materials you'll need are a piece of ½-in. plywood good on both sides for the core of the tray (10x15 in. or whatever size you wish), veneer for the tray top (we used African Bubinga) and tray bottom (a less expensive plain mahogany is fine here), ½ x 1¼-in. cherry or other wood edging strips to size; veneer tape and tung oil.

Tools and equipment needed include a model knife, metal straightedge, plastic resin or yellow glue, short-nap roller, file and sandpaper in grits from 60 to 400. Either glue requires a veneer press made by sandwiching the tray between wax paper, two sheets of plywood the same size as the tray and three 2x2s on either side. Six C-clamps hold the assembly together.

Begin by cutting the veneers for the tray top and bottom the same size as the plywood piece. Cut the veneer so its grain is at right angles to the top layer of plywood to help prevent warping. Tape veneers together with short crosspieces, then with one long vertical strip.

Next apply plastic resin evenly to the back of the veneer that goes on the tray top, facing the tape side up. Now work quickly until the tray is in the press. Place the veneer on the plywood and tape the edges. Glue and tape the tray bottom veneer.

Place the tray in the press with wax paper on each side and start applying pressure with the C-clamps, working from the middle out. After you've turned down all clamps part way, begin from the middle again and tighten them as much as possible. Wait about 12 hours; then remove the tray and peel off the tape.

Sand with the grain, clean, then rub on tung oil. Glue and press the long edging pieces to the tray with bar clamps. Then do the same to the short edgings, round the corners, sand and finish with tung oil.

BACKGAMMON BOARD

■ THIS BACKGAMMON BOARD is made with four wood veneers and inlay banding. Materials you'll need are four pieces of ½ x 14 x 17-in. birch plywood good on two sides (two pieces each for the board and a press), wood strips to make the box and inner compartments, edging for plywood, two 3-in. butt hinges, a box catch, plastic resin or yellow glue, sandpaper from coarse to fine grit; masking tape and tung oil.

You need light and dark veneers for the playing triangles, another for the center of the board face and board back, a fourth for the inner compartments, plus inlay banding.

Tools needed are a plane, glue roller, table saw, sharp model knife, four bar clamps and a press. The veneer press, although larger, is used as it was in the preceding project. It's made of eight 2 x 2s, two plywood sheets, two layers of wax paper and eight C-clamps.

cutting and taping veneer

Mark the veneer layout for the face and back of the backgammon board on two pieces of ply-

wood. Each side of the boards must be completely veneered to prevent warpage. *Be sure to set up a right and left-hand panel with alternating colored triangles.*

Make cardboard templates of the veneer triangles and draw outlines on the veneer. The latter may need trimming later, so make templates slightly larger than required. The jig shown can help you cut the veneer with a model knife. Use moderate pressure and make repeated passes over the veneer. To plane the veneer, brush it lightly with the grain across the plane's cutting edge.

Cut all veneer pieces. Inlay bands can be cut and taped now or glued later in a space cut and chipped out of the veneer after it's pressed.

You can begin taping the face pieces together with short cross-pieces of tape pulled tightly. Then tape the joints lengthwise, covering the cross tapings. Tape the face veneers for both panels, then tape both back inlay and veneers.

Mix the plastic resin and smooth some on a plywood panel; then place the back veneer on the panel (tape side up) and tape edges. Place veneered side down in the press on wax paper; then glue and tape edges of the face veneer to top side of the panel. Cover with wax paper, plywood and the top 2x2s evenly spaced; then apply pressure with C-clamps.

After the proper glue-setting time has elapsed, remove the panel and repeat the process for the second panel. Remove the tape, sand the panels with the grain and oil lightly.

constructing the box

Cut the ¾x1¼-in. pieces and make lap joints. Glue them together; then clamp and glue them to

FIRST STEP OF taping process is shown below. The pieces are held together with tightly pulled cross-pieces of tape. Then longer tape strips are placed lengthwise covering the cross tapings.

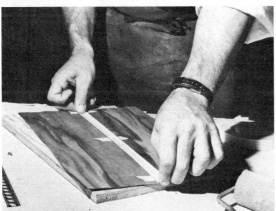

WOOD PIECES that make the box are glued and clamped to the board. Bar clamps apply pressure sideways and C-clamps apply up-and-down pressure. Wax paper and scrap wood are placed between the board and clamps.

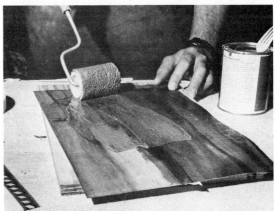

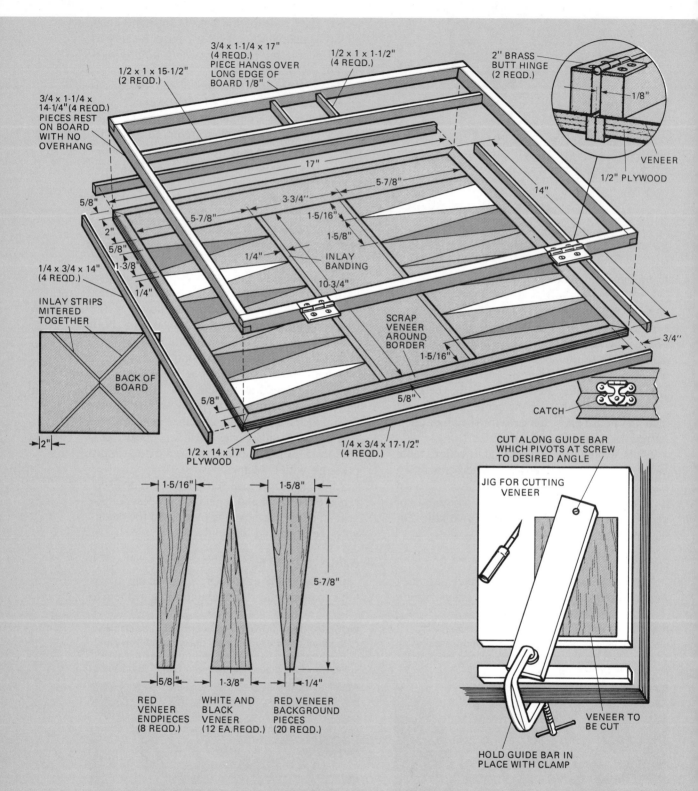

3/4 x 1-1/4 x 17"
(4 REQD.)
PIECE HANGS OVER
LONG EDGE OF
BOARD 1/8"

1/2 x 1 x 15-1/2"
(2 REQD.)

1/2 x 1 x 1-1/2"
(4 REQD.)

2" BRASS
BUTT HINGE
(2 REQD.)

3/4 x 1-1/4 x
14-1/4"(4 REQD.)
PIECES REST
ON BOARD
WITH NO
OVERHANG

1/8"

VENEER

1/2" PLYWOOD

17"

5-7/8"

14"

5/8"

3-3/4"

5-7/8"

1-5/16"

1-5/8"

2"

5/8"

1/4"

INLAY
BANDING

1-3/8"

1/4"

10-3/4"

1/4 x 3/4 x 14"
(4 REQD.)

INLAY STRIPS
MITERED
TOGETHER

SCRAP
VENEER
AROUND
BORDER

1-5/16"

BACK OF
BOARD

3/4"

5/8"

CATCH

2"

5/8"

5/8"

1/2 x 14 x 17"
PLYWOOD

1/4 x 3/4 x 17-1/2"
(4 REQD.)

CUT ALONG GUIDE BAR
WHICH PIVOTS AT SCREW
TO DESIRED ANGLE

JIG FOR CUTTING
VENEER

1-5/16"

1-5/8"

5-7/8"

5/8"

1-3/8"

1/4"

RED
VENEER
ENDPIECES
(8 REQD.)

WHITE AND
BLACK
VENEER
(12 EA.REQD.)

RED VENEER
BACKGROUND
PIECES
(20 REQD.)

VENEER TO
BE CUT

HOLD GUIDE BAR IN
PLACE WITH CLAMP

faces of the panels using bar clamps and eight C-clamps as in the photo. Use wax paper and scrap wood between the board and clamps.

Cut, glue and clamp the edging to the plywood panels, make the box compartments and hinge the box parts together. Sand and chip away any excess glue and lightly oil the box.

You can get a catalog of playing pieces like those shown from Backgammon Headquarters, 669 Madison Ave., New York, NY 10021.

THIS COLLECTION contains designs from Corsican Briar Carve-a-pipe blocks plus briar and meerschaum ready to be worked.

Carve your own dream pipe

By GARTH GRAVES

■ IF YOU'RE A pipe smoker, you've probably dreamed of owning a beautiful one-of-a-kind handmade pipe. Instead of paying a stiff price to purchase one, you can make your own personalized pipe. All you need is a preshaped pipe block, a few tools and a little imagination.

Briar and meerschaum pipe blocks with a shank, prebored bowl and smoke hole fitted with either a straight or curved stem are available at tobacconists. You can buy the blocks alone or in a kit with carving tools.

Briar is the most popular material used for carving pipes. It is hard and close-grained, yet easy to carve and shape. Heat doesn't easily affect it and it won't absorb tar residues from burned tobacco.

The other elegant alternative, meerschaum, is a soft, white mineral that's so light it floats on water. The wax used to finish these pipes turns them to a golden brown that deepens as the pipe is smoked.

Pipe designs that have become classics over the years combine smoking comfort with a pleasing shape and balance. You may want to choose one of the time-tested designs shown on the following page or create your own classic.

Whether you make an ornately carved pipe or a free-form shape, the design should be planned in proportion to the shape and size of the block.

When selecting the block, remember that curved stems tend to reduce the noticeable weight felt at the bit; straight stems accentuate the weight.

Although the designs you carve can be complex, the tools you'll need are not. Use a hacksaw, bandsaw or coping saw to cut away the excess wood to rough-shape the pipe. You can use pipe cleaners to locate and identify the position of the air holes in your predrilled block, and to apply stain.

You'll need a white China marker or pencil, half-round rasp and rattail file. A small electric

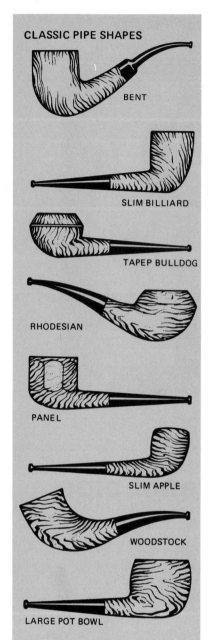

CLASSIC PIPE SHAPES

BENT

SLIM BILLIARD

TAPEP BULLDOG

RHODESIAN

PANEL

SLIM APPLE

WOODSTOCK

LARGE POT BOWL

ROUGH-CUT BLOCK of briar comes with straight stem (shown) or a bent one. Meerschaum blocks are also available.

EXCESS WOOD is trimmed from the block with a hacksaw, bandsaw or coping saw. Be careful not to trim off too much wood.

SAND THE PIPE beginning with coarse and continuing to finer grits of paper while the stem is in the pipe.

THE BASIC PIPE shape is outlined on top and bottom. Portions of the bowl top are also marked to be trimmed.

AS YOU BEGIN to shape the pipe in the vise, attach the stem. It should be in the pipe while fine finishing is done.

BUFFING adds the finishing touch to your pipe. This brings out the grain and texture of the briar.

shaping tool will cut down on your carving time, but there's a lot of satisfaction in cutting your designs by hand.

Use sandpaper in 80, 120, 230 and 400 grits to smooth the pipe surface. A buffing wheel with Tripoli jeweler's rouge gives an ultra-smooth finish.

An alcohol-based stain such as Omega dye from Tandy Leather Co., 2727 W. 7th, Ft. Worth, TX 76107, gives coloring. If your pipe

has a uniformly good grain that you'd like to highlight, simply finish it with a light coat of vegetable oil.

Remove the bit from the briar to keep it from being broken. Place a straight pipe cleaner in the precarved bowl and measure the bowl depth. Also note the approximate position of the air hole entering the bowl from the stem. Using your China marker, transfer these measurements to the outside of the block. Then trace the ap-

WHEN YOU GET the hang of carving, try making a pipe as unique as your imagination allows. These dream pipes are from left: a Sun figure, Swedish chap, a large Sun figure, Zeus, and the North Wind.

proximate shape of the bowl *interior* on one side of the block, using the bowl depth and air hole location as guide lines.

Place a straight pipe cleaner in the predrilled hole in the stem and use a straightedge to mark the location on the outside of the block.

Now you're ready to sketch the basic shape of your pipe. Within the limitations of your block shape there are endless possibilities. Whether you use a classic design or your own, it's a good idea to make a preliminary sketch on paper.

If you want to try some high-relief carving, make sure you leave enough stock to work with. Plan your design so that the bowl thickness is not less than ⅜ in. in order to make a practical smoking pipe. The thicker the bowl, the cooler the smoke.

Trim the excess wood from the block, using a hacksaw, bandsaw or coping saw. It's better to leave too much wood than to risk trimming the pipe too thin.

During the wood-trimming process, you'll start to see the hidden grain on your pipe, the first evidence of its originality. In many cases, hidden flaws in the grain only add to your one-of-a-kind finished product. Large flaws can be filled with Plastic Wood.

Place the briar in a vise and, using the rasp, begin to rough-shape the bowl. Try to avoid getting too enthusiastic and trimming off too much.

Now that the piece is beginning to take form, replace the bit. It will be an integral part of your design and should be attached when you're fine-shaping the bowl. Protect the block as you work on it in the vise by wrapping it in toweling and using a smooth file for final shaping.

Keep checking the bowl thickness to be sure you aren't shaping the bowl too thin. Shape the shank of the pipe to blend with the stem.

You can also use a sanding disc in an electric

drill to fine-shape the pipe. Start with 80-grit paper. The best way to do this is to put the drill in a vise (being careful not to cover the ventilation openings) and move the pipe into the sander. The pipe must be kept moving constantly and lightly to avoid developing flat areas and deep swirl marks.

You can make ornate carvings on your pipe with regular wood carving chisels or those that come in your kit. Don't use thin model-knife blades—they'll break off in the briar.

Gradually work from coarse to fine grits of sandpaper to finish the pipe. Keep the bit in the pipe and sand it as well so its final finish will blend in with the overall pipe design.

Stain the pipe by brushing stain on with a pipe cleaner and allowing it to dry. The more coats you apply, the darker the finish your pipe will have. Use only alcohol-based dyes.

If you have an unusually attractive grain on your pipe, you may want to omit staining it and simply apply vegetable oil for the finish.

Whether stained or left with a natural vegetable oil finish, buffing will put the finishing touch on your pipe. The grain and texture of your pipe will now be brought out to their fullest beauty. Be sure to buff the top of the bowl and the bit. Use plenty of Tripoli on the buffing wheel.

A well-stocked tobacconist should carry rough-cut briar and meerschaum pipe blocks and kits. If you have difficulty in locating pipe supplies in your area, write to A. Oppenheimer and Co., 435 North Midland Ave., Saddle Brook, NJ 07662. They are pipe-kit distributors and can give you the name of a tobacconist in your area who carries the items.

You can also order a rough-cut briar block with a straight stem from The Tinder Box Int'l., Ltd., 1723 Cloverfield Blvd., Santa Monica, CA 90404.

Build a redwood chaise

**Relax in the sun!
Your comfort is assured in this reclining chaise.
Its back can be lowered to the horizontal
position so you can get an even
tan. Here's how to build one
for your family**

■ THIS REDWOOD CHAISE will help you enjoy your outdoor leisure hours this summer. The lift-up section pivots to four different angles or lowers to a full horizontal position.

You can make the chaise with clear heart redwood—good for outdoor furniture—resorcinol or other waterproof glue and the minimal hardware noted in the materials list. You'll need about 68 ft. of ¾ x 3½-in. wood, 20 ft. of 1½ x 3½-in. wood and 10 ft. of ¾ x 1½-in. wood. This includes allowance for waste.

The chaise is made up of four parts: the lounge section, the side (arms and legs) section, the lift-up section and the ratchet section.

Begin by cutting the lumber to size. Label the pieces and separate them into their individual sections as you work.

The legs and arms are joined by mortise-and-tenon joints. Carefully lay out the tenons in the legs and score the shoulder line with a sharp knife. Then secure the work in a vise, repositioning the wood for each cut so it can be made square with the face of the work. Cut the tenons with a backsaw. Then use a ripsaw to make the four cuts parallel to the tenon to remove waste.

Next lay out the mortises in the arms and use a ³/₁₆-in. auger bit to bore out the mortises. Bore each hole ⅛ in. deeper than its mating tenon (to allow space for glue). Secure the wood and clean out all waste with a sharp chisel.

Use a router or table saw to cut the notches in the legs where the side rails attach.

The slats in the lounge and lift-up sections rest in grooves in the side rails. Rout the grooves for the slats on the side pieces using a straightedge guide.

Make the dado cuts for the end piece of the lift-up section. Also cut notches in the lift-up

section to accommodate the ratchet when in the horizontal position. Drill and chisel out the first slat of the lift-up section where the pivot bolts will be attached.

Next, make the rabbet cuts on the lounge side rail ends.

Mark and cut the dadoes and the slots in the ratchet support section and the notches for the ratchet stops. Assemble.

You can use a compass set at 1¾-in. to mark the circle design on the leg bottom. Draw the circle, then measure ⅝ in. down from the circle top. Make a freehand cut inward from the outside of the wood around the mark. Also cut the other rounded corners on the arms, lift-up section and ratchet.

Join all sections with glue. You may need to clamp the sections overnight; check manufacturer's directions on the glue can.

Begin with the lounge section. Spread the glue evenly in the grooves of the side rails and space the slats 1 in. apart. Glue and screw the end pieces and adjust bar clamps.

Glue and clamp the lift-up section in the same manner. Then glue and clamp the two side sections and the ratchet support.

Join the lounge section to the side sections with glue and screws. Fit and bolt the lift-up section into the chaise. Then attach the ratchet support section to the lift-up section and bolt them together.

Attach the lower ratchet pieces by gluing and screwing them to the chaise leg. Then glue and clamp on the ratchet stop covers.

Lounge pads are available in department and home center stores. The one shown is from Crawford Mfg. Co., Inc., Third Ave. and Decatur St., Richmond, VA 23224.

CHAISE SLATS are spaced 1 in. apart. To maintain even spacing, you can make a jig of ¼-in. plywood.

MATERIALS LIST—CHAISE	
No.	**Size and description (use)**
2	¾ x 3½ x 78″ redwood (side rails)
10	¾ x 3½ x 26¼″ redwood (slats, ends)
2	¾ x 3½ x 39″ redwood (lift-up sides)
9	¾ x 3½ x 24¾″ redwood (lift-up slats)
2	¾ x 3½ x 11″ redwood (ratchet cover)
4	1½ x 3½ x 20⅜″ redwood (legs)
2	1½ x 3½ x 44″ redwood (arms)
2	1½ x 3½ x 20″ redwood (ratchet)
1	¾ x 1½ x 27″ redwood (endpiece)
2	¾ x 1½ x 17″ redwood (ratchet sides)
1	¾ x 1½ x 25½″ redwood (ratchet piece)
1	¾ x 1½ x 23¼″ redwood (ratchet piece)
2	¼-20 x 1¼″ fh galv. bolt, acorn nut
2	¼-20 x 1¾″ fh galv. bolt acorn nut
16	No. 8 x 1¼″ brass fh screws
6	No. 8 x 2½″ brass fh screws
	Resorcinol or other waterproof glue

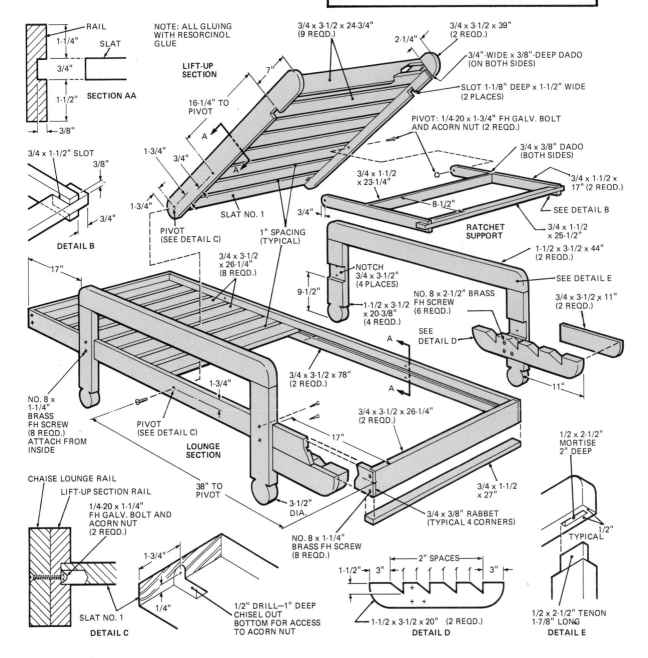

Six wood projects for the outdoors

A contemporary swing with a touch of nostalgia, hanging planter, screens and more. These ideas were designed to make your yard even more comfortable and beautiful

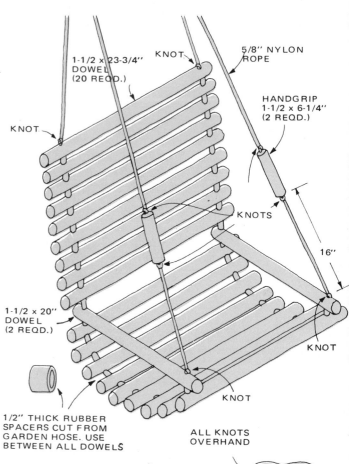

1-1/2 x 23-3/4″ DOWEL (20 REQD.)

KNOT

5/8″ NYLON ROPE

HANDGRIP 1-1/2 x 6-1/4″ (2 REQD.)

KNOT

KNOTS

16″

1-1/2 x 20″ DOWEL (2 REQD.)

KNOT

KNOT

1/2″ THICK RUBBER SPACERS CUT FROM GARDEN HOSE. USE BETWEEN ALL DOWELS

ALL KNOTS OVERHAND

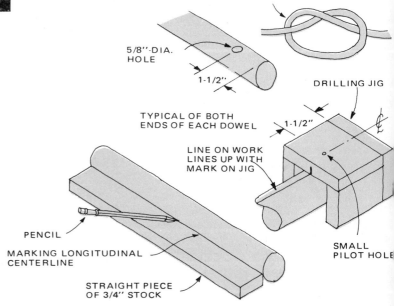

5/8″-DIA. HOLE

1-1/2″

TYPICAL OF BOTH ENDS OF EACH DOWEL

DRILLING JIG

1-1/2″

LINE ON WORK LINES UP WITH MARK ON JIG

SMALL PILOT HOLE

PENCIL

MARKING LONGITUDINAL CENTERLINE

STRAIGHT PIECE OF 3/4″ STOCK

DOWEL SWING

Wood furniture in either yard or garden setting is as natural as the plants themselves. Through careful use of material, life in a backyard can be enhanced considerably—aesthetically and functionally. The dowel swing above is one of six projects we selected from the Ortho book *Wood Projects for the Garden* at most garden centers or directly from Chevron Chemical Co., 575 Market St., San Francisco, CA 94105.

BONSAI BOX

This tabletop planter is a natural for those who are dedicated to the fascinating pastime of creating charming miniature Oriental gardens. The solid box is basically a mallet and chisel chore, but you can save a great deal of sculpting time by boring out a number of 3-in. holes to remove the majority of the waste stock. The holes for the through-dowels at both ends should be made by boring carefully from both sides to assure neat holes. Locate hole centers using rule and pencil.

1. 4 x 9 x 13''
WOOD BLOCK

3/4'' x 11''
DOWEL(4 REQD.)

BONSAI BOX
PROTOTYPE
MADE OF FIR

3/4 x 1-3/4''
DOWEL
(4 REQD.)

3. BORE 3'' DEEP HOLES
TO REMOVE BULK

5. BORE FOR AND
INSTALL 3/4'' DIA.
DOWELS WITH WATERPROOF
GLUE

1''
1''

1-3/4''
BORDER

2. DRAW ROUGH
OUTLINE OF CAVITY

4. 1/2'' MIN.
BOTTOM
THICKNESS

ROUND ALL EDGES

6. BORE 1/2'' DEEP
INSTALL DOWEL
LEGS WITH
GLUE

DRAIN HOLE
(2 REQD.)

1''

1''

LOW TABLE WITH BUTCHER-BLOCK TOP

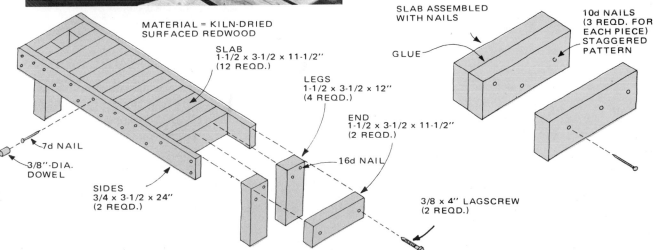

Just as a living room is enhanced by low end tables, patio living is upgraded when a table is conveniently placed for parking drinks, snacks and the like. Create it using scrap 2x4s left over from other projects. If you own bar clamps, assemble with resorcinol glue only. If not, you can put the table together using the glue-and-nail method. Set all exposed nailheads; finish with outdoor sealer.

MATERIAL = KILN-DRIED
SURFACED REDWOOD

SLAB
1-1/2 x 3-1/2 x 11-1/2''
(12 REQD.)

LEGS
1-1/2 x 3-1/2 x 12''
(4 REQD.)

END
1-1/2 x 3-1/2 x 11-1/2''
(2 REQD.)

SLAB ASSEMBLED
WITH NAILS

GLUE

10d NAILS
(3 REQD. FOR
EACH PIECE)
STAGGERED
PATTERN

7d NAIL

3/8''-DIA.
DOWEL

16d NAIL

SIDES
3/4 x 3-1/2 x 24''
(2 REQD.)

3/8 x 4'' LAGSCREW
(2 REQD.)

HANGING PLANTER

Rope and wood used with coleus create a rustic hanging that will complement any patio. The box shown is made of clear all-heart redwood, assembled with waterpoof glue and galvanized finishing nails. Start by cutting the four side pieces the same size, using 45° miters at the corners. For strong joints, assemble the box with corner cleats as shown. To hang it, use screweyes in the box and a screw hook as the hanger. If box will hold a potted plant rather than one in soil, bore holes in bottom.

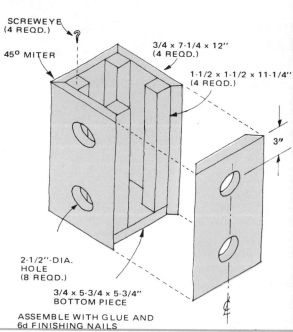

SCREWEYE (4 REQD.)

45° MITER

3/4 x 7-1/4 x 12'' (4 REQD.)

1-1/2 x 1-1/2 x 11-1/4'' (4 REQD.)

3''

2-1/2''-DIA. HOLE (8 REQD.)

3/4 x 5-3/4 x 5-3/4'' BOTTOM PIECE

ASSEMBLE WITH GLUE AND 6d FINISHING NAILS

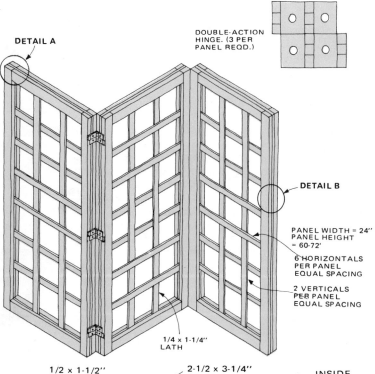

DETAIL A

DOUBLE-ACTION HINGE. (3 PER PANEL REQD.)

DETAIL B

PANEL WIDTH = 24'' PANEL HEIGHT = 60-72'

6 HORIZONTALS PER PANEL EQUAL SPACING

2 VERTICALS PER PANEL EQUAL SPACING

1/4 x 1-1/4'' LATH

FREESTANDING SCREEN TRELLIS

This folding screen is ideal for use as a patio divider. Its double-action (folding-screen) hinges make it flexible enough so it can be arranged to surround a container or be used as a wind screen. Complete directions for building are given below. Finish with a clear sealer to withstand weather.

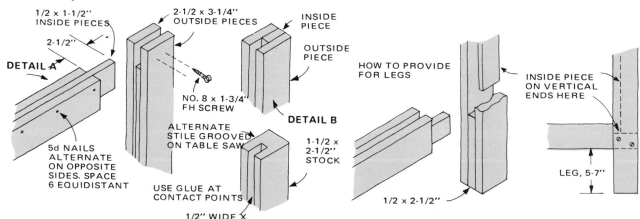

1/2 x 1-1/2'' INSIDE PIECES

2-1/2''

2-1/2 x 3-1/4'' OUTSIDE PIECES

INSIDE PIECE

OUTSIDE PIECE

DETAIL A

NO. 8 x 1-3/4'' FH SCREW

5d NAILS ALTERNATE ON OPPOSITE SIDES. SPACE 6 EQUIDISTANT

ALTERNATE STILE GROOVED ON TABLE SAW

USE GLUE AT CONTACT POINTS

1/2'' WIDE X 1'' DEEP GROOVE

DETAIL B

1-1/2 x 2-1/2'' STOCK

1/2 x 2-1/2''

HOW TO PROVIDE FOR LEGS

INSIDE PIECE ON VERTICAL ENDS HERE

LEG, 5-7''

FOLDING TRELLIS

Reminiscent of safety gates for toddlers, this accordion-like trellis permits adjustment of both its height and width to suit a particular space. The critical dimension is the spacing of the pivot holes; in order for the trellis to work smoothly, these must be accurately located. The safest way to work is to carefully bore the pivot hole in the first piece and then use it as a template for the remaining pieces. The slot in the end posts is a must so the terminal points on the trellis can move freely when you make a size adjustment. You can use stock of a heftier dimension than the lattice shown, but be sure the cotter pins and bolts are long enough to do the job.

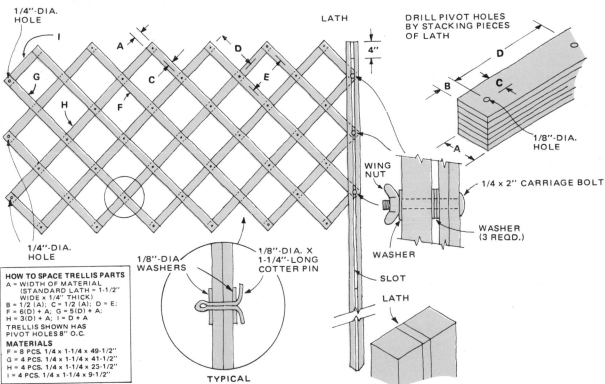

HOW TO SPACE TRELLIS PARTS
A = WIDTH OF MATERIAL
(STANDARD LATH = 1-1/2"
WIDE x 1/4" THICK)
B = 1/2 (A); C = 1/2 (A); D = E;
F = 6(D) + A; G = 5(D) + A;
H = 3(D) + A; I = D + A
TRELLIS SHOWN HAS
PIVOT HOLES 8" O.C.

MATERIALS
F = 8 PCS. 1/4 x 1-1/4 x 49-1/2"
G = 4 PCS. 1/4 x 1-1/4 x 41-1/2"
H = 4 PCS. 1/4 x 1-1/4 x 23-1/2"
I = 4 PCS. 1/4 x 1-1/4 x 9-1/2"

1/4"-DIA. HOLE

1/4"-DIA. HOLE

LATH

DRILL PIVOT HOLES BY STACKING PIECES OF LATH

4"

1/8"-DIA. HOLE

WING NUT

1/4 x 2" CARRIAGE BOLT

WASHER (3 REQD.)

WASHER

SLOT

LATH

1/8"-DIA WASHERS

1/8"-DIA. X 1-1/4"-LONG COTTER PIN

TYPICAL

Three firewood projects

By HARRY WICKS

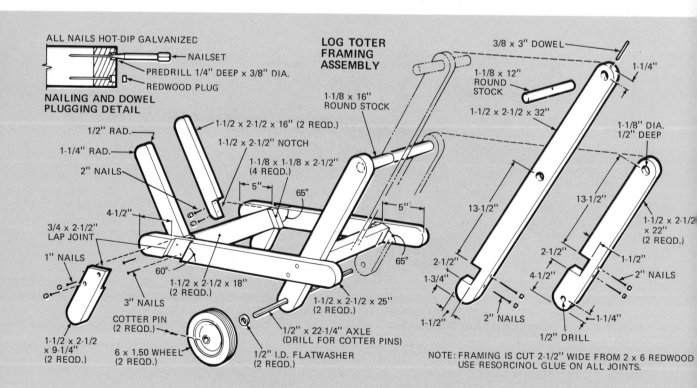

NAILING AND DOWEL PLUGGING DETAIL

ALL NAILS HOT-DIP GALVANIZED
- NAILSET
- PREDRILL 1/4" DEEP x 3/8" DIA.
- REDWOOD PLUG

LOG TOTER FRAMING ASSEMBLY

3/8 x 3" DOWEL

1-1/4"

1-1/8 x 12" ROUND STOCK

1-1/2 x 2-1/2 x 32"

1-1/8" DIA. 1/2" DEEP

1-1/8 x 16" ROUND STOCK

1-1/2 x 2-1/2 x 16" (2 REQD.)

1/2" RAD.

1-1/4" RAD.

2" NAILS

1-1/2 x 2-1/2" NOTCH

1-1/8 x 1-1/8 x 2-1/2" (4 REQD.)

5"

65°

5"

13-1/2"

13-1/2"

1-1/2 x 2-1/2 x 22" (2 REQD.)

4-1/2"

3/4 x 2-1/2" LAP JOINT

1" NAILS

60°

65°

1-1/2 x 2-1/2 x 18" (2 REQD.)

3" NAILS

COTTER PIN (2 REQD.)

1-1/2 x 2-1/2 x 9-1/4" (2 REQD.)

6 x 1.50 WHEEL (2 REQD.)

1/2" I.D. FLATWASHER (2 REQD.)

1-1/2 x 2-1/2 x 25" (2 REQD.)

1/2" x 22-1/4" AXLE (DRILL FOR COTTER PINS)

2-1/2"

1-3/4"

1-1/2"

2-1/2"

4-1/2"

2" NAILS

2" NAILS

1-1/2"

2" NAILS

1-1/4"

1/2" DRILL

NOTE: FRAMING IS CUT 2-1/2" WIDE FROM 2 x 6 REDWOOD USE RESORCINOL GLUE ON ALL JOINTS.

FOR CONVENIENCE, park the log bin by the back door. It keeps dry an evening's supply of wood.

COLONIAL FIRESIDE box blends with all types of decor. Made of pine, it's stained and varnished.

■ THE HIGH PRICE of natural gas, oil and electricity makes it just about a certainty that Americans will burn more firewood in upcoming winters than ever before. To help you store and move the firewood that you've cut and split, here are designs for three projects you can build yourself.

The first is a log toter that lets you haul a healthy supply of fireplace-sized logs from woodpile to back door. The second project is a log bin that permits you to store an evening's supply of firewood to assure its being dry and ready for use. Wood from the log bin is hauled inside and deposited in a practical, yet hand-

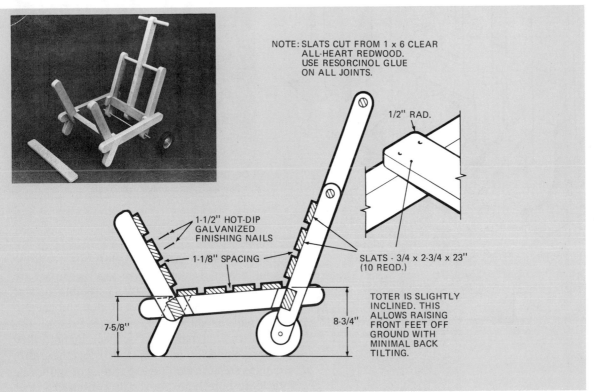

NOTE: SLATS CUT FROM 1 x 6 CLEAR ALL-HEART REDWOOD. USE RESORCINOL GLUE ON ALL JOINTS.

1/2" RAD.

1-1/2" HOT-DIP GALVANIZED FINISHING NAILS

1-1/8" SPACING

SLATS - 3/4 x 2-3/4 x 23" (10 REQD.)

7-5/8"

8-3/4"

TOTER IS SLIGHTLY INCLINED. THIS ALLOWS RAISING FRONT FEET OFF GROUND WITH MINIMAL BACK TILTING.

some, colonial fireside box that holds a good supply of wood.

The outdoor log-bin design is by courtesy of the Georgia-Pacific Co. while the toter and fireside box creations are a joint effort by Rosario Capotosto and the author.

Sound building principles were used to achieve strong construction. Though all projects could be made with hand tools alone, certain power tools do make the task much easier. We avoided intricate and exotic methods of joinery. Our aim was to present projects that both skilled and beginning woodworkers could duplicate with relative ease.

Make certain you use glue on all joints. On the outdoor projects use weatherproof resorcinol glue; on the fireside box yellow carpenter's (aliphatic resin) glue works fine.

Use hardware as specified for the various units on the drawings. For log toter and bin, make certain you use only aluminum or hot-dipped galvanized nails for assembly so that wood surfaces will not be marred by ugly rust stains.

● **Toter.** For looks, the toter shown was built of redwood. Use of this wood simplifies finishing because two coats of outside varnish are adequate. You can, if desired, use less expensive pine, fir or spruce; then seal and prime the piece and finish with a coat of exterior paint.

The toter is simpler to build than a quick look might imply. Start by cutting all parts to size and

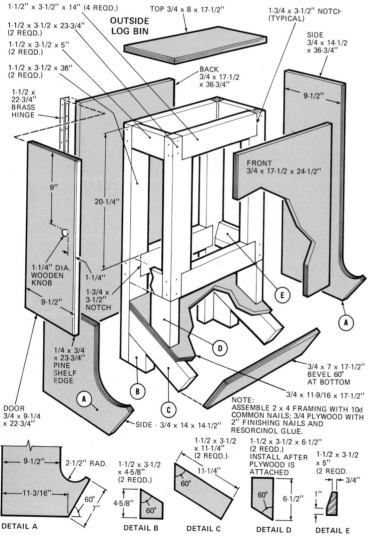

LOG BIN is framed using 2x6s ripped in half (or use 2x3s) and galvanized nails.

shape, marking each part lightly for quick assembly later. Tack the pieces together to be sure you are satisfied with fit, then assemble the cart permanently using waterproof glue and galvanized nails as shown.

Notice that nails are well set in predrilled holes. While the piece is tacked together, affix clamps so parts won't move when you withdraw tacks to bore holes for the dowel buttons (that

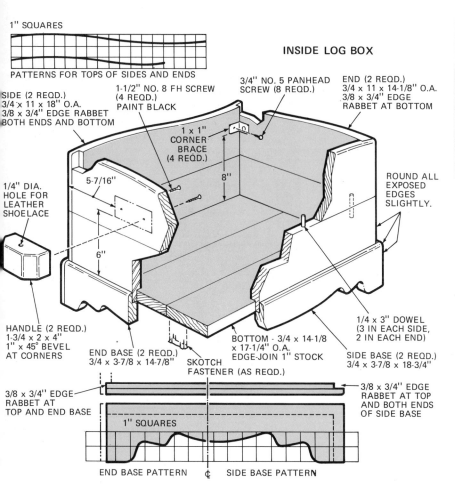

1" SQUARES

PATTERNS FOR TOPS OF SIDES AND ENDS

INSIDE LOG BOX

SIDE (2 REQD.)
3/4 x 11 x 18" O.A.
3/8 x 3/4" EDGE RABBET
BOTH ENDS AND BOTTOM

1-1/2" NO. 8 FH SCREW
(4 REQD.)
PAINT BLACK

3/4" NO. 5 PANHEAD
SCREW (8 REQD.)

END (2 REQD.)
3/4 x 11 x 14-1/8" O.A.
3/8 x 3/4" EDGE
RABBET AT BOTTOM

1 x 1"
CORNER
BRACE
(4 REQD.)

1/4" DIA.
HOLE FOR
LEATHER
SHOELACE

5-7/16"

8"

6"

ROUND ALL
EXPOSED
EDGES
SLIGHTLY.

HANDLE (2 REQD.)
1-3/4 x 2 x 4"
1" x 45° BEVEL
AT CORNERS

END BASE (2 REQD.)
3/4 x 3-7/8 x 14-7/8"

SKOTCH
FASTENER (AS REQD.)

BOTTOM - 3/4 x 14-1/8
x 17-1/4" O.A.
EDGE-JOIN 1" STOCK

1/4 x 3" DOWEL
(3 IN EACH SIDE,
2 IN EACH END)

SIDE BASE (2 REQD.)
3/4 x 3-7/8 x 18-3/4"

3/8 x 3/4" EDGE
RABBET AT
TOP AND END BASE

3/8 x 3/4" EDGE
RABBET AT TOP
AND BOTH ENDS
OF SIDE BASE

1" SQUARES

END BASE PATTERN   ¢   SIDE BASE PATTERN

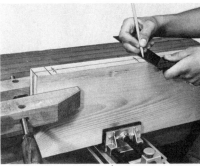

TO EDGE-JOIN boards for sides, clamp and mark mating pieces with pencil.

NEXT, USE DOWELING jig and drill to bore dowel holes.

cover all nailheads). Use a stop on your drill bit to make certain holes are no deeper than ⅜ in.

Mark the location of the three holes for the axle. (Note: The axle stock is a standard hardware item, as are the wheels we used.) Bore the holes to receive the wooden round stock at top and insert the top round and the handle. Secure both parts with glue and pins as shown.

● **Log bin.** Ours is constructed using 1½ x 2½-in. framing stock but 1x3 stock can be substituted without any real sacrifice of structural stability because the outside is covered with ¾-in. exterior-grade plywood. Use house paint—both primer and finish coat—for the bin and a brass continuous hinge to hang its door.

● **Colonial log box.** This project is constructed to simulate primitive Early American furniture. For that reason, corners are joined using 4d common nails which are set with a heavy nailset. The box sides are edge-joined with dowel as in the photos on these pages. The bottom is quickly put together using Skotch connectors (or corrugated nails). To finish, apply stain, following

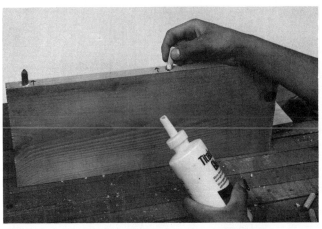

BOARDS ARE JOINED using glue and grooved dowels. Hold the boards with clamps until the glue dries.

manufacturer's directions. Rub a small amount of burnt umber pigment over nail holes and in corners; let this dry and apply a coat of water-thin shellac. When dry, finish with a coat or two of semigloss varnish.

Adjustable candlestand holds high the light

By ROSARIO CAPOTOSTO

AS CANDLES burn down, candlestand's crossbar can be raised to keep light widely distributed.

■ CLOSE-GRAINED, handsomely figured cherry is ideal for this unique, adjustable candlestand, but you can use any hardwood you like.

Start by gluing up stock to form a 5x5x6-in. block for the base. After trimming off corners with the bandsaw, shape the block to a rough cylinder with the gauge. Then use calipers and a full-size drawing to make the initial cuts with a sharp parting chisel, to the depths shown in the drawing. The resulting grooves will guide you in forming contours. Remove excess stock with the gouge, then follow up with round-nose, dia-

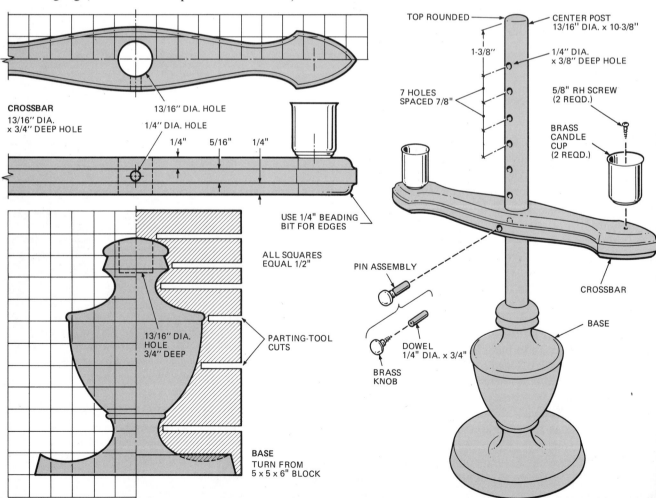

CROSSBAR
13/16" DIA.
x 3/4" DEEP HOLE

13/16" DIA. HOLE

1/4" DIA. HOLE

1/4"   5/16"   1/4"

USE 1/4" BEADING BIT FOR EDGES

ALL SQUARES EQUAL 1/2"

13/16" DIA. HOLE 3/4" DEEP

PARTING-TOOL CUTS

BASE
TURN FROM
5 x 5 x 6" BLOCK

TOP ROUNDED

CENTER POST
13/16" DIA. x 10-3/8"

1-3/8"

1/4" DIA.
x 3/8" DEEP HOLE

7 HOLES
SPACED 7/8"

5/8" RH SCREW
(2 REQD.)

BRASS
CANDLE
CUP
(2 REQD.)

PIN ASSEMBLY

CROSSBAR

BASE

DOWEL
1/4" DIA. x 3/4"

BRASS
KNOB

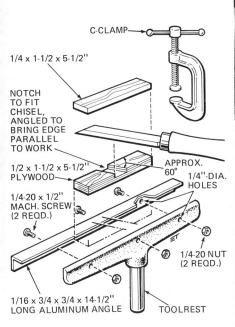

C-CLAMP

1/4 x 1-1/2 x 5-1/2"

NOTCH TO FIT CHISEL, ANGLED TO BRING EDGE PARALLEL TO WORK

1/2 x 1-1/2 x 5-1/2" PLYWOOD

APPROX. 60°

1/4"-DIA. HOLES

1/4-20 x 1/2" MACH. SCREW (2 REQD.)

1/4-20 NUT (2 REQD.)

1/16 x 3/4 x 3/4 x 14-1/2" LONG ALUMINUM ANGLE

TOOLREST

USE A LARGE gouge to rough-turn the round. Work from center of the block outward to prevent splintering.

AFTER YOU MAKE initial cuts with parting chisel, check diameter of each groove. Allow about ⅛ in. for final shaping.

USE A round-nose chisel to finish off the concave curves. Use a skew chisel for the convex curves.

JIG HELPS turn a post accurately and parallel. Notched block holds skew chisel at the proper angle for turning.

mond-point and skew chisels to shape the final contours. With the base still on the lathe, sand it with 220-grit abrasive paper, apply a coat of sanding sealer, and then sand lightly with No. 400 finishing paper. Apply a satin-finish top coat such as Constantine's Wood-Glo or Wipe-On ZAR semigloss. Remove the base from the lathe and bore a $^{13}/_{16}$-in.-dia. hole for the post.

The post is turned from a length of 1x1 stock and is fairly critical as to diameter. Instead of trying to do it freehand, use the simple jig shown on this page. First, put a true straightedge on the outside of the toolrest by attaching a strip of ¾ x ¾-in. aluminum angle to the top as shown in the drawing.

Make a nest for the skew out of scrap wood so that the leading edge is parallel to the cutting edge of the chisel. Use a small C-clamp to lock the chisel securely into the jig as shown.

Use the gouge to rough-form the post's cylindrical shape, then set the toolrest so that the attached straightedge is parallel to the line between live and dead center points. Remove the work for easier measurements. Replace the

work and adjust the skew in the jig so that it projects the right distance to make a $^{13}/_{16}$-in.-dia. cut. Then you can simply slide the jig while holding its front surface firmly against the toolrest's straightedge. The result will be a perfectly parallel cut.

A piece of scrap wood with a V-cut down the center will support the post for boring the ¼-in.-dia. holes for the peg on the drill press. After the holes have been bored, return the post to the lathe and sand it sufficiently to allow it to slide freely through the $^{13}/_{16}$-in.-dia. hole bored in center of the crossbar.

Cut the crossbar to shape with a bandsaw or jigsaw, then tack-nail it through the bottom of a scrap block for edge-shaping with a router and a ¼-in. bead-cutting bit. Finish the crossbar and post in the same way as the base.

The solid-brass candle cups and miniature knob are available as a set from Capro Craft, 9 Griggs Dr., Greenlawn, NY 11740. Similar hardware, brass-plated and less expensive, is sold by Albert Constantine and Son, Inc., 2050 Eastchester Rd., Bronx, NY 10461.

How to hike straight up

By JIM WHITTAKER

■ THE EXHILARATION of climbing does not come cheaply. On May 1, 1963, when I stood on top of Everest, the highest mountain on earth at 29,028 feet above the sea, it was the result of many years of mountaineering. In the 60-mph wind and minus 35°F. cold, I unfurled the American flag to mark the first ascent of Mount Everest by an American team.

I began to learn the mountains as a young boy with my parents and, at 12, with West Seattle's Boy Scout Troop 272. There were hikes and backpacking trips into the forests of western Washington where the trails wind through the dense lowland underbrush of the rain forest. But many of the trails we hiked traversed high into the mountains, up through the sub-Alpine zone, where at 5000 feet the dense forest yields to meadows of heather and flowers. Late-melting snow fields beckon even higher to the ridge tops and to their high points.

I joined the Mountaineers Club of Seattle and signed up for its basic climbing course. Graduation was a climb to the 14,410-foot summit of Mount Rainier, and by that time the lure of the

New equipment and techniques are changing the challenging sport of mountaineering. In this article, one of America's leading authorities and expedition leaders offers some hints on equipment, conditioning and climbing

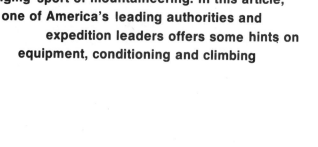

K2, WORLD'S SECOND highest, looms over Himalayan camp set up by Whittaker.

DURING WHITEOUT at 19,500 feet, Jim Whittaker radios the K2 Camp II above.

BALANCED ON narrow corniced ridge at 20,600 feet, Jim Whittaker's Camp II was dug in against continual snowstorms. At the northern end of the Himalayan Karakoram Range the K2 ridge separates Pakistan (at left) from China.

mountains was in my blood. During university summers, my brothers and I operated the Mount Rainier Guide Service and led climbs to its peak. A two-year hitch in the Army with the Mountain and Cold Weather Command in Colorado kept me further involved with rock climbing in the summer and ski mountaineering in the winter. My discharge meant I could guide on Mount Rainier once again until I became employed full time at Recreational Equipment, Inc., the Seattle mountaineering co-op, where I sold—and continue to sell—the equipment I use.

Climbing adventures that followed reached new heights—Mount McKinley in 1960 and in '63, Mount Everest. In 1965 I climbed Mount Kennedy with Sen. Robert F. Kennedy. The 14,400-foot summit of the highest unclimbed peak in the Yukon was named after the late President John F. Kennedy. Robert Kennedy became the first to stand on the summit of the

peak named after his brother. As leader of the 1975 American K2 Expedition to Pakistan and the second highest summit in the world, I was discouraged to see years of dreaming and preparations thwarted by the vagaries of storms, avalanches and porter strikes.

Experience shows that mountaineering success requires gradual and painstaking physical conditioning, climbing skills, and the proper equipment and knowledge of how to use it the right way in the Alpine world. Of the three essentials—conditioning, skills and equipment—the novice will find getting equipment the easiest. You can now walk into most good mountain shops and be superbly outfitted for climbing (a far cry from 20 or 30 years ago).

So now you stand there with hundreds of dollars of exotic gear draped artfully over your body and pack. What next? You take your first day hike and find the $100 Alpine climbing boots

torture your feet because they are not made for trail walking. You find that $80 down parka isn't much good either unless it's below freezing and you're doing nothing more active than sleeping.

And what good is that superlight ice hammer and those 12-point crampons on an afternoon's mushroom hunt? Although it's possible to fit yourself out in a few days for the world's toughest summits, it's much more sensible to accumulate gear gradually. As you enter a new level of climbing ability, make each purchase while asking yourself, "Do I have the skill yet to use it; is it appropriate to my present climbing; will it make the trip safer and more enjoyable?"

choosing boots

Take special care in choosing boots. Do not "over boot." If you're just starting to backpack and are sticking to the trails, select a flexible boot which makes for comfortable walking. Say you're doing a "mixed" climb which involves travel over trails, brush and scree, stepkicking in snow and delicate footwork on steep rock. Then you'll need a boot which is a compromise between conflicting requirements—a type generally called a medium-weight climbing boot.

If you're strictly on steep snow and ice, you may require a very stiff boot. An accomplished mountaineer may even have three pairs of boots (one on his feet and two in his closet). All boots should have a sturdy Vibram lug sole of hard rubber. The Vibram grips on rock and snow and provides excellent insulation from the cold as well as giving traction in the muddy brush-battles.

Clothing also deserves particular care in selection. The key principle here is the "layer system." The clothing worn should preserve body heat and provide sweat-absorbent material next to the skin. Then come insulating layers which trap dead air, followed by outer shells which protect from wind and rain. Layers of garments must be easy to put on or take off even in difficult conditions as changes in temperature, wind and exertion dictate.

A key principle to remember is that thickness is warmth. In insulating the torso, cotton is the killer; it absorbs water and has no insulating

UNDER 100 POUNDS of pack at 17,500 feet up on the world's second highest mountain, leader of the expedition Jim Whittaker climbs toward the base camp on K2. Conditioning and courage, skill and equipment must combine to make a summit assault possible.

ANY TRIP

Ten essentials in pack	Other items in pack
Map of area (in case)	Lunch
Compass	Sunburn preventive
Flashlight with extra	Lip protection*
batteries and bulb	Insect repellent*
Extra food	Handkerchief
Extra clothing (socks,	Toilet paper
mitts, sweaters, long	Canteen
underwear, scarf)	Small insulation pad
Sunglasses	(to sit on)*
Pocket knife	Whistle
Matches in waterproof	Altimeter*
container	Camera, film*
Candle or fire-starter	Emergency shelter
First-aid kit	*Optional item

Clothing: Boots, socks, gaiters, underwear, pants, warm sweater and shirt, parka, hat(s), wool (rain, sun) mittens, gloves, wind pants*, rain gear*, shorts*, hot-weather shirt*.

value when wet. Wool, which is also absorbent, nonetheless retains its warmth retention properties when wet, and is a good choice for the inner layers. Down provides excellent insulation when dry, but is of no value if soaked (in wet, cold conditions).

Spun synthetic filament, like Dacron fiberfill II, is lighter for equivalent dead air thickness than wool and, unlike down, does not collapse when wet. Outer garments should be loose to allow movement and have windproof closures to prevent heat loss.

The basic list of clothing and pack items at the top of this page is from *Freedom of the Hills* by the Mountaineers.

You can see that accumulation of gear depends on the growth of your mountain skills. Careful reading of mountaineering catalogs will help you pick equipment to fit your needs, and experienced sales people at qualified mountaineering stores are valuable.

Choose clothing for each trip depending on the type of weather you expect to encounter, but always allow for the unexpected. Notice that one of the 10 essentials already listed is extra clothing. The extra weight of rain gear and additional wool clothing is never too much to carry, even on a day trip, and will protect you from hypothermia in those sudden mountain storms.

The other major equipment category is the

hardware used for the climbing itself. Once again, the key is to select appropriate gear. Snow flukes and pickets are wonderful implements on steep glacier climbs, but are virtually useless on frozen waterfalls. In some cases, the best way for a novice to learn how to use the equipment is to go on a climb with an experienced group. For me, this occurred naturally in my Boy Scout troop. An older person can join a mountaineering club or climb with experienced friends.

Roped climbing begins at this point. Roping the climbing team together serves to reduce the length of a fall and minimize the dangers of falling. The technique which makes roping up safe is called belaying and, when properly done, the belayer can absorb the impact of a climber's fall and avoid injury to the one climbing and himself.

Along with belaying, another technique which must be mastered is placing protection against a fall. This is the leader's responsibility, and on a steep climb he inserts into the rock or ice the appropriate piece of equipment. The leader is belayed from below by his second, and as he climbs the leader will drive a piton (steel peg) or wedge a chock into an appropriate place in the rock. Next, a runner of woven nylon webbing and a carabiner (oval metal ring) are clipped into the protection. Then the rope is run through the carabiner so that if the leader falls, he will fall only to the point of his last protection. As the leader reaches the end of the available rope, he finds a belay stance and belays the second, who climbs and "cleans" the pitch of the protection. The new ethics of rock climbing demand that most protection be of the chock or nut variety. Pitons scar the route and spoil the pristine nature of the climbs for others who follow.

conditioning program

So you've purchased your gear, taken the courses, and signed with your local climbing club for next month's climb of Mount Molehill. You're all set except for your conditioning. Mountaineering is a stressful sport; it requires sustained periods of severe exertion, and the mountain environment itself subjects the climber to considerable stress. To be a successful climber, you must condition your body to cope with various stresses before you climb.

Your proper conditioning program will be balanced between three areas: aerobic conditioning of the cardio-vascular system, strength training, and flexibility training. The most important is the aerobic conditioning which strengthens the heart and improves the oxygen utilization capability of the lungs and circulatory system. Efficient transport and metabolism of oxygen is the cornerstone of endurance, and is best achieved by regular participation in "huff and puff" sports like distance swimming, running, bicycling, cross-country skiing and hiking.

On the 1963 American Everest Expedition we used the sustained daily exertion of the 185-mile approach march to higher and higher altitudes to sharpen the previous conditioning of the entire team. Similarly, much conditioning of the basic mountaineer occurs in a natural way as he hikes and backpacks in progressively more rugged terrain. Don't depend on hiking to do all your conditioning, though. If you're like most of us who hold five-day-a-week jobs, the weekends of exertion won't make up for the conditioning lost during the week.

If you wish to improve, you must schedule your training so you have at least three days of aerobic activity per week. Assuming you've spent the weekend hiking and climbing, you should have two more days which must have one half-hour or more of aerobic conditioning. If these few hours per week seem too much, remember that the conditioning will not only help

you to climb better but will let you enjoy the climb more. The side benefit is that you will be healthier and live longer.

The two other kinds of training are for strength and flexibility. Strength training consists of any form of resistance exercise. I am a fan of the push-up, pull-up and sit-up routine for general upper body strength, and if you desire you can also get strength improvement for specific muscles with a weight training program. Lastly, any training program should be balanced with stretching exercises to maintain flexibility and agility.

The proper equipment, the proper skills and the proper conditioning can make you a true mountaineer, and to fit this definition you will seek the mountains for their beauties but will also accept their demands. We are living in an age in which the crush of humanity can destroy the fragile Alpine environment. The mountaineer's creed must respect the mountains and leave no trace of his passing.

The rewards of mountain climbing are many. A sensible approach toward learning the sport will enable you to enjoy "this life that is higher than most."

OUTDOOR GEAR especially suitable for mountain sport includes Kletter rucksack in nylon with leather bottom plus 11 auxiliary patches used for attaching strap-on accessories. Approximately $30. R.E.I. 2½-lb. Pol-Over Sack with PolarGuard lining can zip over another sleeping bag or be used alone; about $40. Haute Route ski mountaineering boot for alpine skiing and climbing uses inner wool-lined removable boot; about $115 a pair. Down-filled ultralight Summit Parka, around $70. R.E.I. Grand Hotel expedition tent sleeps four and sells for approximately $190.

Tips for better boating

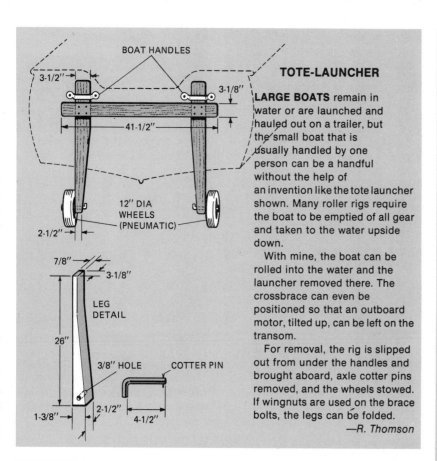

TOTE-LAUNCHER

LARGE BOATS remain in water or are launched and hauled out on a trailer, but the small boat that is usually handled by one person can be a handful without the help of an invention like the tote launcher shown. Many roller rigs require the boat to be emptied of all gear and taken to the water upside down.

With mine, the boat can be rolled into the water and the launcher removed there. The crossbrace can even be positioned so that an outboard motor, tilted up, can be left on the transom.

For removal, the rig is slipped out from under the handles and brought aboard, axle cotter pins removed, and the wheels stowed. If wingnuts are used on the brace bolts, the legs can be folded.
—*R. Thomson*

BOAT DOCK BUMPERS

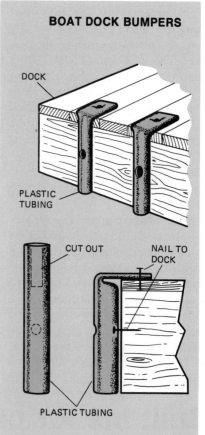

OIL/GAS MIX RATIO

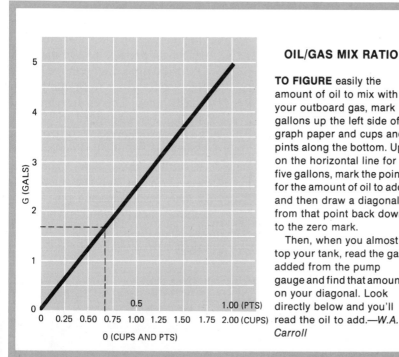

TO FIGURE easily the amount of oil to mix with your outboard gas, mark gallons up the left side of graph paper and cups and pints along the bottom. Up on the horizontal line for five gallons, mark the point for the amount of oil to add and then draw a diagonal from that point back down to the zero mark.

Then, when you almost top your tank, read the gas added from the pump gauge and find that amount on your diagonal. Look directly below and you'll read the oil to add.—*W.A. Carroll*

WHEN WE replaced the plastic water line from the pump house to our summer cottage, we used the old pipe to protect our boat and dock from chafing.

Lengths of pipe were cut to the depth of the dock facing plus an extra four inches. The pipe was then cut in half lengthwise for the top four inches so that only half the pipe remained to form a tongue at the top that was easy to fold over.

One or more holes were drilled in the outer side of the pipe and galvanized nails were used to secure the tongue to the top decking of the dock, while nails positioned through the holes and driven with a nailset fasten the pipe to the up-right face of the dock. Our boat is no longer scarred.—*Q. Kirk Davis*

CATALYTIC HEATER FOR MORE WARMTH

■ BIG MOTOR HOMES come with furnaces for warmth when the engine heater is off. Vans and small camp rigs aren't that lucky, but it's easy to install a catalytic heater. The Therm'X Mark 2A, from Therm'X Corp., Box 268, Reedley, CA 93654, is thin enough to fit flush in a door panel and can be installed in one afternoon. Catalytic heaters work at temperatures far below those necessary to support flame-type combustion. Leaving a window slightly open provides necessary air.

Installation requires a sabre saw with metal-cutting blade and some quick-disconnect hardware which avoids any flexing problems of a permanent gas line. Trace the heater outline on a cardboard template and cut the opening for the heater. Using Teflon pipe tape on threaded joints, secure the fittings to the door and hook up for a test.—*Joseph P. Greeves*

THE SHAPE of the heater is traced on a pattern for marking and cutting the door.

QUICK-DISCONNECT fittings make permanent gas line unneeded.

A BALANCING ACT allows the hookup of lines and securing the heater.

THE INSTALLED HEATER, inset from latches, can be covered when not in use.

Built-ins for campers

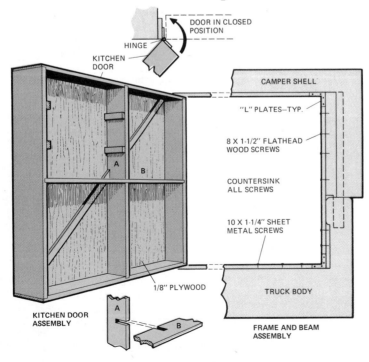

DOOR IN CLOSED POSITION

HINGE

KITCHEN DOOR

CAMPER SHELL

"L" PLATES—TYP.

8 X 1-1/2" FLATHEAD WOOD SCREWS

COUNTERSINK ALL SCREWS

10 X 1-1/4" SHEET METAL SCREWS

1/8" PLYWOOD

TRUCK BODY

KITCHEN DOOR ASSEMBLY

A

B

FRAME AND BEAM ASSEMBLY

BACK-DOOR KITCHEN

■ MOUNT A storage door at the back of the camper shell enclosure in your pickup truck and there is no need to unpack every mealtime. With the stock door removed, notch pine or fir beams to fit into the rear stake holes. Then a frame of 1x4-inch pine is assembled and screwed to these supports and the truck bed. Some spacer blocks may be necessary. The door, built ½-inch narrower and ¼-inch shorter than the frame, is of 1x6-inch pine backed with ⅛-inch plywood and hung with a piano hinge. The tailgate holds the door closed.—*Bud Tassano*

CLAMPING BLOCKS attached to the rain gutter hold set-up rods securely but allow quick removal.

Rod carrier for your car

By SID STALL

■ HAVE YOU EVER heard the sickening crunch of a $60 fishing rod being crushed by a slammed car door? It's an unpleasant sound and a high price to pay for having a rod ready.

Here's a carrier you can build for as little as $2 that gives quick access to a pair of rods, yet holds them snugly at highway speeds. You will have to drill two holes in your car's rain gutter, but these are inconspicuous.

Begin by cutting an 8 or 10-in. length of ash, oak or other hardwood to about 1⅛x1⅝ in. Mark off two 3½-in. lengths on the wider side and locate the centers of two rod-holding holes on each length.

My two fly rods needed a ⅜-in. and a 1-in. hole in each section, with centers spaced 1¾ in. apart. *Your requirements may differ.*

Note that hole locations for the second assembly are the reverse of those in the drawing. After the four holes are drilled, halve the piece lengthwise by ripping it down the center of the 1⅝-in. side. Crosscut the two halves to make four blocks, each with two half-holes. Sand and finish the blocks with several coats of exterior paint or varnish.

A 2-ft. length of ⅛x1¼-in. steel bar stock will provide the metal parts of the sandwiches. Top pieces are just hacksawed to 3⅝-in. length; the bottom pieces with their doglegs are heated with a torch and bent. If you bend them cold, allow at least 3/16 in. extra length for each bend or cut them to length after bending.

To make the ¼-in. bolt holes, clamp the top and bottom metal pieces together and drill through both, then clamp the wood blocks between them, align them carefully and drill halfway through the wood from each side.

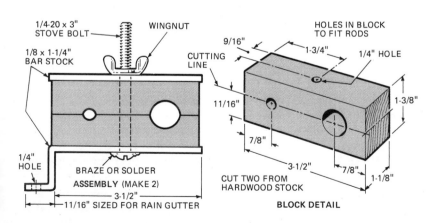

1/4-20 x 3" STOVE BOLT
WINGNUT
1/8 x 1-1/4" BAR STOCK
CUTTING LINE
9/16"
HOLES IN BLOCK TO FIT RODS
1-3/4"
1/4" HOLE
11/16"
1-3/8"
1/4" HOLE
7/8"
BRAZE OR SOLDER
ASSEMBLY (MAKE 2)
3-1/2"
3-1/2"
7/8"
1-1/8"
11/16" SIZED FOR RAIN GUTTER
CUT TWO FROM HARDWOOD STOCK
BLOCK DETAIL

TO MOUNT or remove rods, loosen wingnut, lift the top block and twist a quarter turn. A single screw fastens the carrier securely to the rain gutter.

Tips for wildlife photographers

By JAMES TALLON

Moose, coyotes, hawks, zoo animals or just some of the wild birds in your back yard can all be good subjects for the wildlife photographer. It can take as much cunning as hunting— and is just as rewarding and exciting

GOOD SHOTS depend on good lighting, good composition and good luck. It's also essential to know wildlife habits—where to find a mountain lion, when the swans migrate, the feeding times of various birds.

■ IT WAS a shirt-sleeve fall morning and Bob Hirsch and I were on the Papago Indian Reservation in Arizona trying to lure coyotes into photo range. Bob sat under an ironwood tree, wrapped in camouflage netting. I was stationed about 75 feet away, more netting covering me and my tripod-mounted reflex with its 400-mm telephoto lens, so that only the lens's glass eye was exposed to the outside world.

Suddenly the morning stillness was shattered by the scream of a rabbit in trouble—it was Bob, using a commercial predator call, a tube of wood with a tuned reed inside. (This mouth-blown instrument will draw in quite a few animals and birds, including such nonpredators as deer, javelinas, wild burros, and even songbirds.) The screech from these calls always makes the back hairs on my neck stiffen, and they were just starting to get limber again when I saw something that stiffened them in earnest: a coyote, traveling full-bore toward Bob's back.

The initial idea—getting Bob and the coyote in the same shot—seemed a shoo-in. But my friend seemed unaware that the animal had zeroed in on his back. And callers *have* been bitten by their callees.

I wanted the picture badly—but I didn't want Bob hurt. I made a split-second decision to snap off a couple of fast shots the instant both Bob and the coyote were in my viewfinder, then shout a warning. I swung the camera to follow the animal.

But as I swung, it did a tricky two-step. Instead of my expected side view, I now had a front view of it—*front* view? Yikes! The coyote had picked a new target: me. Its supersensitive hearing had picked up the slight rustle of the camouflage material, and it no doubt assumed its easy meal had moved.

I was using a follow-focus lens, one with a pistol-grip, squeeze-focusing device that lets you pop the lens from its 27-foot minimum focus to infinity in a fraction of a second. But the coyote was coming at me so fast my adrenalin valve had opened all the way. I was shaking so badly I couldn't get a sharp image on the ground glass.

The wind was coming from the coyote's direction; the animal couldn't smell me. When it was just a few feet from me, I screamed—not from fear, mind you, but to let the critter know a human, not a rabbit, occupied the camouflage.

The coyote's intent expression turned to one of pure shock. It performed a half-gainer and

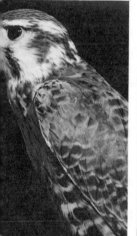

ACTION, like the two bull moose above, makes good wildlife shots. And static shots are appealing, if they are well composed. If possible, choose a simple background that will make your subject stand out.

LONG TELEPHOTO LENSES are a wildlife photographer's most useful tool, keeping you far enough away so that you won't frighten your subjects—nor can they frighten you! Keep them handy.

then sped off, spending more time in the air than on the ground. Bob howled in laughter.

That was just one of my many wildlife adventures in more than a decade of outdoor shooting. Nearly every trip afield produces some kind of excitement—including that of the pictures I bring back.

As with any vocation, certain tools and knowledge are needed to break into wildlife photography. I know wealthy people who were able to start with sophisticated motor-driven cameras and thousand-dollar lenses—but you can give them a lot of competition for about $200 and some know-how.

Once you have camera and lens, all you need add is film and you're equipped to take wildlife pictures. I recommend, however, that you buy a tripod and a bellows, as soon as possible. Both are relatively inexpensive. The former will enable you to take sharper pictures and the latter lets you break the close-focusing barrier inherent in most telephoto lenses.

The best places to shoot wildlife pictures are national parks and monuments and other sanctuaries. Wildlife in them becomes, in varying degrees, adjusted to man's presence. Often these birds and animals will pose for portraits better than children do. It must be remembered, though, that animals are unpredictable. A deer, for example, may pause for pictures one day but take flight the next.

Wildlife refuges of some sort exist in every state in the Union. In those where the bigger animals—bear, elk, moose, buffalo—roam free, the pursuit of wildlife photography can be hazardous. In a less wild environment, birds and animals become less afraid of man.

Yellowstone National Park is one of my favorite spots for wildlife photography. A big animal habitat visited by thousands of people who have been raised on a diet of Disney's talking animals, the park is an excellent place to see the chances novice photographers will take.

Near Mount Washburn one summer day, I

AUTHOR USES many tricks to get his shots. He uses his car as a rolling tripod and wildlife blind. Hidden bait drew the pinyon jay to perch on the author's follow-focus 400-mm lens. Loudspeaker broadcasts wildlife cries from a portable tape recorder to bring the animals within close camera range.

found a road blocked by a "bear-jam," a pile-up of vehicles whose drivers have stopped in the middle of the road to see or photograph a bear. The culprit who caused it all was a two-thirds-grown female black bear, a roadside beggar. Despite red-printed National Park Service warnings not to feed bears or approach them too closely, dozens of people were in flagrant violation. One young man grabbed an ear of the bear while his friend tried to snap a shot of him doing it. The animal whirled and lashed out with four-inch-long claws at the man's face. I expected to see horrible mutilation, but the bear missed him by a scant fraction of an inch.

The bear-approachers on Mount Washburn exhibited sheer foolishness, but shooting pictures of wildlife always involves some risks, no matter how careful or how experienced the photographer may be.

Approaching Brooks Lake in northwestern Wyoming's Rocky Mountains, I followed a cow moose into the forest and lost track of it. Then I saw a pair of eyes hurtling my way with 1000 pounds of animal attached to them. I stepped behind a Douglas fir and the critter passed close enough to touch. I didn't get its picture, but I was all right.

Cow moose are quick to charge when they think their young are threatened. So when a curious calf saw me trying to shoot it and its mother against a background of Yellowstone Park spectators, I shooed it away. Luckily, mother had her head down, feeding. But the calf came back, and this time the cow saw me.

Again I had a half ton of irate animal thundering toward me. I had an escape route planned: back into the safety of the woods at the edge of the meadow. But just inside, I jumped on a damp deadfall and my feet went out from under me. I expected skillet-size hooves to redesign my body. But the moose had stopped at the forest's fringe and now stared at me, apparently entranced (or maybe even amused) by my performance. This time, though, I got the shots.

a long lens is best

The importance of at least 400-mm worth of telephoto lens for wildlife photography cannot be overemphasized. If a 400-mm forces you to back away to get the whole scene in your finder, remember you're less likely to spook wildlife by backing away from it than approaching it, as you might have to with a shorter focal length. A 400-mm telephoto magnifies eight times. This figure is arrived at by dividing the focal length of your normal 50-mm lens into the longer lens's focal length. The value of this as a *minimum* focal length has proved itself to me time and time again.

A good example took place in Rainy Mountain Provincial Park in Manitoba, Canada. Chance had put me at the head of a caravan of competitive outdoor writer-photographers. My wife spotted a black bear tearing chunks from the rotting carcass of a whitetail deer.

A feeding bear can make an interesting shot. But bears are almost as touchy about defending their dinners as they are about their young, so I cautiously broke out my 400-mm lens to shoot with.

The others laughed at my timidity—but they stood just as far back from the bear as I did. And since they all were using 200-mm or shorter lenses, I alone was able to fill my frame with the bear from our common shooting spot. The

200-mm users had to settle for half-filled frames, and the rest for even less.

read before shooting

Once you decide to get into wildlife photography, start building up a library of books and articles. And read them—don't just store them on your shelf. A few minutes before retiring each night will soon give you an insight into wildlife behavior, where animals range, the best time of year to photograph them.

One of the important things you'll learn is that often you need go no farther than your back yard to photograph wildlife. And you can devise simple tricks to bring *them to you*. Once I thought it would be nice to have a picture of a bird standing on my follow-focus lens. I put it on a camera and a tripod in my back yard and taped a tiny box of bird seed to the far side of the lens barrel. In minutes some pinyon jays were using the lens for a runway and pecking at the seeds. I shot pictures of them with a second camera and telephoto lens through a partially opened window of my house. A tape recorder playing the calls of the animals you're trying to shoot or their prey will help, too. But be sure your bait equipment doesn't show in the photo.

easy blinds

Houses and cars make excellent blinds; I've shot hundreds of wildlife pictures from them. Expose as little of yourself as possible, and the odds go up for your getting good shots.

When I can't use a house or car, I resort to my light, super-portable mini-blind: a 9-foot square of camouflage netting—the one that fooled the coyote—and a small, folding camp stool. Drape the netting over you, and its loose weave allows fairly good vision out. Just remember to secure the netting to the lens's sunshade with a rubber band, so it doesn't fall in front of the lens.

The blind can be set up in seconds, and really works. Driving the highway toward Grand Canyon one summer day, I saw several hummingbirds sipping nectar from roadside flowers. The birds flew away when I approached, of course, but returned after I had rigged the blind and crawled inside. Some of them flew within inches of the netting.

If you want a 100-percent guarantee, try your nearest zoo. Even the pros occasionally depend on zoos for shots of certain animals (they'll kill me for telling). Recently a wildlife publication sent me on assignment to the Phoenix zoo to photograph a mustached tamarin, a member of the New World monkey family. It was a lot cheaper than sending me to South America to photograph them in the wild.

Although shooting through bars, screens and fences would seem to be a problem at a zoo, you can often photographically eliminate them. Put a long-focal-length telephoto on your camera—the 400-mm is often ideal—and change distances a few times, refocusing on your subject until the barriers blur out of focus enough to disappear.

more equipment tips

As mentioned earlier, insects are a part of the wildlife scene. A picture of a butterfly on a flower can have as much impact as a grizzly-bear portrait. Since many telephoto lenses focus no closer than 25 or 30 feet (some go down to less than 12 feet, but they're usually very expensive), a bellows must be put between the lens and the camera to extend the focusing range. Now you can fill the frame with tiny subjects, yet remain far enough away not to frighten them off.

When you get deeper into wildlife photography, you'll want a second camera body. Nothing can be more frustrating than to work for hours to get into position, then have a camera malfunction, and not have a spare. It also speeds up lens-switching if you keep a different lens on each of your two bodies.

Investigate the big zoom lenses, too. Using a 200-500-mm zoom in southern Montana, I was able first to take pictures of several bighorn sheep together, then zoom in on individual herd members. The lens virtually eliminated the need to move about and perhaps spook the animals into flight.

Because telephotos are slower lenses, transmitting less light, many wildlife photographers standardize on high-speed films. Under the best of conditions, these films are not too bad; in poor light, when you really need them, they leave a lot to be desired. My standard is Kodachrome 64 for wildlife photography.

If you want to take wildlife pictures to sell, you must be much more demanding than one who shoots for personal enjoyment only. You'll quickly learn that pictures of animals or birds, just standing or sitting are doomed to sit forever in your files. To sell, they must show action or unusually attractive composition.

All my life I have been a hunter. But I find wildlife photography just as exciting and rewarding. The photographer must often approach closer than the hunter to bag his trophy; and he usually has no gun to defend himself.

Photo-hints

PAINTED CAP SAVES MISSED SHOTS

THE USUAL BLACK or chrome lens cap blends in with a black-and-chrome camera so it's easy not to notice it's on. Paint your lens cap a bright color so you won't forget to remove it. It'll be easier to find if you drop it, too.

RACK FOR NEGATIVES

THOSE HANDY slide-storage pages of pockets, sold by photo dealers and mail-order houses, made dandy racks for negatives during an enlarging session. The transparency of the plastic storage pages permits you to see quickly just which negatives are in your selection.

Holes that are punched along their edges for ring binders make the pages easy to hang up on a line near your enlarger with a wide variety of wire hangers. You will find it easy and convenient to retrieve them when you need them.

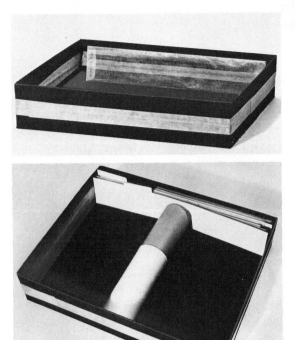

EASY COST-FREE NEGATIVE FILE

WITH FILM coming in 20 or 36 shots per roll, many 35-mm photographers wind up with a lot of negatives to file.

One suggestion is to file them in storage files made from empty 100-sheet 8x19 enlarging-paper boxes. It takes two such boxes to make a file. Cut the bottom out of one and stack it over the other, then carefully tape the two together (top), both inside and out. That makes a box just the right size to hold six-negative strips of 35-mm film in glassine envelopes.

To keep the envelopes from shifting in the box, prop them up with a telescoping tube made from two toilet-paper roll cores, one crimped down to jam into the other. As the box fills, simply cut the tube shorter. When it's full, take the tube out.

You can even organize your files by sticking labeled cards between the envelopes. In this way you can quickly locate any group of negatives.

KEEP YOUR WASHER DRAIN CLEAR

STANDPIPE DEVICES like the Gantz De-Hypo turn your sink into a print washer. But if the prints should float over the pipe's drain opening and block it, as they often do, they could turn your kitchen into a wading pool. To prevent that, roll a 2x3-inch piece of hardware cloth (chicken wire mesh) into a tube, and insert it in the device's drain hole. The water will still flow, but the prints won't be able to block it.

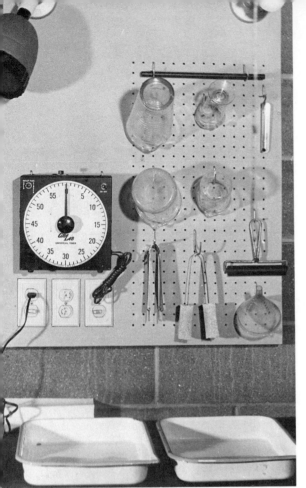

UNCLUTTERING A DARKROOM is easy with this simple panel which combines most of my wiring and switching with storage space for odds and ends. The wiring diagram below explains my setup—but feel free to make yours differently if another arrangement suits you better.

An organizer panel for your darkroom

By WILL FITZ

type with a U-ground plug to minimize shock hazards.

The panel's wiring should suit your needs; my circuit is just a suggestion. The two end switches control the safelight and the white light visible in the picture, while the switch for the radio (good darkroom company) separates the other two to minimize mistakes. (The radio, on a shelf when this shot was taken, is now built into the panel with the back of its case removed; that gives me better bass response as well as a neater look.)

Note that the safelight gets its power from the enlarger timer (not shown); the timer turns the light off when the enlarger's on for easier focusing. Outlets are not switched, as I use them chiefly for timers which I prefer to control directly. If your setup includes equipment you'd like to switch on and off at the panel, just wire in a switch for that outlet.

■ ALL THE ELECTRICAL devices in a modern darkroom can easily turn it into a clutter of electric cords. This panel centralizes all my darkroom's wires and controls, and it's ready to move to another house whenever I am.

Construction is simple: The basic panel is a 2½ by 3-ft. hardboard sheet framed with 2x2-in. lumber and fastened to the wall with 1-in. angle brackets.

The perforated storage section was drilled, using a piece of perforated hardboard as a template, and a ⅛-in. bit. Make sure none of the wiring runs behind the perforated section so there's no chance of wires being dripped on when wet equipment is hung up to dry. Pegboard hooks hold the equipment.

The panel's main power source is a 25-ft. No. 12 cable. It enters from the top of the panel, away from wet trays, and is a three-conductor

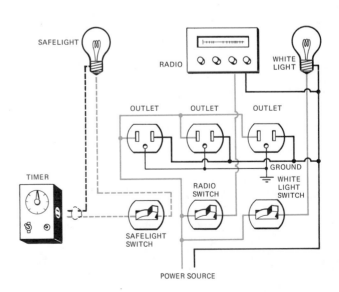

Build a crystal set— the original solid-state radio

By CONRAD MILLER

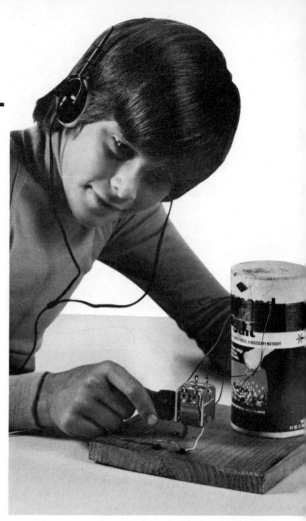

■ RETURN WITH US now to those thrilling days of yesteryear, when radio listeners crouched over crystal sets, black headphones clamped over their ears, as they adjusted a "cat's whisker" and a coil in the hopes of hearing one of the few stations then on the air.

But don't laugh. Because those crystal sets, simple as they were (any child could build one—and most boys did), were forerunners, in their way, of today's solid-state radios. In fact, you can build one today around a modern, solid-state crystal diode.

You've certainly heard about those crystal sets of yesteryear, but you may never have realized exactly what they were. They were very popular, though, back when radio was young.

The ingredients of a crystal set were—and remain—simplicity itself: There's nothing to one but a coil, a variable condenser, a crystal and a headset, plus a long, plain wire as an antenna.

Just for fun, and to rehear the kind of reception that our fathers and grandfathers heard, try building a crystal set. Using inexpensive, store-bought parts, you can build this receiver for about $5. All prices on the price list were in effect when this article was written.

You'll be surprised at the purity of its tone, too. Since the crystal set has no amplification, no tubes and no transistors, its distortion is just about zero. Voices and music sound pure.

However, it has its drawbacks. Since there's no amplification of the incoming signal, the set is not too sensitive—it can only receive strong signals from powerful or nearby stations. And since it has but a single untuned circuit and no intermediate-frequency (i.f.) amplifier to act as a filter, it's unselective—it has a hard time separating signals from different nearby stations unless their frequencies are quite far apart.

But we can forgive its weaknesses. After all, it uses no power, has no batteries, no tubes or integrated circuits, so there's nothing to wear out, and no expense beyond the original cost of building it.

The crystal set's theory of operation is as simple as its construction: The coil and condenser together make a tuned circuit that resonates within the broadcast band. The diode acts as a detector, rectifying the signal to strip off the radio-frequency carrier and leave only the audio information. The schematic shows how little there is to it. Hooked up as shown and attached to a long antenna and a good ground, the set should pull in several stations.

In the good old days, the coil would have been hand-wound, and the detector would have been an open crystal of galena, touched lightly by a fine wire called a "cat's whisker." Since open galena crystals are hard to find these days, we opted for a modern germanium diode (1N34 or similar), costing about a quarter.

We did roll our own coil, the good, old-fashioned way. Our coil form was a Diamond Crystal salt box, (which seemed appropriate).

Salt or oatmeal boxes were standard ingredients of crystal sets, and any round box or cardboard tube of 3¼-inch diameter will do. But avoid boxes or tubes with metal ends or end rings.

The coil is basically one piece, tapped at both ends and in the middle. The primary portion comprises 14 turns of No. 24 AWG enameled wire, and the secondary takes 24 turns. Both coils are tightly wound, with no space between turns or between the primary and secondary windings. Use Scotch tape to hold the windings in place.

The precise number of turns on the primary winding isn't critical. But the number of turns on the secondary determines what part of the broadcast band the set will receive. Test your coil in your set. Should the rig receive only stations toward the bottom of the AM band (550 kHz), remove a few secondary turns as required to receive the entire band.

If you don't want to wind your own coil, you can use a factory-made broadcast-band antenna coil or ferrite loop stick of about 240 microhenries inductance, such as a Miller No. 2004 antenna coil (about $2.80). But the signal is much louder with the hand-wound, salt-box coil than

with the commercial one (which, frankly, delighted us).

The variable tuning condenser should have a value of about 365 picofarads (pF)—a standard value—such as Calectro's No. A1-227 or Radio Shack's No. 272-1344.

The headphones must be high-impedance types—2000 ohms or more—not hi-fi headphones, which are typically 8 ohms, and rarely more than 600. We used a Saxon No. 285, priced at $3.35; you could also use Cannon BA-2 (Lafayette 40 P 81071, $4.15) or BA-5 (40 P 81097, $4.70) or Lafayette's lightweight, stethoscope-type 99 P 25504 ($2.59).

One more thing is essential: a good, long antenna, the longer the better. 50 feet is about the minimum, 100 feet is very good, and 150 or 200 feet is great. String the antenna between buildings, poles or trees and bring a lead-in to the set. Since the antenna could attract lightning, it's a good idea to provide a lightning arrester, or to ground the lead-in wire to a water pipe when you're not listening to the set.

A good ground connection is also required: Attach the ground to a water pipe or radiator, keeping the lead as short as practicable.

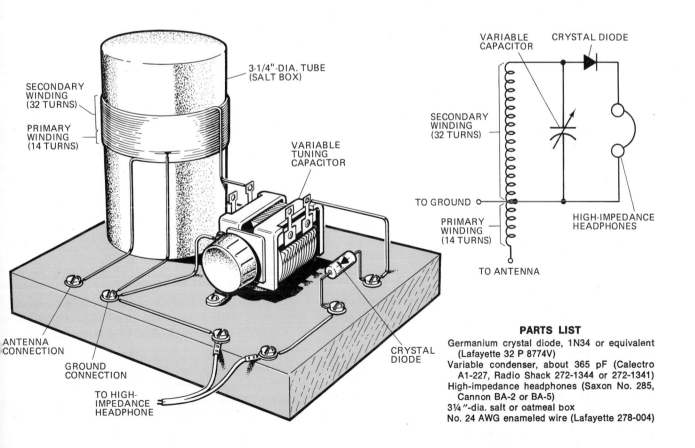

3-1/4"-DIA. TUBE (SALT BOX)

SECONDARY WINDING (32 TURNS)

PRIMARY WINDING (14 TURNS)

VARIABLE TUNING CAPACITOR

ANTENNA CONNECTION

GROUND CONNECTION

TO HIGH-IMPEDANCE HEADPHONE

CRYSTAL DIODE

VARIABLE CAPACITOR   CRYSTAL DIODE

SECONDARY WINDING (32 TURNS)

TO GROUND

PRIMARY WINDING (14 TURNS)

TO ANTENNA

HIGH-IMPEDANCE HEADPHONES

PARTS LIST

Germanium crystal diode, 1N34 or equivalent (Lafayette 32 P 8774V)
Variable condenser, about 365 pF (Calectro A1-227, Radio Shack 272-1344 or 272-1341)
High-impedance headphones (Saxon No. 285, Cannon BA-2 or BA-5)
3¼"-dia. salt or oatmeal box
No. 24 AWG enameled wire (Lafayette 278-004)

Check your own transistors

By ANDY MORGAN

■ REMEMBER WHEN TV sets had tubes and you had a fighting chance of fixing them if they went on the blink? You took the back off, pulled the tubes out, then tested them on a checker at the corner drugstore.

Now TV sets are solid-state (except for their picture tubes). And when something goes dead and you look at the back of the set, you find a label reading:

No user-serviceable parts
inside. Refer servicing
to a qualified technician.

Is that really true? Do you have to pay a repairman for a house call if the problem is a single bad transistor?

No, you don't. You can sometimes fix the set yourself, and often track the problem down far enough to keep a check on the repairman. All you need is some knowledge of transistor-testing methods, plus some relatively inexpensive test equipment. (All prices listed here were in effect at the time this article was written.) Then you'll be on your way to saving money on repairs of your TV and all your other transistorized equipment.

method No. 1: check voltages

Transistors rarely get sick, but they often die. A bad transistor nearly always has a short or an open circuit between its leads, not some subtle change in its performance. That makes the first step very simple: Check voltages at each lead of the suspect device. (Of course, this assumes that the TV doesn't pop its fuse or circuit breaker every time it's turned on.)

Almost any voltmeter can be used for this purpose, including inexpensive volt-ohm-milliammeters (VOMs). Or you may prefer a digital multimeter (DMM) or digital voltmeter (DVM).

IS THAT TRANSISTOR good or bad? What's wrong with it? Is it shorted? Open? Leaky? Transistor testers can answer these questions and more, and you can perform many checks without specialized equipment, using an ordinary voltage and resistance meter.

Luckily (since transistors are usually soldered into place, not plugged in, as tubes were), you make this check without removing the transistor from the circuit. But you must observe safety precautions when working on any equipment which, like television, may contain hazardous high voltages.

Clip one test lead (usually the black, ground lead) to the set's metal chassis. Then, for safety's sake, *use only one hand* to probe into the unit with the other lead. (If you keep your other hand in your pocket, you're less likely to touch another point completing a circuit through your body.)

If the transistor is good, the voltage on each of its leads will usually be at least slightly different from those on the others. If any two leads test the same, suspect a shorted transistor.

method No. 2: check resistance

If the equipment you're testing won't turn on or stay on, the first step is to check resistances. And if you've narrowed down the suspects by checking voltages, this is a good second step.

Remember that transistors can generally be thought of as two diodes—circuit elements that conduct current in only one direction—in series, with leads of like polarity wired together and this junction brought out as the third lead. The resistance between the base and either of the other two leads should be very high in one direction and very low in the opposite one; and resistance between the collector and emitter should be very high in both directions.

You can use this fact—and your VOM or DVM—to determine if a transistor is shorted or open. If the resistance between any two leads is less than a few ohms in *both* directions, suspect a short; if resistance between the base and either other lead is very high in both directions, suspect an open transistor.

With a VOM, this test is telling—but tedious, because you have to keep switching the test leads around. So if you spend much time troubleshooting, you might consider a specialized transistor tester like the Hickok 215 ($138); you simply connect its three test leads to the transistor, and light-emitting diodes tell you whether the device is good or bad, whether it's an NPN or PNP type, and which of its three leads is the base.

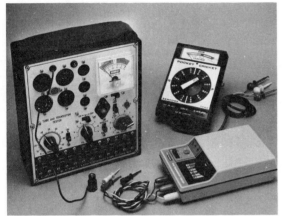

THE LAFAYETTE, Sencore and B&K meters shown above check a.c. gain. The Lafayette model also checks tubes.

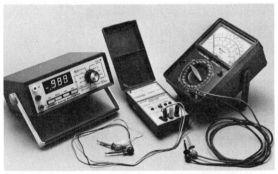

THE HEATH digital voltmeter (DVM), Hickok 215 transistor tester and Triplett VOM check resistance.

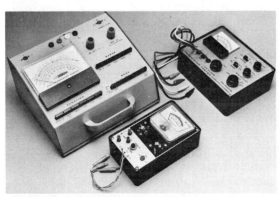

THESE HEATHKIT, Mura and VIZ ($33) units check d.c. gain (d.c. beta).

method No. 3: check d.c. gain

If you've determined that none of the transistors is shorted or open, but the circuit still doesn't work, you may have to test for more subtle problems.

A transistor's amplifying ability, called its "beta," is the ratio between its input current and its output current. You can measure this, too, with a simple meter, but it's not a simple job. It's much better if you can use a meter designed specifically for this test.

There are a lot of these around, including the Mura 375-M ($50), the Heath IT-121 ($63 in kit form), and the VIZ Instrument's WUC-506B ($33). Hook them up as directed, and you can read beta directly from a meter scale. But you'll need to know the beta the transistor should have before you know if it's working correctly. Here again, a schematic diagram is very helpful.

method No. 4: check leakage

Sometimes impurities in the transistor make it conduct continuously, never completely shutting off. This causes hard-to-diagnose failures in transistor circuits. To be accurate, leakage current tests require that you remove the transistor from the circuit. If it's tested in-circuit, other components connected to it will conduct some current and throw the test off; the meter can't tell whether current is leaking through the transistor or whether part of the current is coming back through the rest of the circuit.

method No. 5: amplify real signals

A transistor's a.c.-signal gain—its a.c. beta—tells you more about how it will handle real signals than any other test. As with d.c. beta, an a.c. beta check compares the output and input current, but this time the current is an a.c. signal.

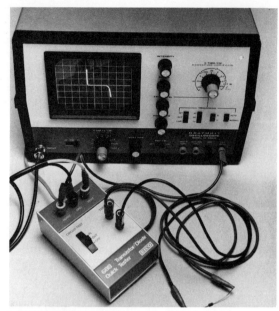

A BREAKDOWN voltage test requires just an oscilloscope and an a.c. signal source—but this Eico checker simplifies this test.

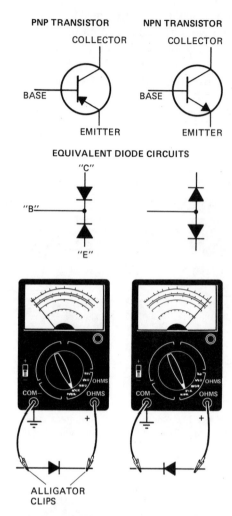

TREAT A TRANSISTOR as a pair of diodes, and you can check it with an ohmmeter: Resistance should always be high between the transistor's emitter and collector, but only in one direction between the base and the other two leads (collector and emitter).

About the least expensive instrument for this is the Lafayette 38-01123 tester kit ($35), also available wired as 38-01131 ($50)—it also tests vacuum tubes. To use it, you have to know the correct lead orientation for the transistor you're checking. In most cases, that's no problem, but it can be in the event that your transistors are unmarked or housebranded.

Both the B&K Precision 510 ($90) and the Sencore TF 40 Pocket Cricket ($98) eliminate this problem and speed testing even when you know which lead is which. As with the Hickok, you connect either instrument's three leads to the transistor in random order; then you move a switch through six positions. If the transistor is good, either tester will beep in at least one of these positions; and the tester will also show you whether the transistor is an NPN or PNP type, which lead is the base, and sometimes which of the other two leads is which.

using an oscilloscope

It's not completely true that diodes and transistors conduct in only one direction between leads. Put a high-enough reverse voltage across a diode or transistor junction, and that junction will conduct backward. The voltage necessary to cause this is called "breakdown voltage."

Breakdown-voltage troubles occur when circuit voltages rise high enough to cause reverse conduction in a normal transistor, or when a sick

transistor's breakdown voltage is low enough to conduct backward with the voltages normally present in the circuit.

If you know the transistor's normal breakdown voltage, you can check to see if abnormally high voltages exist. If they don't, you can check your transistor's actual breakdown voltage by removing it, putting an a.c. signal across two of its leads, and looking at the voltage output on an oscilloscope. If the input signal drives the scope's horizontal scan, and the output signal drives the scope's vertical, a curve will be traced on the screen. With proper calibration, you can read the breakdown voltage right off the screen. Eico's Model 688 Kit ($15) simplifies the connections for this test.

Build an easy auto circuit checker

By RUDOLF F. GRAF and GEORGE F. WHALEN

■ FOR A QUICK DIAGNOSIS of car wiring problems, this compact handful is just what the doctor ordered. Combining a polarity indicator with a continuity checker, it can tell you which wires carry 12 volts and which are connected to ground; it can tell you whether wires that *should* show +12 volts are accidentally grounded; and it can help you find broken wires or open circuits.

Our quick circuit checker isn't fragile or bulky like a meter and needs no outside light for you to read it. Just clip a lead to ground or to one side of the circuit you want to check, touch the probe to any other point you're checking, and a light-emitting diode (LED) flashes on—red if the probe tip is at +12 volts, green if the point is grounded or there's continuity between the probe and clip lead.

The circuit is simple, using the car's own 12-volt power for the red LED, and a 9-volt battery in the checker for the green one.

Compactness and a package that fits your hand are features of the checker's design. But, of course, you can vary the packaging.

The author's version is packaged in a 1¼-in. dia. x 2⅞-in.-long plastic pill vial with a snap-on top. Emptied of its medication, the vial easily accommodates the 9-volt battery, LEDs, transistors, resistors and switch. The probe tip is a 1¼-in. finishing nail. (If you want an insulation-piercing probe, sharpen the tip to a fine point on a bench grinder.) Components, mounted on a scrap of perforated board, nestle snugly into the bottle. The LEDs and switch are mounted in the snap-on cap. The accompanying drawing shows the parts and how they are laid out.

Clip the lead wire to one end of the car's circuit to be checked (ground to chassis, for example) and use the probe to touch significant points in the rest of the circuit, pressing S1 as you do so. Where there's a positive voltage, the red LED will light; where there's ground, the green LED will light. Neither will light with an open circuit.

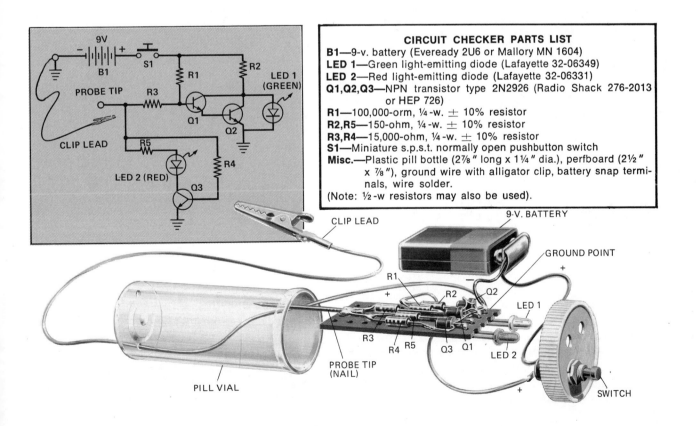

CIRCUIT CHECKER PARTS LIST
B1—9-v. battery (Eveready 2U6 or Mallory MN 1604)
LED 1—Green light-emitting diode (Lafayette 32-06349)
LED 2—Red light-emitting diode (Lafayette 32-06331)
Q1,Q2,Q3—NPN transistor type 2N2926 (Radio Shack 276-2013 or HEP 726)
R1—100,000-orm, ¼-w. ± 10% resistor
R2,R5—150-ohm, ¼-w. ± 10% resistor
R3,R4—15,000-ohm, ¼-w. ± 10% resistor
S1—Miniature s.p.s.t. normally open pushbutton switch
Misc.—Plastic pill bottle (2⅞″ long x 1¼″ dia.), perfboard (2½″ x ⅞″), ground wire with alligator clip, battery snap terminals, wire solder.
(Note: ½-w resistors may also be used).

TODDLER'S ROCKING HORSE

Great gifts you can make

By HARRY WICKS

■ THERE'S A GIFT for just about everyone on your list in this great collection of project ideas from our workshop. Many of them can be created for less than $10, and even the most sophisticated project—the wine rack—costs less than $50 to build. Complete directions for the construction of all projects shown on these pages start on page 172.

1. Toddler's rocking horse is sized to suit age 3 or under. It's created by using sugar pine and stock lattice from the lumberyard. The rocker design is carefully worked out to assure safe rocking for your active youngsters. **2.** Our elegant wine rack holds 18 bottles, measures 29 in. high, 13 in. wide and 32 in. long. **3.** Free-form fir and pine vases, fashioned on a bandsaw, hold

WINE RACK

FREE-FORM VASES

CASSEROLE CARRIER

continued

5

TOY TRUCK

CHILDREN'S CLOTHES HANGER

7

PINE DISPLAY SHELF

CANDLESTAND

8

OAK KNIFE BLOCK

SANDWICH BOARDS

9

SPOOL CANDLEHOLDERS

10

11

TRINKET CHEST

PINE CUTTING-SERVING BOARD

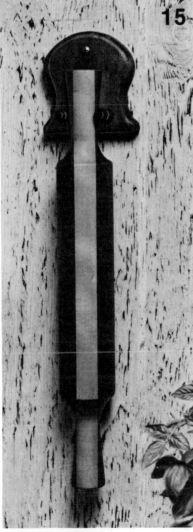

CASTLE PUZZLE

continued

CLOTHES RACKS   **ROLLING PIN**

17

18

19

STEM-GLASS RACK   MIRROR CANDLE SCONCE   PINE STEAM ROLLER

dried flowers, small candles. **4.** Casserole carrier lets you move hot pots safely from oven to table. **5.** Toy truck can be of scrap wood or pine, left natural. **6.** Children's clothes hangers of ¼-in. plywood add whimsical, but functional, touch to the nursery. **7.** Pine wall display shelf has rosewood knob, will hold a collection. **8.** Oak knife block can be sized to suit your kitchen set; ours measures about 5x5x10 in. **9.** Antique flax spools inspired these candleholders. **10.** Candlestand project for lathe buffs calls for both spindle and faceplate turning. **11.** Festive sandwich boards feature a "crate" made of textured wood lath. **12.** For young lady's jewelry, there's an acrylic plastic trinket chest with painted-pine drawer fronts. **13.** Simple pine cutting-serving board is equally good for cold cuts and cheese. **14.** The clean-cut lines of these clothes racks may help junior hang his clothes—at least, they'll make it easier. **15.** Multicolor rolling pin is made by laminating birch and walnut layers and turning them on a lathe. Its walnut bracket has a pair of small turned pegs. **16.** Castle puzzle looks easy to put together, but cuts are made at color edges rather than through colors, so the task takes longer than you'd think. (Small parts rule out this one as a game for toddlers.) **17.** Stem-glass wall rack is stained a mellow honey tone, measures 4x18x32 in. and holds 20 glasses. **18.** Mirror candle sconce decorates a wall, gives pleasing effect when candle is burned. **19.** Pine steamroller is

made by cutting a glued-up clear pine block on a bandsaw and adding slices of dowel for roller, wheels and seat. This toy, left natural, was finished with two coats of white shellac.

General building directions

Except for a couple of lathe turnings, you can create all projects included in this roundup of gifts to make using hand tools only. Of course, with power tools, the building will go faster.

Most of the projects are constructed using clear pine (or carefully selected common pine). In some cases, a hardwood is called for such as in the walnut and birch rolling pin. In all cases, carpentry and joinery have been kept relatively easy. To assure professional-looking results, give extra attention to finishing techniques. In general, the projects shown were either stained or left natural, sealed with a coat of shellac (thinned 50 percent with denatured alcohol) and then completed with a coat of varnish. For smooth finishes, rub between coats with double 0 steel wool, dust and *wipe with a tack cloth.*

CREDITS

Project designs: Truck (No. 5), Andrew Cummins; Hangers (No. 6), sandwich boards (No. 13), Stanley Dunaj; Castle puzzle (No. 18), Kari Lonning. All other designs were constructed in the PM Workshop by Rosario Capotosto, John Wicks and Harry Wicks, PM photos by George Ratkai and R. Capotosto; technical art, Eugene Thompson.

Wine cart

Start by ripping lengths of 6/4-in. pine to the thicknesses indicated, then rip the mahogany to size. To create the mortises in the underside of the top, assemble the laminations in sections as shown below. As an aid when gluing the laminations, drive a pair of small nails partly into each alternate edge, then clip off the heads to leave a small protruding point. Press each successive edge together before applying glue; the indents will prevent sliding during gluing.

The best way to cut the notches on the uprights is on a bench saw as shown. To get clean scallops in the bottle racks, use a circle cutter in a drill press to bore holes in 5-in.-wide boards. (Clamp boards for drilling.) Then rip the boards on the bench saw. Use varnish to finish.

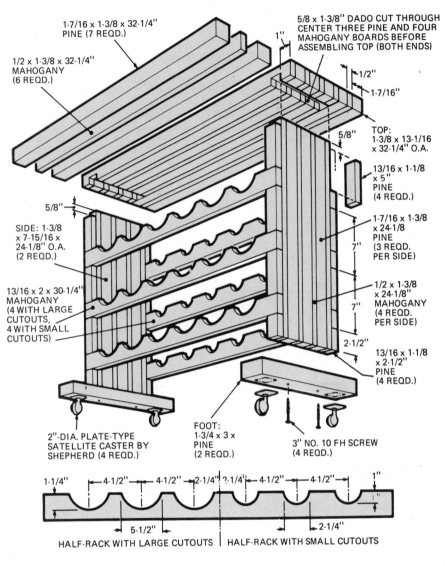

1-7/16 x 1-3/8 x 32-1/4" PINE (7 REQD.)

1/2 x 1-3/8 x 32-1/4" MAHOGANY (6 REQD.)

5/8 x 1-3/8" DADO CUT THROUGH CENTER THREE PINE AND FOUR MAHOGANY BOARDS BEFORE ASSEMBLING TOP (BOTH ENDS)

1"

1/2"

1-7/16"

5/8"

TOP: 1-3/8 x 13-1/16 x 32-1/4" O.A.

13/16 x 1-1/8 x 5" PINE (4 REQD.)

1-7/16 x 1-3/8 x 24-1/8 PINE (3 REQD. PER SIDE)

7"

1/2 x 1-3/8 x 24-1/8" MAHOGANY (4 REQD. PER SIDE)

7"

2-1/2"

13/16 x 1-1/8 x 2-1/2" PINE (4 REQD.)

5/8"

SIDE: 1-3/8 x 7-15/16 x 24-1/8" O.A. (2 REQD.)

13/16 x 2 x 30-1/4" MAHOGANY (4 WITH LARGE CUTOUTS, 4 WITH SMALL CUTOUTS)

2"-DIA. PLATE-TYPE SATELLITE CASTER BY SHEPHERD (4 REQD.)

FOOT: 1-3/4 x 3 x PINE (2 REQD.)

3" NO. 10 FH SCREW (4 REQD.)

1-1/4" 4-1/2" 4-1/2" 2-1/4" 2-1/4" 4-1/2" 4-1/2" 1"

5-1/2" 2-1/4" 1"

HALF-RACK WITH LARGE CUTOUTS | HALF-RACK WITH SMALL CUTOUTS

TO FORM mortises in top's underside, cut dadoes across partially assembled top.

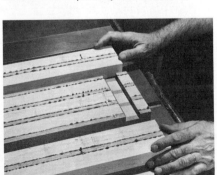

THREE SECTIONS are glued up using hidden nail points to avoid slipping.

USE A SLOW-SETTING glue and at least four pipe (or bar) clamps.

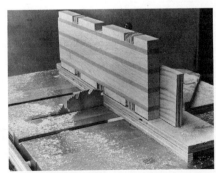

A MAKESHIFT high-fence miter gauge helps you cut notches and tenons.

continued

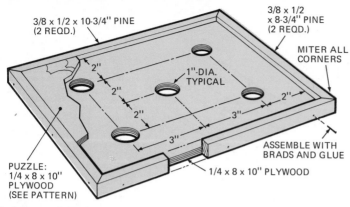

3/8 x 1/2 x 10-3/4" PINE (2 REQD.)

3/8 x 1/2 x 8-3/4" PINE (2 REQD.)

MITER ALL CORNERS

2"

1"-DIA. TYPICAL

2"

2"

2"

3"

3"

ASSEMBLE WITH BRADS AND GLUE

PUZZLE: 1/4 x 8 x 10" PLYWOOD (SEE PATTERN)

1/4 x 8 x 10" PLYWOOD

PUZZLE PATTERN (1" SQS.)

Castle puzzle

Since this puzzle has a number of small pieces that could fit into a toddler's mouth, plan on giving it to an older child or adult. Draw the design on ¼-in. birch plywood and cut the pieces, using a fine blade in a jigsaw, a coping saw. The stars are cut from a second piece of plywood to suit cutouts made in the puzzle. Paint the parts as shown, build the frame, and seal the parts with shellac.

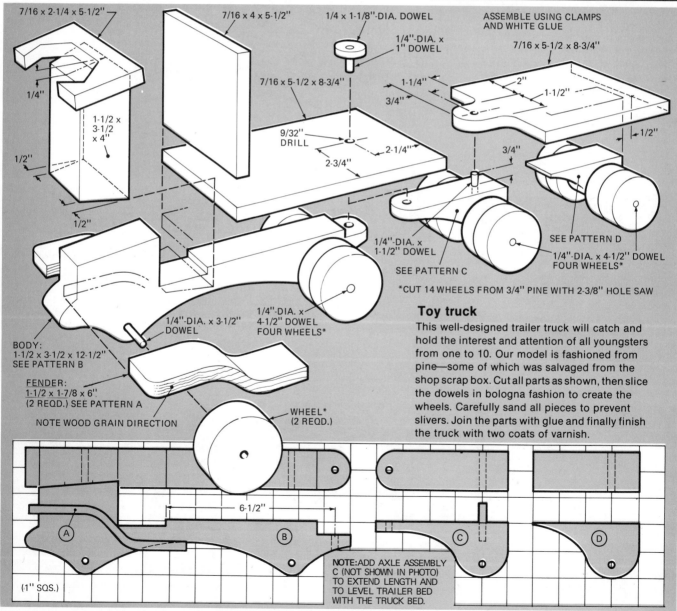

7/16 x 2-1/4 x 5-1/2"

7/16 x 4 x 5-1/2"

1/4 x 1-1/8"-DIA. DOWEL

ASSEMBLE USING CLAMPS AND WHITE GLUE

1/4"-DIA. x 1" DOWEL

7/16 x 5-1/2 x 8-3/4"

1/4"

1-1/2 x 3-1/2 x 4"

7/16 x 5-1/2 x 8-3/4"

1-1/4"

2"

1-1/2"

3/4"

1/2"

9/32" DRILL

2-1/4"

3/4"

1/2"

2-3/4"

1/2"

1/4"-DIA. x 1-1/2" DOWEL

SEE PATTERN D

1/4"-DIA. x 4-1/2" DOWEL FOUR WHEELS*

SEE PATTERN C

1/2"

1/4"-DIA. x 3-1/2" DOWEL

1/4"-DIA. x 4-1/2" DOWEL FOUR WHEELS*

*CUT 14 WHEELS FROM 3/4" PINE WITH 2-3/8" HOLE SAW

Toy truck

This well-designed trailer truck will catch and hold the interest and attention of all youngsters from one to 10. Our model is fashioned from pine—some of which was salvaged from the shop scrap box. Cut all parts as shown, then slice the dowels in bologna fashion to create the wheels. Carefully sand all pieces to prevent slivers. Join the parts with glue and finally finish the truck with two coats of varnish.

BODY: 1-1/2 x 3-1/2 x 12-1/2" SEE PATTERN B

FENDER: 1-1/2 x 1-7/8 x 6" (2 REQD.) SEE PATTERN A

NOTE WOOD GRAIN DIRECTION

WHEEL* (2 REQD.)

6-1/2"

A

B

C

D

NOTE: ADD AXLE ASSEMBLY C (NOT SHOWN IN PHOTO) TO EXTEND LENGTH AND TO LEVEL TRAILER BED WITH THE TRUCK BED.

(1" SQS.)

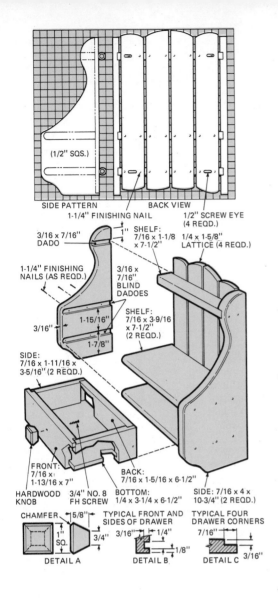

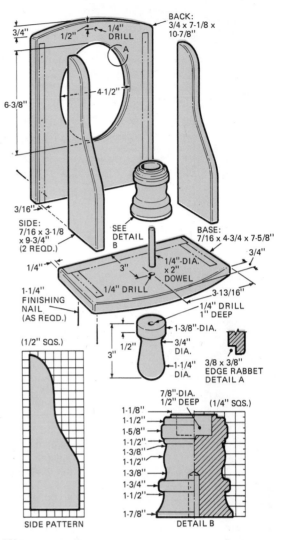

Pine shelf

This shelf is extra-easy to build because all of the parts are made from stock lumberyard material. The case is ½-in. pine, the back is ¼-in. lattice. Cut the parts as shown in the drawing above, test-assemble them for close fit, then do the permanent assembly using glue and brads. Check all shelves and sides for squareness, then install the back slats. Build the drawer and cut the knob on your bench saw or purchase a commercial knob. Stain, seal with shellac and apply varnish.

Mirror sconce

This is another project that is easier to build than its looks imply. Start by cutting out the bottom, sides and back. Lay out the oval and cut it out with your sabre saw being careful to follow your layout. Sand the inner edges and, using a router, cut the mirror-holding edge rabbet. Have the mirror cut to suit by a professional glazier. Turn the candleholder and handle on a lathe; then fasten both of them to the shelf using glue and dowel. Stain and varnish the assembled sconce.

Cutting board

The board shown was fashioned of 1¾-in. thick pine laminated to form a 1¾ x 5⅞ x 11⅜-in. chopping block. After joining the pieces, adjust the bench-saw blade to a setting of 20° and a depth of ⅝-in., and use your miter gauge to make the four angled cuts on the top's underside. While the blade is still set at this angle make the four angle cuts on the feet. Return the blade to the 0° setting and remove waste from all three pieces. Join the pieces with glue, screws and dowel buttons as shown. Rub all parts with two coats of mineral oil.

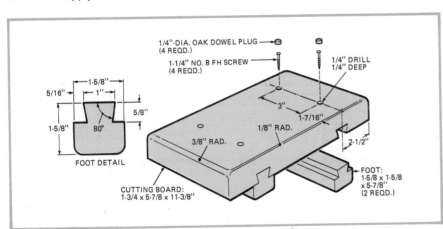

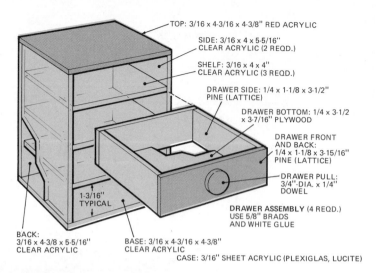

TOP: 3/16 x 4-3/16 x 4-3/8" RED ACRYLIC

SIDE: 3/16 x 4 x 5-5/16"
CLEAR ACRYLIC (2 REQD.)

SHELF: 3/16 x 4 x 4"
CLEAR ACRYLIC (3 REQD.)

DRAWER SIDE: 1/4 x 1-1/8 x 3-1/2"
PINE (LATTICE)

DRAWER BOTTOM: 1/4 x 3-1/2
x 3-7/16" PLYWOOD

DRAWER FRONT
AND BACK:
1/4 x 1-1/8 x 3-15/16"
PINE (LATTICE)

DRAWER PULL:
3/4"-DIA. x 1/4"
DOWEL

DRAWER ASSEMBLY (4 REQD.)
USE 5/8" BRADS
AND WHITE GLUE

1-3/16"
TYPICAL

BACK:
3/16 x 4-3/8 x 5-5/16"
CLEAR ACRYLIC

BASE: 3/16 x 4-3/16 x 4-3/8"
CLEAR ACRYLIC

CASE: 3/16" SHEET ACRYLIC (PLEXIGLAS, LUCITE)

AFTER REMOVING protective paper, tape parts together, apply solvent as shown.

Casserole carrier

The carrier shown is shaped from a single wide oak plank. If preferred, narrow boards can be edge-joined to achieve desired width. Carefully round the corners and then lay out and bore holes to receive the dowels. Finish the board with a polyurethane varnish. Attach handles, cut eight lengths of dowel.

Trinket chest

To make this little chest, you will need ³/₁₆-in. clear sheet acrylic, plus a small opaque colored piece for the top. Cut out three 4 x 4-in. pieces with fine-tooth blade, then tape them together to sand all edges perfectly smooth. Repeat for the two sidepieces and the top, bottom and back sections. Finish all edges with 220-320 wet-or-dry paper—but do *not* polish the edges at this time. Remove protective masking paper and apply solvent to each joint using the special solvent applicator (available from Plexiglas dealers). Keep joints being glued horizontal. When box is dry, polish exposed edges with DuPont auto polishing compound. Construct drawers of lattice and paint the fronts as shown. Then spray-varnish all drawer parts.

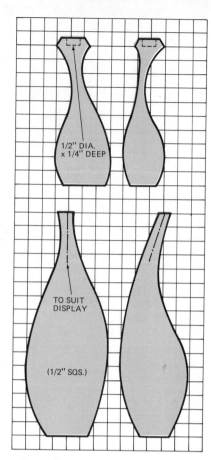

1/2" DIA.
x 1/4" DEEP

TO SUIT
DISPLAY

(1/2" SQS.)

Free-form vases

We illustrate two vase shapes here, but you can create your own designs if preferred. Draw the front and side views of the desired shape on a suitable-size block of wood. Cut out the first side on the bandsaw, tack scrap back on to cut the second side. Bore hole in neck.

Rolling pin

Start by laminating two pieces of walnut and one piece of birch. Note: ⅞ in. is actual thickness for hardwoods. Use carpenter's (yellow) glue and clamp parts securely while glue dries. Cut or plane the laminated block octagonal and mount it in your lathe in conventional manner and turn the rolling pin to diameters shown. Make bracket from walnut. Finish all parts by rubbing with mineral oil.

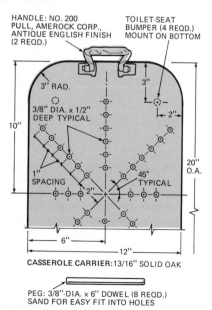

HANDLE: NO. 200
PULL, AMEROCK CORP.,
ANTIQUE ENGLISH FINISH
(2 REQD.)

TOILET-SEAT
BUMPER (4 REQD.)
MOUNT ON BOTTOM

3" RAD.

3/8" DIA. x 1/2"
DEEP TYPICAL

3"

2"

10"

1"
SPACING

45°
TYPICAL

2"

20"
O.A.

6"

12"

CASSEROLE CARRIER: 13/16" SOLID OAK

PEG: 3/8"-DIA. x 6" DOWEL (8 REQD.)
SAND FOR EASY FIT INTO HOLES

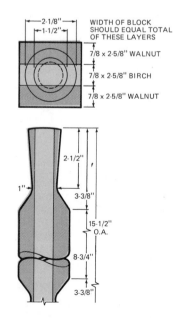

2-1/8"

1-1/2"

WIDTH OF BLOCK
SHOULD EQUAL TOTAL
OF THESE LAYERS

7/8 x 2-5/8" WALNUT

7/8 x 2-5/8" BIRCH

7/8 x 2-5/8" WALNUT

2-1/2"

1"

3-3/8"

15-1/2"
O.A.

8-3/4"

3-3/8"

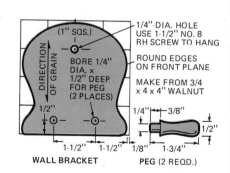

(1" SQS.)

DIRECTION
OF GRAIN

1/2"

BORE 1/4"
DIA. x
1/2" DEEP
FOR PEG
(2 PLACES)

1/4"-DIA. HOLE
USE 1-1/2" NO. 8
RH SCREW TO HANG

ROUND EDGES
ON FRONT PLANE

MAKE FROM 3/4
x 4 x 4" WALNUT

1/4"   3/8"

1/2"

1-1/2"   1-1/2"   1/8"   1-3/4"

WALL BRACKET

PEG (2 REQD.)

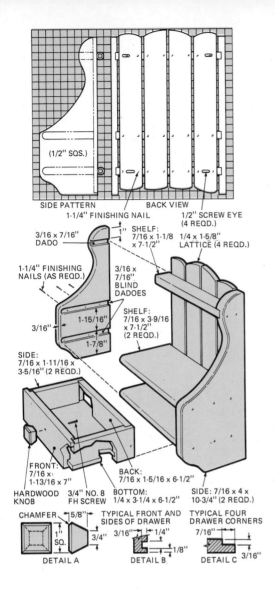

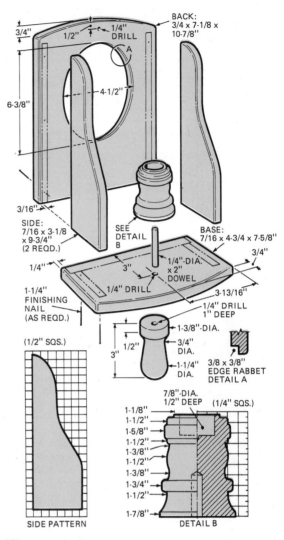

Pine shelf

This shelf is extra-easy to build because all of the parts are made from stock lumberyard material. The case is ½-in. pine, the back is ¼-in. lattice. Cut the parts as shown in the drawing above, test-assemble them for close fit, then do the permanent assembly using glue and brads. Check all shelves and sides for squareness, then install the back slats. Build the drawer and cut the knob on your bench saw or purchase a commercial knob. Stain, seal with shellac and apply varnish.

Mirror sconce

This is another project that is easier to build than its looks imply. Start by cutting out the bottom, sides and back. Lay out the oval and cut it out with your sabre saw being careful to follow your layout. Sand the inner edges and, using a router, cut the mirror-holding edge rabbet. Have the mirror cut to suit by a professional glazier. Turn the candleholder and handle on a lathe; then fasten both of them to the shelf using glue and dowel. Stain and varnish the assembled sconce.

Cutting board

The board shown was fashioned of 1¾-in. thick pine laminated to form a 1¾ x 5⅞ x 11⅜-in. chopping block. After joining the pieces, adjust the bench-saw blade to a setting of 20° and a depth of ⅝-in., and use your miter gauge to make the four angled cuts on the top's underside. While the blade is still set at this angle make the four angle cuts on the feet. Return the blade to the 0° setting and remove waste from all three pieces. Join the pieces with glue, screws and dowel buttons as shown. Rub all parts with two coats of mineral oil.

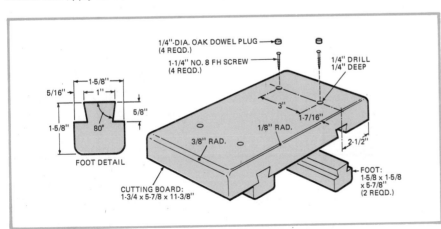

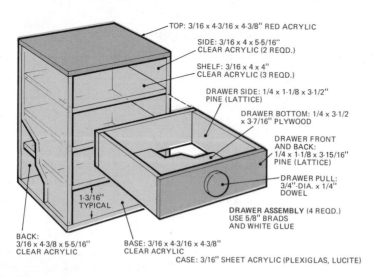

TOP: 3/16 x 4-3/16 x 4-3/8" RED ACRYLIC

SIDE: 3/16 x 4 x 5-5/16"
CLEAR ACRYLIC (2 REQD.)

SHELF: 3/16 x 4 x 4"
CLEAR ACRYLIC (3 REQD.)

DRAWER SIDE: 1/4 x 1-1/8 x 3-1/2"
PINE (LATTICE)

DRAWER BOTTOM: 1/4 x 3-1/2
x 3-7/16" PLYWOOD

DRAWER FRONT
AND BACK:
1/4 x 1-1/8 x 3-15/16"
PINE (LATTICE)

DRAWER PULL:
3/4"-DIA. x 1/4"
DOWEL

1-3/16"
TYPICAL

DRAWER ASSEMBLY (4 REQD.)
USE 5/8" BRADS
AND WHITE GLUE

BACK:
3/16 x 4-3/8 x 5-5/16"
CLEAR ACRYLIC

BASE: 3/16 x 4-3/16 x 4-3/8"
CLEAR ACRYLIC

CASE: 3/16" SHEET ACRYLIC (PLEXIGLAS, LUCITE)

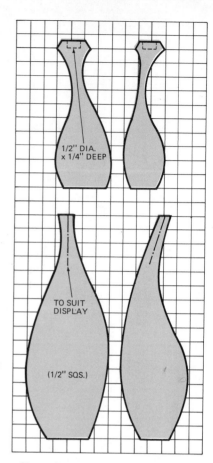

1/2" DIA.
x 1/4" DEEP

TO SUIT
DISPLAY

(1/2" SQS.)

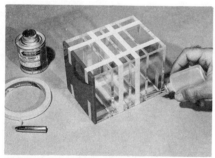

AFTER REMOVING protective paper, tape parts together, apply solvent as shown.

Casserole carrier

The carrier shown is shaped from a single wide oak plank. If preferred, narrow boards can be edge-joined to achieve desired width. Carefully round the corners and then lay out and bore holes to receive the dowels. Finish the board with a polyurethane varnish. Attach handles, cut eight lengths of dowel.

Trinket chest

To make this little chest, you will need ³/₁₆-in. clear sheet acrylic, plus a small opaque colored piece for the top. Cut out three 4 x 4-in. pieces with fine-tooth blade, then tape them together to sand all edges perfectly smooth. Repeat for the two sidepieces and the top, bottom and back sections. Finish all edges with 220-320 wet-or-dry paper—but do *not* polish the edges at this time. Remove protective masking paper and apply solvent to each joint using the special solvent applicator (available from Plexiglas dealers). Keep joints being glued horizontal. When box is dry, polish exposed edges with DuPont auto polishing compound. Construct drawers of lattice and paint the fronts as shown. Then spray-varnish all drawer parts.

Free-form vases

We illustrate two vase shapes here, but you can create your own designs if preferred. Draw the front and side views of the desired shape on a suitable-size block of wood. Cut out the first side on the bandsaw, tack scrap back on to cut the second side. Bore hole in neck.

Rolling pin

Start by laminating two pieces of walnut and one piece of birch. Note: ⅞ in. is actual thickness for hardwoods. Use carpenter's (yellow) glue and clamp parts securely while glue dries. Cut or plane the laminated block octagonal and mount it in your lathe in conventional manner and turn the rolling pin to diameters shown. Make bracket from walnut. Finish all parts by rubbing with mineral oil.

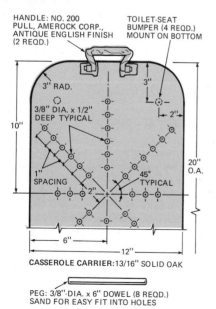

HANDLE: NO. 200
PULL, AMEROCK CORP.,
ANTIQUE ENGLISH FINISH
(2 REQD.)

TOILET-SEAT
BUMPER (4 REQD.)
MOUNT ON BOTTOM

3" RAD.

3"

3/8" DIA. x 1/2"
DEEP TYPICAL

10"

2"

1"
SPACING

45°
TYPICAL

2"

20"
O.A.

6"

12"

CASSEROLE CARRIER: 13/16" SOLID OAK

PEG: 3/8"-DIA. x 6" DOWEL (8 REQD.)
SAND FOR EASY FIT INTO HOLES

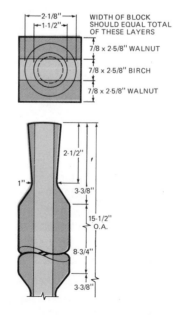

2-1/8"
1-1/2"
WIDTH OF BLOCK
SHOULD EQUAL TOTAL
OF THESE LAYERS

7/8 x 2-5/8" WALNUT

7/8 x 2-5/8" BIRCH

7/8 x 2-5/8" WALNUT

2-1/2"

1"

3-3/8"

15-1/2"
O.A.

8-3/4"

3-3/8"

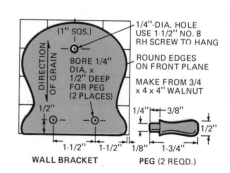

(1" SQS.)

1/4"-DIA. HOLE
USE 1-1/2" NO. 8
RH SCREW TO HANG

DIRECTION
OF GRAIN

BORE 1/4"
DIA. x
1/2" DEEP
FOR PEG
(2 PLACES)

ROUND EDGES
ON FRONT PLANE

MAKE FROM 3/4
x 4 x 4" WALNUT

1/2"

1/4"   3/8"

1/2"

1-1/2"   1-1/2"   1/8"   1-3/4"

WALL BRACKET

PEG (2 REQD.)

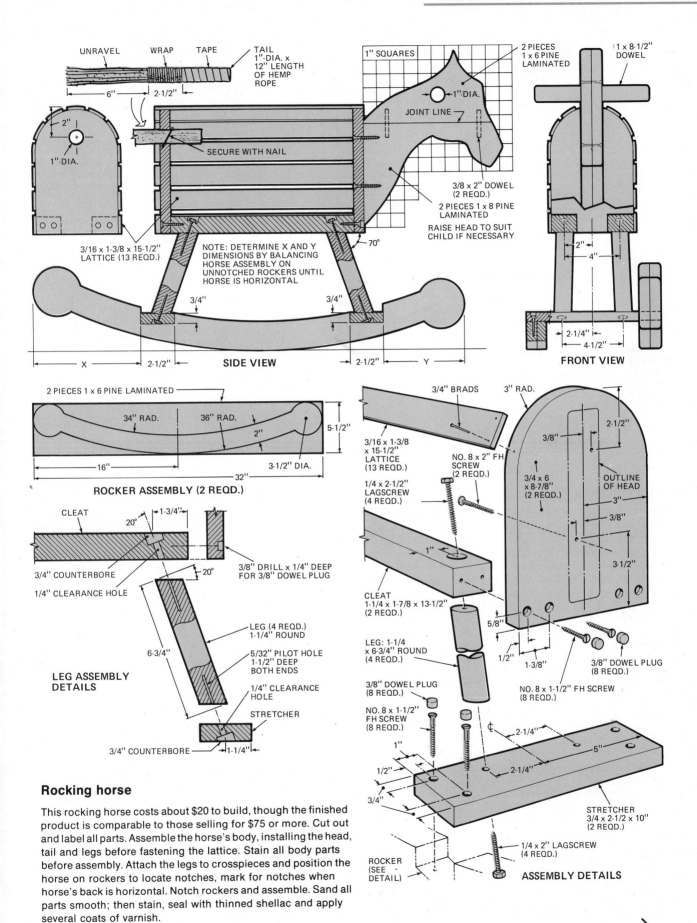

UNRAVEL   WRAP   TAPE   TAIL 1"-DIA. x 12" LENGTH OF HEMP ROPE

6"   2-1/2"

2"
1"-DIA.

SECURE WITH NAIL

1" SQUARES

1"-DIA.
JOINT LINE

2 PIECES 1 x 6 PINE LAMINATED

1 x 8-1/2" DOWEL

3/8 x 2" DOWEL (2 REQD.)

2 PIECES 1 x 8 PINE LAMINATED

RAISE HEAD TO SUIT CHILD IF NECESSARY

3/16 x 1-3/8 x 15-1/2" LATTICE (13 REQD.)

NOTE: DETERMINE X AND Y DIMENSIONS BY BALANCING HORSE ASSEMBLY ON UNNOTCHED ROCKERS UNTIL HORSE IS HORIZONTAL

70°

3/4"   3/4"

X   2-1/2"   **SIDE VIEW**   2-1/2"   Y

2"
4"

FRONT VIEW

2-1/4"
4-1/2"

2 PIECES 1 x 6 PINE LAMINATED

34" RAD.   36" RAD.
2"
5-1/2"

16"   3-1/2" DIA.
32"

ROCKER ASSEMBLY (2 REQD.)

3/4" BRADS   3" RAD.

3/16 x 1-3/8 x 15-1/2" LATTICE (13 REQD.)

NO. 8 x 2" FH SCREW (2 REQD.)

1/4 x 2-1/2" LAGSCREW (4 REQD.)

2-1/2"
3/8"

3/4 x 6 x 8-7/8" (2 REQD.)

OUTLINE OF HEAD

3"
3/8"
3-1/2"

CLEAT

20°   1-3/4"

3/4" COUNTERBORE
1/4" CLEARANCE HOLE
20°

3/8" DRILL x 1/4" DEEP FOR 3/8" DOWEL PLUG

LEG (4 REQD.) 1-1/4" ROUND

6-3/4"

5/32" PILOT HOLE 1-1/2" DEEP BOTH ENDS

1/4" CLEARANCE HOLE

STRETCHER

3/4" COUNTERBORE   1-1/4"

LEG ASSEMBLY DETAILS

1"

CLEAT 1-1/4 x 1-7/8 x 13-1/2" (2 REQD.)

LEG: 1-1/4 x 6-3/4" ROUND (4 REQD.)

3/8" DOWEL PLUG (8 REQD.)

NO. 8 x 1-1/2" FH SCREW (8 REQD.)

5/8"

1/2"
1-3/8"

3/8" DOWEL PLUG (8 REQD.)

NO. 8 x 1-1/2" FH SCREW (8 REQD.)

1"
1/2"
3/4"

2-1/4"
2-1/4"
5"

STRETCHER 3/4 x 2-1/2 x 10" (2 REQD.)

1/4 x 2" LAGSCREW (4 REQD.)

ROCKER (SEE DETAIL)

ASSEMBLY DETAILS

Rocking horse

This rocking horse costs about $20 to build, though the finished product is comparable to those selling for $75 or more. Cut out and label all parts. Assemble the horse's body, installing the head, tail and legs before fastening the lattice. Stain all body parts before assembly. Attach the legs to crosspieces and position the horse on rockers to locate notches, mark for notches when horse's back is horizontal. Notch rockers and assemble. Sand all parts smooth; then stain, seal with thinned shellac and apply several coats of varnish.

continued

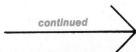

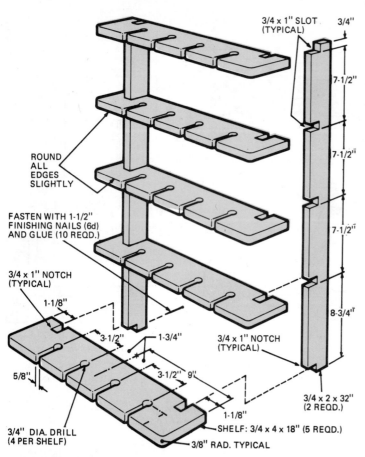

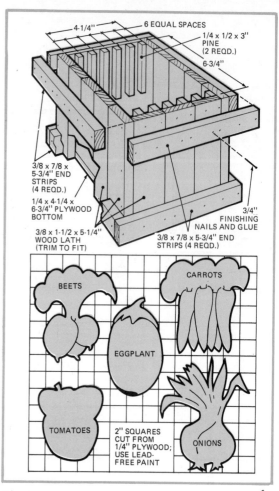

Stem-glass rack

Start by cutting both sides and shelves. Then tack-nail the five shelves together to expedite the cutting of the notches for the cross-lap joints. Using a dado cutter which is set for a width equal to the thickness of the stock and a depth of 1-in., make the notch cuts. While the shelves are still bundled together, insert a $9/16$-in. bit in your drill and bore all of the holes for the stems. Separate the pieces and remove the brads. Use either a bench saw or a sabre saw and carefully cut out the slots from the edge to the bored holes. Sand all of the surfaces, then assemble using glue and 6d finishing nails. Install two screweyes which will hold the rack on the wall. Finish the entire rack with several coats of a quality semigloss varnish. Rub with steel wool between coats.

Sandwich boards

Start by building the vegetable crate of wood lath. Sand lightly to remove whiskers, but leave texture. Cut parts of the four sides. Then assemble the box using glue and brads. When glue has dried, seal the porous wood with a coat of white shellac thinned 50 percent with denatured alcohol. Next day apply semigloss varnish.

Using 1-in. squares, lay out vegetables on ½-in. pine or birch plywood and cut out parts. As you cut each one, check its fit in box and make additional cuts if needed. Next sand all pieces smooth—rounding edges slightly—and seal with a prime coat of paint. To finish, apply colors using *nontoxic* water-base paints.

Kid's clothes hangers

The hangers shown were cut from ¼-in.-thick pine plywood (because fir plywood does not take paint evenly). Start by drawing the hanger design (one shown here or your own design) on a piece of light tracing paper. Flop the drawing over and rub soft pencil on the back side. Tape tissue to plywood and redraw the lines to transfer your artwork to the wood. If necessary, go over the lines on the wood with a dark felt marker to prevent smudging. Cut the hanger using a sabre saw or a jigsaw. At this stage it is a good idea to test the fit of the hanger on a clothes bar. When satisfied, sand the hanger smooth, dust off and seal with a coat of white shellac thinned with denatured alcohol. When thoroughly dry, lightly redraw the designs with charcoal, then fill in with paint. Use your imagination and bright colorful paint to give each one a distinctive appearance.

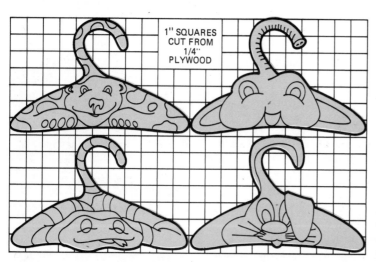

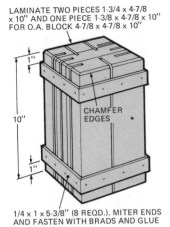

LAMINATE TWO PIECES 1-3/4 x 4-7/8 x 10" AND ONE PIECE 1-3/8 x 4-7/8 x 10" FOR O.A. BLOCK 4-7/8 x 4-7/8 x 10"

1"

CHAMFER EDGES

10"

1"

1/4 x 1 x 5-3/8" (8 REQD.). MITER ENDS AND FASTEN WITH BRADS AND GLUE

TOP VIEW OF BLOCK

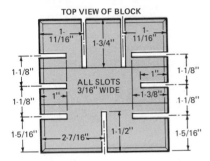

1-11/16"   1-3/4"   1-11/16"

1-1/8"   1"   1-1/8"

1-1/8"   1"   1-3/8"   1-1/8"

1-5/16"   2-7/16"   1-1/2"   1-5/16"

ALL SLOTS 3/16" WIDE

Knife block

In order to create the size block needed here, it is necessary to laminate three oak boards as shown. Note: two pieces are 1¾ in. and one is 1⅜ in. thick. Clamp the block until the glue dries. Meanwhile, you can be cutting the strips that encircle the block at top and bottom. With a dado blade mounted on your bench saw, cut ³/₁₆-in. grooves to suit your knife set. Attach strips and apply varnish.

Flax spool candleholders

This is a super-easy project because the candlestand body is simply a 6-in. length of ready-made dowel. Cut the top and bottom circles from ½-in. clear pine; bore the mortises and attach to dowel. At top, bore a ¾-in.-dia. hole (or size to suit) to receive candle. To finish, seal with a very thin coat of shellac. For natural look, apply stain, wipe off excess, finish with varnish. For antique look, apply paint, rub off at center.

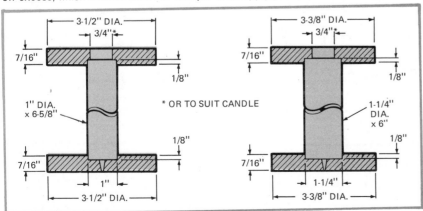

3-1/2" DIA.
3/4"
7/16"
1/8"
1" DIA. x 6-5/8"
* OR TO SUIT CANDLE
1/8"
7/16"
1"
3-1/2" DIA.

3-3/8" DIA.
3/4"
7/16"
1/8"
1-1/4" DIA. x 6"
1/8"
7/16"
1-1/4"
3-3/8" DIA.

Clothes rack

Because of simplicity of design, the clothes trees shown are particularly easy to build. In fact, the toughest part of the job is boring the angled holes for the dowels. Use a guide to assure accuracy. Sand all parts before assembling as shown below. Seal with shellac and finish with either varnish or enamel.

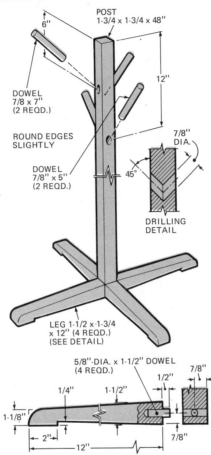

POST 1-3/4 x 1-3/4 x 48"

6"

12"

DOWEL 7/8 x 7" (2 REQD.)

ROUND EDGES SLIGHTLY

DOWEL 7/8" x 5" (2 REQD.)

45°

7/8" DIA.

DRILLING DETAIL

LEG 1-1/2 x 1-3/4 x 12" (4 REQD.) (SEE DETAIL)

5/8"-DIA. x 1-1/2" DOWEL (4 REQD.)

1/4"   1-1/2"   1/2"   7/8"

1-1/8"

2"   12"   7/8"

7/8"

LEG DETAIL

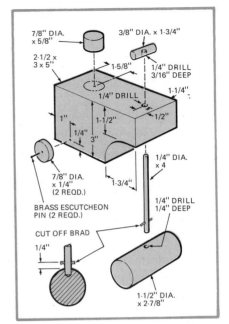

7/8" DIA. x 5/8"   3/8" DIA. x 1-3/4"

2-1/2 x 3 x 5"   1-5/8"   1/4" DRILL 3/16" DEEP

1/4" DRILL   1-1/4"

1"   1-1/2"   1/2"

1/4"   3"

7/8" DIA. x 1/4" (2 REQD.)

1-3/4"

1/4" DIA. x 4

1/4" DRILL 1/4" DEEP

BRASS ESCUTCHEON PIN (2 REQD.)

CUT OFF BRAD

1/4"

1-1/2" DIA. x 2-7/8"

Pine steamroller

The chassis is created by gluing up pieces of pine. The curve at front is cut with a coping saw or bandsaw and should be shaped to suit the dowel roller. Note: To simplify finishing task, spray parts with clear varnish *before* assembly.

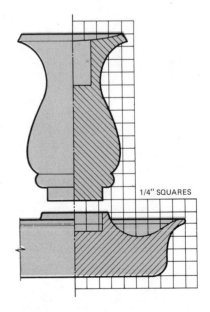

1/4" SQUARES

Candlestand

Size blocks of walnut for both spindle and faceplate turnings (turn spindle first). Mount the faceplate block and shape bottom, then reverse piece to finish top. Cut mortise on spinning plate to suit tenon. Finish parts while they're still in the lathe.

Motorize your bicycle

By BILL HARTFORD

Just about any bicycle can be turned into a 'moped' by adding this friction drive helper motor. It's easy to mount on your bicycle and allows you to pedal or go with power

BIKEBUG ENGINE from AquaBug International easily mounted on this Schwinn Suburban 10-speed in a few steps. The engine design is carefully planned throughout.

■ EVER TRY TO PEDAL a moped? You can do it, but it's difficult—and surely it isn't any fun. If you enjoy bicycling pleasures, the way to go is 10-speed with a helper motor.

For our "Project Moped" we started with a Schwinn Suburban 10-speed. For upright riding position, comfort and versatility, we selected the women's model with tourist handlebars. It's a '76 model so it doesn't have the Shimano Front Freewheeling (FF) system of later models. Don't motorize an FF machine because it would be annoying to have the chainwheel revolving constantly.

The Suburban with front and rear caliper brakes was our choice, but any bike will accept the front-wheel-drive motor we installed.

Designed to clamp onto the front fork of your bike without interfering with the front-fender or brake calipers, the BikeBug is an impressive 22-cc engine and drive unit. We ordered the BikeBug QBM-23 engine from AquaBug International, 100 Merrick Rd., Rockville, Centre, NY 11570. (A price of $170 was in effect when this article was written.) Another QBM-23 distributor is TAS Industries, 12728 N.E. 15th Pl., Bellevue, WA 98005.

The high quality of the BikeBug is apparent as

SLIP MOTOR into position with clamp over front fork of the bike.

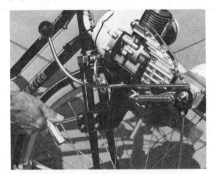

TIGHTEN THE rubber-faced clamps on front fork with tool provided.

SUPPORT ROD adjusts roller ¼ inch over tire, and positions muffler.

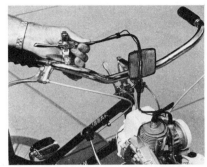

CLAMP THROTTLE lever/kill switch to the handlebars.

FILL FUEL TANK with liter of gas/oil mix and get ready to ride!

TO START the BikeBug, lift the engagement lever which lowers the drive roller against front tire. Engine starts with throttle at idle; choke is automatic.

WINGNUT on support rod adjusts roller on wheel. Rollers can be replaced.

soon as you unpack it. An example of well-thought-out design is the rubber-faced fork clamps. Instructions are thorough.

We mounted the air-cooled motor in a few minutes, as shown, topped off the tank with a liter of gas/oil (25:1)—good for 50 miles, easily.

Pedal up to a few miles per hour, pull the engagement lever to drop the driving roller against your front wheel and—*voila!*—you're on your way. With 1.39 cu. in. putting out .8 hp, you can cruise about 15 mph. (We don't plan to do it,

but if you remove the governor, engine power is boosted to 1.2 hp and top speed to 24 mph.)

At first we were alarmed at how rapidly the grooved rubber drive roller was wearing, but it is designed to shape itself to your tire quickly and then wear itself instead of the tire. It never slipped or spun during our tests which included pulling a Cannodale Bugger bicycle trailer with two kids on board. The BikeBug puts an extra 15 pounds on your front fork, but is easily manageable.

Build a puppet theater

By PENELOPE ANGELL

Puppetry is a hobby the whole family can share. There's lots to do.
Make the stage! Design the backdrops! Fashion the puppets! Write the script! Rehearsals!
Hurry, the show's about to begin!

■ DIM THE HOUSE LIGHTS and let the show begin. The curtain opens and two puppets appear. You've just entered the puppet world.

Preparing for a puppet production actually does involve creating a miniature world—building a stage where puppets perform, making the puppets and supplying them with props and scenery.

The production can provide entertainment for your family and friends, as puppets act out stories and funny family happenings.

The puppet's world is the theater. This colorful theater has been designed to aid the puppeteers (persons who work the puppets behind the scenes). It can be folded for easy storing after use.

materials for the theater

The theater is made with two sheets of ⅜-in. A-A (good two sides) plywood and 1x1-in. framing on the side panels. Curtains are hung on a traverse rod and the backdrop is a window shade.

We applied fabric and star appliques to the shade for an outer space setting. You can use fabric or paint the window shade to achieve the proper setting for your production. Scenery is easily changed by changing shades.

The hardware you'll need includes three 1⅛-in.-wide piano hinges, two for the stage sides so they can be closed for storing and one for the stage door on the side. Four 4-in. barrel bolts lock the stage sides open when in use. A fifth barrel bolt can be placed inside the stage door to keep fans and friends out when the theater is backed against the wall. A knob is screwed onto the outside of the door. Wooden brackets support the performing stage and an inside ledge that is used to store puppets and the props.

Bright paint in four colors, glue and nails for construction and fabric for curtain and bottom cutout are the materials you'll need.

constructing the theater

The basic theater consists of seven pieces of plywood as shown on the cutting diagram. The 7 and 9-year-olds pictured in the theater can work the puppets comfortably. You might want to change the theater dimensions to fit your family's needs.

You can draw the cutouts on the stage front, then saw them out with a fine blade before assembling.

Since the stage door is cut directly from the side of the stage, then reattached with a hinge,

take special care to make a clean cut. Also make a ⅛-in.-deep recess along the side of the door for the hinge.

There are several extra steps to take in gluing and nailing the parts together to make the attractive theater easy to store. After you attach the theater front, small side panels and inside ledge, saw a notch in the ledge to fit the hinge for the larger side panels. When you hinge the stage door to the side, add a 1x1-in. support strip to the door.

It's good to paint the theater in bright colors to add to the festivity, as long as the theater isn't so flamboyant it detracts from the stage action.

After you add hardware, paint scenery on the window shade and install the stage and kick curtains, the theater is ready for use. You might also want to clamp lights to the theater top to light the stage.

Your puppets are the life of the production. They can be glove puppets, hand puppets or rod puppets. Our space monster is a glove puppet and the space man and woman are rod puppets, which have great freedom of movement. You can make your own type of rod and glove pup-

AN ADVANTAGE of rod puppets over glove puppets is that they have freer arm movement. Rod puppets can also have feet that enable them to sit, kick or run.

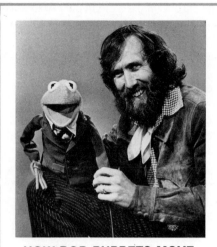

HOW ROD PUPPETS MOVE

Kermit the Frog is moved by Jim Henson of Sesame Street. Kermit and his Muppet friends are rod puppets like those in our theater. The puppeteer moves the head with one hand and works the rods attached to the puppet's left and right arms with the other hand.

Two people can also work a rod puppet. One moves the head and right arm while the other works the left arm. The person who moves the head acts as the puppet's voice. Two people working together need coordination, but they allow the puppet greater movement.

When you move the puppets, exaggerate their movements. Your puppets can bow until their head touches the stage floor. They can keel over backward in a dead faint. Use your fingers, wrist and arm in the process. Practice making your puppet sneeze, cry and hiccup. Try making it wave, rub its hands or tap its head to show thought.

Vary the pitch of your voice when talking through your puppet.

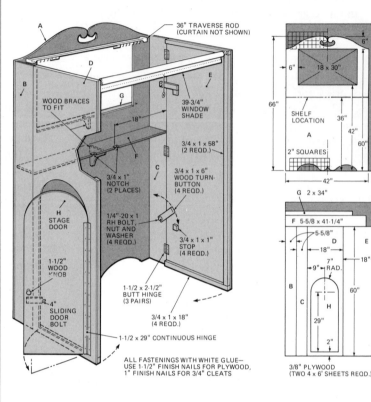

pets following the basic patterns here. When you're painting the faces, remember that delicate details won't be seen by the audience.

making the puppets

The head of a rod puppet is a hard Styrofoam ball with a hole cut out for your index finger. A strip of elastic is glued around the finger hole to which clothes can be sewn. The face is made of wrapping-paper strips moistened and applied with wheat paste and smoothed over moistened tissue wadded to make facial features. When dry, the face is lightly sanded smooth and

painted. Felt is glued to the head where the hair will be attached. You can make the curly hair by wrapping a strand of yarn around your finger, then running a securing thread through each curl and gluing the strand to the felt.

Bodies of the rod puppets are made with two thicknesses of material stuffed with polyester fiber fill. Old umbrella spokes make good rods; they have holes for attachment to the puppet. Stiff wire can also be used.

Small Styrofoam balls should be fitted to the rod end that rests in the palm of your hand for safety reasons and for easy manipulation.

Puppet boots and gloves are made with a stiff interlining and cardboard soles covered with black vinyl used in garbage bags. Tubing on arms and legs is fabric stuffed with fiber fill.

The space monster is a simple glove puppet made from the pattern with button eyes and antennae of small 2-in. fabric-covered springs.

After you've made your puppets and practiced with them, all you need is a story and an audience—then let the show begin.

A SLIT IS CUT in back of lining for puppeteer's hand. Then the lining pieces are stitched together.

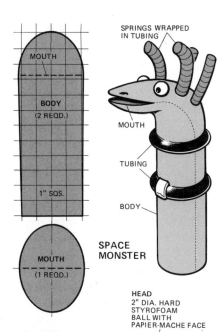

SPACE MONSTER

MOUTH

BODY (2 REQD.)

1" SQS.

MOUTH (1 REQD.)

SPRINGS WRAPPED IN TUBING

MOUTH

TUBING

BODY

STAGE-DOOR hinge is placed in ⅛-in. recess sawed out of door. A 1x1-in. support strip will be attached later.

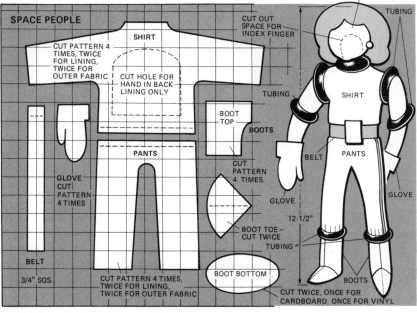

SPACE PEOPLE

SHIRT

CUT PATTERN 4 TIMES, TWICE FOR LINING, TWICE FOR OUTER FABRIC

CUT HOLE FOR HAND IN BACK LINING ONLY

GLOVE CUT PATTERN 4 TIMES

PANTS

BELT

3/4" SQS.

CUT PATTERN 4 TIMES, TWICE FOR LINING, TWICE FOR OUTER FABRIC

BOOT TOP

BOOTS

CUT PATTERN 4 TIMES.

BOOT TOE — CUT TWICE

BOOT BOTTOM

CUT TWICE, ONCE FOR CARDBOARD, ONCE FOR VINYL

HEAD 2" DIA. HARD STYROFOAM BALL WITH PAPIER-MACHE FACE

CUT OUT SPACE FOR INDEX FINGER

TUBING

TUBING

SHIRT

BELT

PANTS

GLOVE

GLOVE

TUBING

BOOTS

12-1/2"

A NOTCH IS SAWED into the ledge for the hinge attaching the side panels to the front.

THE PUPPET FACE is a Styrofoam ball with strips of wrapping paper moistened and applied with wheat paste.

THE HEM of the shirt back is stitched, but the slit is left free for the puppeteer's hand.

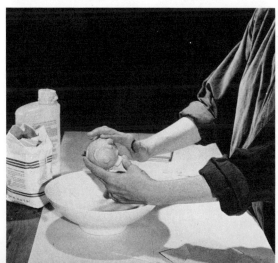

■ EXPERIENCE the exhilaration of flight by setting sail with your own kite. Both the Indian Fighter and the Marconi-Jib kites shown here have unique qualities that make them a pleasure to fly. The Fighter kite can streak and loop across an almost windless sky. The Marconi-Jib kite, named after the Marconi-rigged sailing yachts, allows you to set sail in gusty winds.

You can make the Fighter in less than an hour for about $1. The Marconi-Jib, a good all-day project, will run you $25 including material which is actually sail material. You can make it for under $10 if you substitute nylon or tightly woven cotton.

As you work, remember that the key to a good kite is *symmetry*.

the Indian Fighter kite

When other kites can't get off the ground, the Indian Fighter is the terror of the skies. In India (where this kite originated) combatants coat part

Two exciting kites you can build

By MAXWELL EDEN

THE INDIAN FIGHTER KITE (below) is a sleek variation of the ones handcrafted in India. It is a highly maneuverable kite that needs very little wind to fly.

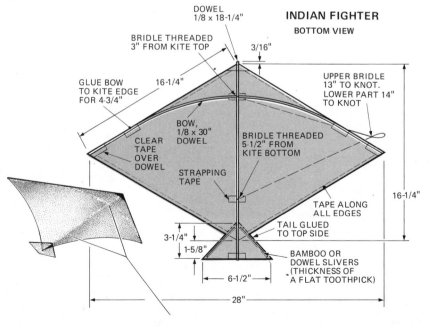

DOWEL
1/8 x 18-1/4"

BRIDLE THREADED
3" FROM KITE TOP

3/16"

INDIAN FIGHTER
BOTTOM VIEW

GLUE BOW
TO KITE EDGE
FOR 4-3/4"

16-1/4"

UPPER BRIDLE
13" TO KNOT.
LOWER PART 14"
TO KNOT

BOW,
1/8 x 30"
DOWEL

CLEAR
TAPE
OVER
DOWEL

BRIDLE THREADED
5-1/2" FROM
KITE BOTTOM

STRAPPING
TAPE

TAPE ALONG
ALL EDGES

16-1/4"

TAIL GLUED
TO TOP SIDE

3-1/4"

1-5/8"

BAMBOO OR
DOWEL SLIVERS
(THICKNESS OF
A FLAT TOOTHPICK)

6-1/2"

28"

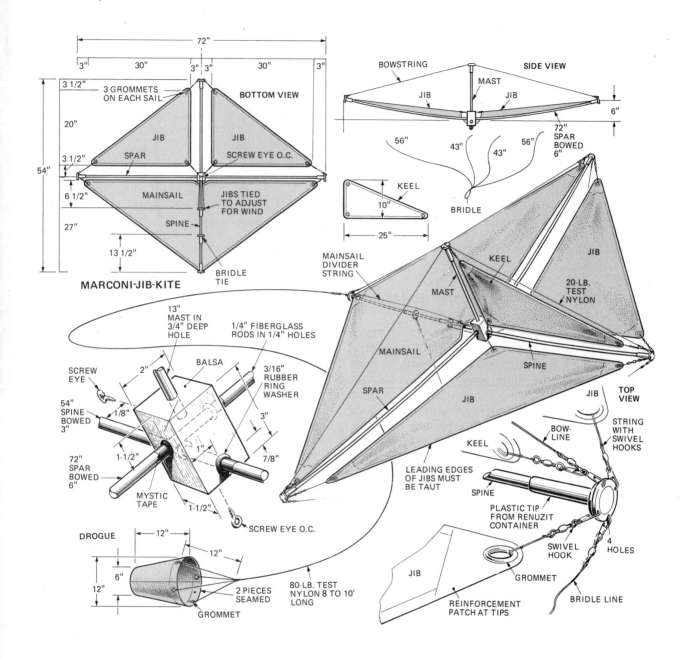

BOTTOM VIEW

72"

3" 30" 3" 3" 30" 3"

3 1/2"
3 GROMMETS
ON EACH SAIL

20"

JIB   JIB

SPAR   SCREW EYE O.C.

3 1/2"

54"

6 1/2"

MAINSAIL   JIBS TIED
TO ADJUST
FOR WIND

SPINE

27"

13 1/2"

BRIDLE
TIE

MARCONI-JIB-KITE

SIDE VIEW

BOWSTRING

MAST

JIB   JIB

6"

72"
SPAR
BOWED
6"

56"   43"   43"   56"

KEEL

10"

BRIDLE

25"

13"
MAST IN
3/4" DEEP
HOLE

1/4" FIBERGLASS
RODS IN 1/4" HOLES

2"   BALSA

SCREW
EYE

3/16"
RUBBER
RING
WASHER

54"
SPINE
BOWED
3"

1/8"

3"

72"
SPAR
BOWED
6"

1-1/2"

1"

7/8"

MYSTIC
TAPE

1-1/2"

SCREW EYE O.C.

MAINSAIL
DIVIDER
STRING

KEEL

MAST

JIB

20-LB.
TEST
NYLON

MAINSAIL

SPAR

SPINE

JIB

TOP
VIEW

JIB

STRING
WITH
SWIVEL
HOOKS

BOW-
LINE

KEEL

SPINE

PLASTIC TIP
FROM RENUZIT
CONTAINER

SWIVEL
HOOK

LEADING EDGES
OF JIBS MUST
BE TAUT

4
HOLES

JIB

GROMMET

BRIDLE LINE

REINFORCEMENT
PATCH AT TIPS

DROGUE

12"

12"

6"

12"

2 PIECES
SEAMED

GROMMET

80-LB. TEST
NYLON 8 TO 10'
LONG

of their kite string with ground glass then attempt to cut each other's flying line. Here's a variation of the Indian kite.

Materials. You'll need: two ⅛-dia. hardwood dowels, one 18¼ in. long and one 30 in. long; heavy tissue paper (Crystal brand is a heavyweight paper that comes striped in a variety of colors); two 4-in. dowel slivers the diameter of a flat toothpick (or slivers from bamboo shoe trees can be used); clear tape; strapping tape; rubber cement and string for the bridle and flying line. Use a light kite line or carpet thread for the bridle and fly line.

Construction. Lightly fold the tissue paper in half to assure symmetry, then measure and cut out the diamond shape shown in the diagram. Cut the small triangle stabilizer and glue it to the front of the kite. Apply clear tape reinforcement along the kite edges.

Flex the longer dowel to be sure it bends evenly to form a symmetrical bow, then glue about 4¾ in. of both ends along the edge of the

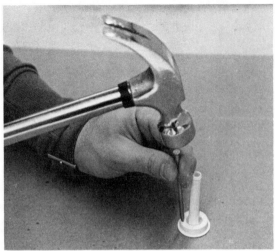

USE A HAMMER and nail to punch holes in the top of the plastic Renuzit cores to anchor swivel hooks and strings.

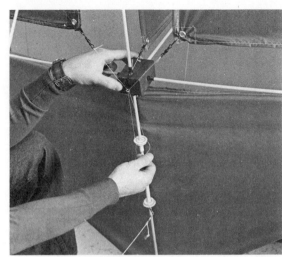

A SLIP KNOT is used to tie the jib strings to the top plastic core on the lower spine.

kite. Add two pieces of clear tape reinforcement to the bow.

Place strapping tape in both places where the bridle strings will go through the paper. Then glue the spine dowel to the kite body, *between* paper and bow. Spine and bow should hold the tissue paper taut.

Glue both dowel slivers to the stabilizer on the same side as the bow. Attach bridle to the opposite side. The top bridle ties around the bow and

HOLD THE HANDLE in your left hand and wind clockwise away from you.

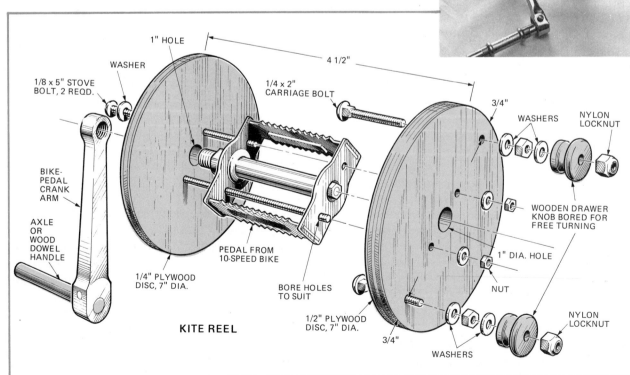

1" HOLE

4 1/2"

WASHER

1/8 x 5" STOVE
BOLT, 2 REQD.

1/4 x 2"
CARRIAGE BOLT

3/4"

WASHERS

NYLON
LOCKNUT

BIKE-
PEDAL
CRANK
ARM

AXLE
OR
WOOD
DOWEL
HANDLE

PEDAL FROM
10-SPEED BIKE

1/4" PLYWOOD
DISC, 7" DIA.

BORE HOLES
TO SUIT

WOODEN DRAWER
KNOB BORED FOR
FREE TURNING

1" DIA. HOLE

NUT

KITE REEL

1/2" PLYWOOD
DISC, 7" DIA.

3/4"

WASHERS

NYLON
LOCKNUT

spine. Finally, reinforce the tip and tail with clear tape.

Flying the kite. The Fighter flies best in winds of 1 to 5 mph. With practice you can launch it yourself. But begin by having a friend facing you, lightly holding kite pointed upward about 100 ft. downwind. *Pull* the kite out of his fingers with long, steady pulls of the string.

The Fighter will go in the direction its nose is pointed, as long as you pull its string hand over hand smoothly. Once you stop pulling, the kite will start to spin and seek a new direction. If you add a 10-15-ft. crepe-paper tail, the kite will be less frisky.

Marconi-Jib kite

The Marconi-Jib kite is made for sky sailing. You can adjust both jibs to suit winds of 8 to 25 mph.

Set loosely in light winds, the jibs will luff and feed needed air to the mainsail. In heavier winds, you trim the sails by setting the jibs more tightly. The jibs are set properly if the flying line is at a 60° angle to the ground.

The kite pulls relatively hard, so you should use a sturdy reel such as that shown for full control.

Materials. You'll need three ¼-in.-dia. fiberglass rods cut from bicycle safety flag poles (available at bike and hobby shops); a 1½ x 2 x 3-in. balsawood block; cloth tape such as Mystik; inner plastic cores from Renuzit Solid Air Freshener available at supermarkets (lightweight stainless-steel fishing rod tops can be used in place of five cores). If you can't find Renuzit in your supermarket, write for the nearest supplier to: Consumer Relations, Drackett Products, 5020 Spring Grove, Cincinnati, OH 45232. Sail material is Stabilkote III from Howe and Bainbridge, 220 Commerce St., Boston, MA 02109.

Hardware you'll need includes: 17 ½-in.-dia. grommets; four $^3/_{16}$-in. rubber washers; two lightweight 1-in.-dia. key rings; 21 No. 1 swivel hooks; and two $^3/_{16}$-in. screw eyes.

Use 80-lb.-test nylon or Dacron string for the bridle and flying line. Lightweight 20-lb. nylon cord is best for bowstrings and sail attachments.

Construction. Wearing gloves and a filter mask, score then cut the fiberglass rods with a razor saw or fine-tooth hacksaw. Cut the balsa block and drill the needed holes. Put rods and washers in place on the wood block. A piece of colored Mystik tape behind each washer is a good visual check to keep the rods in alignment.

The plastic Renuzit cores serve to anchor swivel hooks and strings. With a ¼-in. bit, drill center holes through the tops of two of the plastic cores so they can slide onto the spine. Using a hammer and nail, punch two equidistant holes on the top of one of these cores. String attached to the right angles of the jibs passes through a screw eye centered on the bottom of the balsa block and attaches to this core. Use a slip knot to attach the jib strings so they can be adjusted according to wind conditions. The second plastic core requires only one small hole to anchor the bridle.

Punch four equidistant holes on each of the remaining five plastic cores. These will be located at the tips of the fiberglass rods. Next add the bowstrings. They're attached with swivel hooks from the spar and spine tips and pass through holes at the mast tip where they intersect.

Cut and sew the sail and drogue material, allowing for ½-in. seams. Cut the small V on the mainsail ½-in. inward, fold back the material and seam it. Then sew small triangular reinforcements at each tip and on the mainsail V. Fasten grommets on the triangles and mainsail V.

Attach sails to the rods with string tied around the grommets and fastened to swivel hooks that attach to plastic cores. The right angle of the keel attaches to the screw eye that holds the jib lines with a string and swivel hook. The mainsail attaches to spar cores by key rings through the mainsail grommets.

Attach a line with swivel hooks on both ends from the lower spine tip, across the mainsail and hooked to the V-grommet and screw eye above the spine. This line should be relatively taut as it keeps the mainsail symmetricaly in flight. *Also check to see that the leading edges of the jibs are taut.*

Set the bridle by attaching one line from the top tip of the spine to the other bridle point on the spine. Attach the other line from tip to tip of the spar. The two lines should meet roughly one-third down from the top of the spine. Tie a loop at that point so all lines are equally taut.

Attach your flying line with a swivel hook to the bridle tie. Then attach drogue with a swivel hook.

Flying the Marconi-Jib. Rest the kite on the bottom spine tip about 50 ft. away from you. When the wind gusts, pull the kite toward you.

To haul in the kite, it's helpful to have a friend stand 20 ft. in front of you pulling the kite in by hand as you reel it in.

Make a back-yard skating rink

By TOM E. MAHL

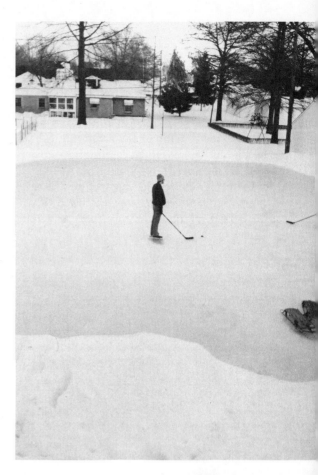

■ YOU CAN MAKE a really big back-yard ice-skating rink without the bother and expense of a 2x4 frame and sheet plastic just by watering a flat piece of lawn, if you have the right weather—temperature below 20° F.

The ideal base is about a 2-in. cover of snow. You can make do with less, but the process takes longer; more than 4 in. means packing or removal. Soak the snow to slush with your hose and let it freeze, then keep adding coats to build up the surface and as needed for maintenance. With good conditions and enthusiasm, you'll have a usable rink in two days, and a fine one in five.

The only effect on next year's turf will be slightly retarded growth—but *don't* put your rink over a septic tank or leach bed. Best watering time is night, at 10° F. or less. Leave the outdoor faucet on, regulated by the indoor valve; after attaching your hose, thaw the faucet with hot water.

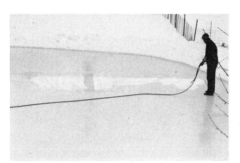

ON A LARGE RINK, it's best to water back and forth in sections approximately 6 ft. wide across the width of the pool.

A STRONG RIM is important. Manicuring it with a snow shovel will keep it hard; removing chips will prevent porosity.

A BASE of more than 4 in. of snow will have to be packed down. It's more easily done with a lawn roller than with feet. To get a flat surface, take the nozzle off your garden hose and let the water run to cover the area evenly, finding its own level.

Index

The page number refers to the first page on which specific information can be found.